Queen Victoria's Cousins

Christina Croft

A Hilliard & Croft Book

Front Cover: *Queen Victoria and her cousin, Victoire, Duchesse de Nemours* by Franz Xavier Winterhalter

Contents

Prologue

Deprived of companions of her own age, Queen Victoria spent much of her childhood with only her dogs and dolls for company. Her lonely and isolated existence was brightened by visits from her cousins, many of whom she came to regard as surrogate brothers and sisters.

From the newly-created Empire of Mexico to the largely undiscovered African Congo, their influence crossed continents; and their lives, spanning more than a century, were interwoven with some of the most significant events of the age. They experienced wars, revolutions, personal tragedies and national disasters, and their characters were as varied as their fortunes. Among them were princes, potentates and dukes; dutiful wives and desperate daughters; an Empress; three Kings; the consorts of Queens; and the spouses of theatre performers and a circus artiste.

With several, Queen Victoria maintained a lifelong correspondence, while others were gradually distanced from her. All, however, contributed something to her life's experience, and many repaid her devotion with love.

List of Queen Victoria's Paternal Cousins

Daughter of King George IV

Charlotte (1796-1817)

Son of Ernest, Duke of Cumberland, King of Hanover

George (1819-1878)

Children of Adolphus, Duke of Cambridge

George (1819-1904)

Augusta (1822-1916)

Mary Adelaide (1833-1897)

List of Queen Victoria's Maternal Cousins

Children of Sophie of Saxe-Coburg-Saalfeld; Countess of Mensdorff-Pouilly

Hugo (1806-1847)

Alfonse (1810-1894)

Alfred (1812-1814)

Alexander (1813-1871)

Leopold (1815-1832)

Arthur (1817-1904)

Children of Antoinette of Saxe-Coburg-Saalfeld; Duchess of Württemberg

Marie (1799-1860) Duchess of Saxe-Coburg-Gotha

Paul (1800-1801)

Alexander (1804-1881) Duke of Württemberg

Ernest (1807-1888) Duke of Württemberg

Frederick (1810-1815)

Sons of Duke Ernest I of Saxe-Coburg-Gotha

Ernest (1818-1893) Duke Ernest II of Saxe-Coburg-Gotha

Albert (1819-1861) Consort of Queen Victoria

Children of Ferdinand of Saxe-Coburg-Saalfeld; Saxe-Coburg Kohary

Ferdinand (1816-1885) King Ferdinand II of Portugal

Augustus (1818-1881)

Victoire (1822-1857) Duchess of Nemours

Leopold (1824-1884)

Children of Leopold of Saxe-Coburg Saalfeld; King Leopold I of the Belgians

Louis Philippe (1833-1834)

Leopold (1835-1909) King Leopold II of the Belgians

Philippe (1837-1905) Count of Flanders

Charlotte (1840-1927) Archduchess of Austria; Empress of Mexico

Part I – The Hanoverians & The Coburgs

Chapter 1 – 'A Hoyden Schoolgirl'

George – Prince of Wales; Prince Regent; King George
IV; Queen Victoria's paternal uncle
Caroline of Brunswick – Wife of George IV; Princess
of Wales; Queen of the United Kingdom
Charlotte of Wales – Queen Victoria's cousin; daughter
of George IV
George III – Queen Victoria's grandfather; King of the
United Kingdom
Charlotte – Queen Victoria's grandmother; wife of
George III; Queen of the United Kingdom

Throughout his twenties and early thirties,
George, Prince of Wales, eldest son of King George III,
had stubbornly withstood the exhortations of his
mother, Queen Charlotte, to marry and father an heir.
Despite pressure from Parliament and his awareness of
his duty to the dynasty, he had neither the strength of
character to abandon his self-indulgent lifestyle nor the
willingness to accept his responsibilities as the future
King. Besides, although he could not openly admit it,
he already had a wife – a twice-widowed Roman
Catholic, Maria Fitzherbert, for whom he had
developed such an infatuation in his early twenties that
he had contracted an illegal marriage in contravention
of the Royal Marriages Act and the Act of Settlement.

This gesture, however, was not as romantic as it
might have appeared, for, despite his initial obsession
with Maria, he had no intention of sacrificing his
position in the line of succession. Moreover, since the
contract was invalid in the eyes of the law, he did not
consider himself bound by the vows that he had taken
and had happily enjoyed affairs with other women. By
the time that George was thirty-two, Maria had been

supplanted in his affection by the cunning wife of the fourth Earl of Jersey, Frances Villiers, who, attempting to draw her paramour's attention further away from her rival, joined the chorus of those who were urging George to contract a legal marriage. He could, she believed, easily find a respectable and malleable bride, who would prove suitably complaisant to allow them to continue their liaison.

It was neither, however, Lady's Jersey's encouragement nor a sense of duty to his country that ultimately prompted the lackadaisical prince into action. It was rather financial necessity that propelled him into a decision which he would regret to the end of his life.

King George III was notoriously parsimonious when it came to his sons' allowances, and, as George had extravagant tastes, it did not take long for him to amass so many debts that, by 1794, he was being hounded by creditors, refusing to supply him with further goods until his bills were paid. The only solution to his pecuniary crisis was to yield to the will of parliament by marrying an appropriate princess, in return for which he would receive a substantial increase in his annuity.

Seeing marriage as merely a matter of necessity, he had little interest in the choice of a bride and therefore duly accepted his family's recommendation of his first cousin, twenty-six-year-old Caroline of Brunswick. The couple had never seen one another when, in the summer of 1794, they were betrothed by proxy, so, a few months later, John Harris, the 1st Earl of Malmesbury, was sent to Hanover to prepare the bride for her future role before accompanying her back to London for the wedding.

On his arrival in Germany, Malmesbury was somewhat surprised to discover that Caroline was positively ecstatic at the prospect of becoming the Princess of Wales. Although she had never visited Britain, she had seen flattering portraits of the prince, and gushed with garrulous excitement about her eagerness to meet him. Unfortunately, neither her appearance nor her manners matched her enthusiasm, and initially Malmesbury struggled to portray her in a favourable light. Her pretty face, he thought, lacked softness; her teeth were 'tolerable but going'; and her figure was anything but graceful. Nonetheless, he stressed her willingness to acquaint herself with the mores of England, and, a few days after their first meeting, he observed optimistically that she 'improves on acquaintance, is gay and cheerful, with good sense'[1].

His optimism was premature, for, in the weeks that followed, he could not fail to notice the warning signs of what was to come. Her father, the Duke of Brunswick, confided in him that he was aware of George's many foibles, and understood that this was not to be a love-match, although he hoped that, given time, the Prince of Wales might at least grow to *like* his daughter. Other members of the household were more explicit, advising Malmesbury of 'the necessity of being very strict with the Princess Caroline — that she was not clever, or ill-disposed, but of a temper easily wrought on, and had no tact.'[2]

More disconcertingly it soon became clear that she was fickle; talked incessantly; loved to gossip; and, although she had an 'innate morality', she had no 'strong notions of its value and necessity.'[3] It was even reported that her conversation and behaviour were so impolite that her father had ordered a chaperone to accompany her at all times, particularly if she attended a ball, to prevent her from 'making an exhibition of herself by her indecent conversations with men.'

Malmesbury's drastic solution to her effusiveness was to counsel her to express no opinions whatsoever throughout her first six months in England. Relieved that she accepted his advice with good grace, he then prepared himself to tackle the more delicate matter of her lack of personal hygiene. Tactfully, he explained that the Prince of Wales was a man of fastidious tastes, and thus it would please him if she would take a little more care over her toilette and cleanliness. His words made an impact, for the next time he saw her he observed that she had washed herself thoroughly *all over,* and, he could only hope that her greater attention to her dress would be sufficient to impress her fiancé when she finally arrived in England.

Following an arduous sea-crossing, during which her courage and good spirits had endeared her to the sailors, Caroline reached Greenwich in April 1795, and was immediately greeted by Lady Jersey, whom George had appointed as one of her Ladies of the Bedchamber, and had sent to accompany her back to London. Unaware that her companion was her fiancé's mistress, Caroline instantly forgot Malmesbury's warnings and spent the entire journey carelessly divulging information about her former amours – all of which Lady Jersey was quick to recount to George as soon as they reached the capital.

It was, however, neither her indiscretion nor her past misdemeanours which prompted George to behave so unchivalrously at their first encounter, but rather the excess of rouge on her cheeks, her ungainly manner and the unpleasant odour emanating from her old-fashioned clothes. The moment that he set eyes on her struggling through a graceless curtsy, he called desperately to Malmesbury, 'Harris, I need a brandy,' before rudely turning his back upon Caroline and swiftly exiting the room.

The feeling of disappointment was mutual. Perplexed by his appalling manners, Caroline gasped to Malmesbury, "My God! Is the Prince always like that? I find him very fat and not at all as handsome as his portrait."

Within a matter of hours, she had discovered that her erstwhile travelling companion was George's mistress and, at dinner that evening, she talked incessantly, making jokes at George's expense and interspersing her monologue with 'vague vulgar hints' about him and Lady Jersey. The Prince sat silently throughout the meal with such an air of disgust that bets were taken in London clubs on the likelihood of his failing to attend his own wedding.

George might well have found an excuse to absent himself from the ceremony were it not for the lure of the increased annuity, the fact that guests had already arrived, and his mother's insistence that:

"It is not for you, George, to say whether you can marry the Princess, or not."[4]

On 8th April, fortified by brandy and noticeably trembling as he acknowledged the posse of his mistresses who stood waving their handkerchiefs towards him, George managed to utter the marriage vows that he had no intention of keeping. During the subsequent reception at Carlton House, he continued to steady his nerves with alcohol to the point where it was widely rumoured that he stumbled over the hearth and spent his wedding night curled up in the fireplace in an intoxicated stupor.

George later denied the allegations, and his protests appeared to be justified when, nine months after the wedding Caroline gave birth to a healthy daughter who, in honour of her paternal and maternal grandmothers, was christened Charlotte Augusta[a].

His duty completed, George was eager to discard his unwanted wife as quickly as possible, and, barely had Charlotte been born than he pointedly made a will leaving virtually all his possessions to Maria Fitzherbert, while bequeathing the Princess of Wales only one shilling. In spite of this insult, Caroline, who, for all her faults, was notably kind-hearted, felt nothing but sympathy for the chief beneficiary, whom she described as 'the Prince's true wife' and 'an excellent woman.'

> "It is a great pity for [George] that he ever broke with her," she told one of her ladies-in-waiting. "Do you know I know the man who was present at his marriage, the late Lord B. He declared to a friend of mine, that when he went to inform Mrs Fitzherbert that the Prince had married me, she would not believe it, for she knew she was herself married to him."[5]

Lady Jersey, however, was far more difficult to forgive, for, unlike Mrs Fitzherbert, she seized every opportunity to publicly humiliate Caroline, taking particular pleasure in flaunting the jewellery that George had given to his bride on their wedding day, before withdrawing it to hand to his mistress.

Her husband's blatant infidelity was far less wounding to Caroline than his refusal to allow her to be involved in their daughter's upbringing. Three months after the birth, he sent her letter informing her that he had no intention of ever resuming marital relations with her, and she would only be permitted to see their child once a day in the presence of a nursery-maid or

---

[a] Caroline's mother, Augusta, Duchess of Brunswick, was a sister of King George III

governess. Viewing the note as confirmation that she was no longer bound by her wedding vows, Caroline moved to Blackheath where, much to the delight of London society, she embarked on a hedonistic lifestyle which ministers and members of her father-in-law's court watched with fascinated horror. Hosting parties at which she reputedly danced naked to the waist, she was said to have taken numerous lovers and even to have given birth to a son by a footman.

Rather than damaging her reputation, these tales served only to increase the public's interest in her plight, and wherever she travelled she was met with cheers from the crowds who viewed her as the wronged wife of a self-indulgent buffoon. Jealous of her popularity, George was so horrified when she threatened to announce that he was not Charlotte's father, that he pressed for the establishment of a parliamentary committee to carry the 'Delicate Investigation' into her alleged immorality, in the hope that the outcome might permit him to obtain an annulment of their marriage.

The process was traumatic for eight-year-old Charlotte, who not only saw her mother facing complete humiliation but was also denied any access to her until the inquiry was completed. Until then, George had been attached to his daughter but, from the time the investigation began, he began to distance himself from her even to the point of moving her into a separate household under the supervision of governesses[b].

In her despair, Charlotte turned for comfort to Mrs Fitzherbert, who could not restrain her tears as the child pleaded with her to persuade her father to show her greater affection. The King, who was sympathetic

---

[b] Ultimately the Delicate Investigation concluded that Caroline was innocent of the charges levelled against her.

to both Charlotte and her mother, was delighted by the news that his granddaughter was to have her own household as he believed it would enable him to play a greater part in her upbringing. He eagerly began preparing rooms at Lower Lodge in Windsor, and was incensed when, at the last minute, George changed his plans, insinuating that he had been forced to take such a stand on account of his father's increasing insanity. The dispute between father and son deprived Charlotte of the guidance of her beloved grandfather, for, as he told the Prince of Wales, he:

> "...must either have the whole care and superintendence of the person and education of the Princess or entirely decline any interference or expense."[6]

Worse was to follow in 1810 when the King suffered a serious bout of porphyria that so affected his mind that he was deemed unfit to continue his duties. The following year, George was created Prince Regent, which gave him unlimited control of his nine-year-old daughter. Denying her free access to her mother, he had Charlotte confined at Windsor, under the constant supervision of her maiden aunts, and her grandmother, Queen Charlotte, who made no secret of her antipathy towards her. Fearing that if she were seen in public, her popularity would far exceed his own, George gave strict instructions that she should be kept out of sight. On the rare occasions when she was permitted to visit the theatre, she was forced to sit at the back of the box out of view of the audience, for, as he made clear, she had no right to a will of her own but must remain subservient to his wishes in every aspect of her life.

> "While I live," he stated, "she must be subject to me as she is at present, if she were thirty or forty or even forty-five."[7]

In spite of so many restrictions and her father's insensitivity, nothing, it seemed, could crush Charlotte's naturally cheerful disposition or her kind-heartedness. The very public wrangling between her parents had, it seemed, given her wisdom beyond her years, and an unshakeable loyalty to those who showed her affection. Her isolation did not blind her to her mother's unsavoury reputation but she came to the conclusion that Caroline's faults were exacerbated by George's cruelty. 'My mother was wicked,' she confided in a friend, 'but she would not have turned so wicked had not my father been much more wicked still.'[8]

Boisterous and tomboyish, she had inherited not only her mother's generosity but also her stubbornness, lack of tact and, at times, her ungainly bearing.

> "She is very clever," observed a lady-in-waiting, "but has at present the manners of a hoyden school girl. She talked all sorts of nonsense to me. She is a fine piece of flesh and blood, but can put on dignity when she chooses, though it seems to sit uneasily upon her."[9]

More worryingly, it seemed to George that she had also inherited her mother's lack of discretion and when her openly flirtatious behaviour became more apparent, he feared the only means of preventing a scandal was to find her a suitable husband as soon as possible.

Chapter 2 – 'The Young Frog'

Charlotte of Wales – Queen Victoria's cousin; the daughter of George IV of the United Kingdom

George – Prince of Wales; Prince Regent; King George IV; Queen Victoria's paternal uncle

Caroline of Brunswick – Wife of George IV; Princess of Wales; Queen of the United Kingdom

George III – Queen Victoria's grandfather; King of the United Kingdom

Queen Charlotte – Queen Victoria's grandmother; wife of George III; Queen of the United Kingdom

William – Duke of Clarence; later King William IV; son of George III; Queen Victoria's paternal uncle

William – Hereditary Prince of Orange; later King of the Netherlands

Augustus – Duke of Sussex; son of George III; Queen Victoria's paternal uncle

By the time of her fifteenth birthday in January 1811, Charlotte had begun to rouse the interest of several would-be suitors. Her physical attractions were debatable but, apart from her proximity to the throne, her charming unpredictability was rapidly become a source of fascination.

"She surprises everybody who has not been told beforehand of her ways," wrote the Austrian Archduke John. "A well-set, young, beautiful woman with the features of a man in her conversation, intelligence, knowledge and wit; for the rest unrestrained merriment, disingenuousness, even a bluntness that is astonishing. She seems to have a good disposition, but is self-willed and quite indifferent to the knowledge that is required of a woman of distinction. A curious mixture."[10]

At the same time, Charlotte, too, was becoming aware of the attractions of the opposite sex, particularly in the form of her recently-appointed tutor, a forty-three-year-old clergyman named Doctor George Frederick Nott. Sadly for Charlotte, when her uncle, the Duke of York, learned of her infatuation, he reported it to her father who duly passed on the information to his mother. The unsympathetic Queen summoned Charlotte to her rooms for an interrogation but Charlotte refused to answer her questions and ultimately stated boldly that she would not be ill-used by her father as her mother had been, and, as Doctor Nott was the only man who had ever paid her any genuine attention, she did not care if it would displease the Prince Regent to hear that she felt great affection for him. Not a little put out by her insolence, Queen Charlotte reminded her that she owed allegiance to her father, who always had her best interests at heart.

> "Can I believe my royal father so great and good, when I have so long witnessed his unremitted unkindness to my neglected mother?" Charlotte retorted. "Neither do I receive much attention from the prince; and my uncle of York is always preaching to me about virtue and submission, and your Majesty well knows he does not practise either. Mr. Nott practises every amiability which he enjoins, and I esteem him exceedingly more than I do any other gentleman."[11]

Before the horrified Queen had time to reply, Charlotte hastened to her rooms and drew up a deed bequeathing all her worldly goods to the astonished tutor. If she hoped that Nott would reward the gesture with uncompromising loyalty, she was soon to be disappointed. Nott sold the deed to the Prince Regent and shortly afterwards resigned his post in return for a more lucrative position arranged for him by Charlotte's father. His considerable financial gains, however, were tempered by the damage that had been done to his reputation as it was widely rumoured that he had manipulated the princess into promising him an Archbishopric on her accession. He became the subject of caricatures in various popular papers, and even Lord Byron parodied him in a nine-stanza poem, entitled '*The New Vicar of Bray*':

> "Do you know Doctor Nott?
> With 'a crook in his lot,'
> Who seven years since tried to dish up
> A neat Codicil
> To the Princess's Will
> Which made Dr. Nott not a bishop."

It did not take long for Charlotte to recover from her disappointment and to develop a new infatuation with her illegitimate cousin, Captain George Fitzclarence. As the eldest of ten children of her uncle, the Duke of Clarence, and his long-term mistress, the actress Dorothea Jordan, the captain had been raised like a prince and mixed freely with the Royal Family, but his illegitimacy barred him from the succession and made him an inappropriate suitor for the daughter of the heir to the throne. When George discovered Charlotte's latest attachment, he berated her for entertaining such ridiculous notions and sent her the details of the 'Delicate Investigation' as a warning of what would happen if she dared to disobey him.

The object of her attraction was soon replaced by another young officer and allegedly illegitimate cousin – Captain Charles Hesse, the putative son of her uncle, the Duke of York. This time George put an end to the matter by having Hesse posted to his regiment in

Spain, unaware that Charlotte had already switched her attention to William Cavendish – the twenty-three-year-old son of the renowned Georgiana, Duchess of Devonshire. Having inherited his father's estates and title, the Duke was a wealthy and respectable young man, but, since he was neither a king nor a prince, the Prince Regent had no intention of permitting him to marry his daughter.

Irked by Charlotte's consecutive infatuations and increasing popularity, George resolved to marry her off to a foreign prince who would take her out of the country at the first possible opportunity. By chance or design, this decision coincided with plans to create stronger ties between Britain and the Netherlands, and there could be no better way to cement an alliance than by the union of two heirs to the two thrones.

Aware that the 'bandy-legged' and 'sickly-looking', 'Young Frog' – Prince William of Orange – would hold little appeal for a headstrong and passionate princess, George insisted that every precaution should be taken to prevent her from developing any more romantic notions of her own, while he began secret negotiations with the prince's family, without revealing to Charlotte anything of his plans. In this, though, as in so many matters, he underestimated her intelligence for she quickly realised what he was doing and thwarted him at every opportunity. She declined invitations to receptions and balls which the prince would attend; and, when George arranged a dinner for her to meet her intended suitor, she feigned illness at the last moment to excuse her absence. Her first encounter with Prince William's father did little to improve her enthusiasm for the match, as, in the middle of the Prince Regent's birthday party at Carlton House, the Dutchman disappeared along with his host and several of

Charlotte's uncles, all of whom, were later discovered under a table, too inebriated to move.

Tired of the subterfuge, George took a more direct approach by telling his daughter that, for the sake of the country, she must marry the Prince of Orange. Unmoved and unyielding, she replied that she could not do so as she had already given her heart to William Cavendish. Incensed by her stubbornness, George launched into a violent tirade, warning her of the dire consequences of such disobedience, but, though shaken, she stood her ground before faithfully recounting every detail of their meeting to her mother, who urged her to continue to resist her father's threats and pleading.

As George's temper began to cool, he came to the sensible conclusion that, if Charlotte could not be swayed by coercion, she might be more willing to yield to flattery and kindness. Over the next few weeks he spoke more gently to her and, allowing her slightly more freedom, explained that he understood better than anyone the pain of a loveless marriage and had no desire to inflict such a situation on her.

The ruse was so successful that when he invited her to a ball at which a portrait of Prince William was prominently displayed, she confessed that he was more handsome than she had been led to believe and she would raise no objections to making his acquaintance. Seizing the opportunity, George lost no time asking the prince to dinner at Carlton House, and this time Charlotte graciously accepted the invitation.

"The Princess Charlotte has completely altered her language as to the Prince of Orange," an observer informed the Lord Chancellor, "and I am quite clear she will take him if they offer him to her."[12]

To George's immense gratification, the young couple spent the entire evening in each other's company, and when Charlotte told her father that she 'liked [Prince William's] manner very well', he was so overjoyed that he clasped the couple's hands together as a symbol of their betrothal.

Whether Charlotte had been caught up in the excitement of the moment or was filled with a sudden desire to please her father, her compliance was short-lived. The following morning, when Prince William cheerfully told her that they would live in the Netherlands for much of the year, she burst into tears at the prospect of leaving her friends and all that was familiar. Distressed by her reaction and keen to appease her, William immediately altered his stance, assuring her that, as soon as his duties permitted, he would look for a house in England, which would become their permanent home; and he was willing to accept her stipulation that a clause be inserted into their marriage contract, guaranteeing that she would never be compelled to live abroad without her consent.

In spite of his eagerness to please, Charlotte, already regretting her decision, told her mother that:

"I think him so ugly that I am almost obliged to turn my head away in disgust when he is speaking to me."[13]

Even as she signed the official marriage contract in June 1814, she was urgently seeking a means of escape from an agreement which she felt had been forced upon her; and, when her father suggested that she should omit the clause about remaining in England, since a wife's duty was 'to follow her husband', she was utterly convinced that he had engineered the match solely to remove her from the country.

"My own family," she confided in a friend, "and the head of it, too, is very desirous I should leave [England], which I cannot say I am, as I feel naturally excessively attached to the country I was born and educated in. You must be sensible, too, that I have been as yet so very little out, and so little known, that I am nearly a stranger, and leaving it with that impression would, I think, never do." [14]

Having achieved his aim, George abandoned the façade of kindness and resumed his former dictatorial manner. When William resumed his duties in the Netherlands, George, fearing that Charlotte might indulge in her former flirtations or renege on her promise, prevented her from attending any social gatherings by reducing her allowance with the excuse that she had been spending too freely and too generously and purchasing items without his express permission. Worse was to follow when she heard from an aunt that he was pressing the Dutch Royal Family to have the wedding take place as soon as possible, despite the fact that Prince William had not yet acquired an English property.

Charlotte's mother happily fuelled her fears, aware that, if her daughter were forced to live abroad, her own position in England would be untenable and her heartless husband would probably turn her out of her home. For her own protection, she persuaded Charlotte to tell her fiancé that she could only marry him on condition that her mother would always be welcome to live with them for as long as she wished. As both Charlotte and Caroline had anticipated, this stipulation placed Prince William in an extremely awkward position. Knowing that any concession to Caroline would enrage her estranged husband, the Dutchman was too much in awe of the Prince Regent to dare to defy his wishes. Falteringly, he told Charlotte that he could not acquiesce to this demand, to which she replied that he must think it over for the rest of the day and, if she had not heard from him by that evening, he must consider their engagement at an end.

While William retired to his rooms, Charlotte nervously spent the afternoon awaiting his response but when, by eleven o'clock that night, she had heard nothing, she wrote him a letter stating plainly that they were no longer betrothed and he should inform her father of what had transpired. For almost forty-eight hours she anxiously waited for a reply but it was not until late on the afternoon of Saturday 18th June that his missive finally arrived:

> "I found the night before last your letter, and have lost no time to acquaint my family with its contents, but I cannot comply with your wish by doing the same with regard to the Regent, finding it much more natural that you should do it yourself; and it is, besides, much too delicate a matter for me to say anything to him on the subject. Hoping that you shall never feel any cause to repent of the step you have taken…"[15]

William's refusal to approach the Prince Regent allowed Charlotte to tailor the story to her own advantage, and, in a note to her father, she claimed that her fiancé was entirely responsible for this sudden turn of events. George was not to be deceived and, when he eventually deigned to respond, he not only told her of his 'deepest concern' at what had occurred but also sent the Bishop of Salisbury to explain to her how greatly she had offended him. The Bishop advised her to write a humble and apologetic letter to her father, assuring him that she was prepared to reconsider her position but, with typical stubbornness, she agreed to express her regret for distressing her father but insisted that she could not alter her decision. Angered by her defiance, George vindictively dismissed her closest companions, blaming them for having persuaded her to flout his authority, and informed her that she would be confined in Warwick House until he could make arrangements for her to be taken to Windsor, where she would be allowed to see no one except her antipathetic grandmother.

Frustrated and anxious, Charlotte flew into a tantrum of despair, and, fleeing unceremoniously from the house, ran down the street to Charing Cross where, climbing into a hackney carriage, she handed the coachman a sovereign and ordered him to take her full-speed to her mother at Connaught House. From there, she sent a message to Caroline's champion, Lord Brougham, who, greatly alarmed, raced to the scene only to find her 'in high spirits…like a bird set loose from its cage'.[16] Unable to persuade her to return home and uncertain how to deal with the situation, Brougham sent for Charlotte's favourite uncle, the Duke of Sussex, who immediately concurred that she had no choice but to return to Warwick House. Even her mother understood the gravity of the situation, advising her that she had a duty to obey her 'unnatural father', who under the law had every right to manage her life and education. Charlotte, strong-willed as ever, retired to bed leaving an anxious Brougham to contemplate the best means of bringing her to her senses.

The following morning, realising that his only hope was to frighten her into compliance, Brougham spoke of the potential consequences of her actions if the public learned of her plight. The masses, he said, would riot on her behalf and:

> "Carlton House will be attacked – perhaps pulled down; the soldiers will be ordered out; blood will be shed; and if your Royal Highness were to live a hundred years, it never would be forgotten that your running away from your father's house was the cause of the mischief;

and you may depend upon it, such is the English people's horror of bloodshed, you never would get over it."[17]

Faced with such a terrifying prospect, Charlotte agreed to go home but not until Brougham and the Duke of Sussex promised that they would make it be widely known that she did not wish to marry the Prince of Orange and, if she were forced to do so, it would be without her consent.

Although it appeared that Charlotte had yielded, her father dared not risk the public outcry that would inevitably ensue, and was forced to abandon all hope of a match with the Prince of Orange. Nonetheless, as word of her escapade spread, George's reputation sank to its nadir and his only hope of regaining public support was by attempting some form of reconciliation with his daughter. Once again, he made kindly overtures towards her by permitting her to take a holiday by the sea, but still she was kept under strict supervision and, shortly before her seventeenth birthday, she wrote to the Prime Minister, urging him to finally grant her freedom by providing her with a home of her own and ladies of her choice to attend her. On hearing what she had done, her father exploded in anger, and, supported by his mother, called her an 'incorrigible girl, and a stupid fool,' whom he ought to have locked up for treason.

Charlotte had had little time to enjoy the triumph of her escape from the Prince of Orange for, within a matter of weeks, she was left with the sense of having been betrayed for a second time. Just as she had discovered that Nott had left her in return for a lucrative pension, now she was told that her mother had negotiated a substantial annuity of £35,000 from Parliament on condition that she would leave the country. Distraught at the prospect of being abandoned

31

once more, Charlotte was unimpressed by Caroline's explanation that she had accepted the money to tour the Continent because she was:

> "...now so much an object of hatred to the Prince that he will not tolerate her presence either in private or in public, and henceforth she cannot submit to disdain of this kind nor allow herself to be treated as a guilty woman when her innocence has been recognized by the ministers and by the Parliament and the accusations of her enemies and betrayers have been disproved."[18]

While appreciating that Charlotte would be saddened at being deprived of her mother's love, Caroline was sure that she would soon recover from the loss since they had often not seen one another for months at a time and had therefore grown used to the separation.

The prediction proved to be accurate for, in spite of her initial reaction, Charlotte was soon distracted from her grief by the courtly attentions of two German princes, one of whom she would ultimately decide to marry.

Chapter 3 – 'So Poignant a Sense of Grief

George – Prince of Wales; Prince Regent; King George IV; Queen Victoria's paternal uncle
Caroline – Wife of George IV; Princess of Wales; Queen of the United Kingdom
Charlotte of Wales – Queen Victoria's cousin; daughter of George IV
George III – Queen Victoria's grandfather; King of the United Kingdom
Queen Charlotte – Queen Victoria's grandmother; wife of George III; Queen of the United Kingdom
Leopold – Prince of Saxe-Coburg-Saalfeld; husband of Charlotte of Wales
Edward – Duke of Kent; son of George III; Queen Victoria's father
Frederick – Duke of York; son of George III; Queen Victoria's uncle

Between midsummer and Christmas 1815, Charlotte's lonely existence was cheered by a clandestine romance with her second cousin, Prince Frederick of Prussia, with whom she maintained a secret correspondence, in full knowledge that her father was firmly opposed to the affair. In January 1815, however, the dalliance came to an abrupt and unexpected conclusion when Prince Frederick informed her that he could no longer continue their relationship as he was about to become engaged to Princess Louise of Anhalt.

The termination of the brief romance was not too traumatic for Charlotte, since, by then, a second suitor had appeared in the form of Leopold of Saxe-Coburg-Saalfeld, the ambitious youngest son of a relatively minor German duke, described by a former mistress as, 'a tall young man, with a false look and a disagreeable, sentimental smile.'[19]

Despite his somewhat humble origins and his mistress's less than flattering description, Leopold had acquired an excellent reputation, charming the future Queen of France with his exquisite manners, and coming to the attention of Tsar Alexander I for his skill and courage in service with the Russian army. So impressed was the Tsar by Leopold's demeanour that in 1814 he invited him to accompany him to the Congress of Vienna – an international convention designed to negotiate a lasting peace in the wake of the Napoleonic Wars and the French revolutions.

En route to the Congress, the Russian party visited London and, at the home of the Tsar's sister-in-law, the Duchess of Oldenburg, Charlotte first made Leopold's acquaintance and was instantly enraptured. Once again, the Prince Regent objected to his daughter's latest infatuation and insisted that he would not sanction a marriage between the second-in-line to the British throne and the son of an impoverished duke whose dukedom had still to recover from the ravages of Napoleon's armies. Leopold, however, was more astute and determined than any of Charlotte's previous suitors and refused to be deterred by the whims of her cantankerous father. Using all of his legendary charisma and cunning, he cultivated a series of friendships with several prominent politicians and with Charlotte's uncle, the Duke of Kent, all of whom began to impress on George the benefits of allowing his daughter to marry a man whom she truly loved.

Under pressure from Parliament, George yielded and, in January 1815, invited Leopold back to England where he grudgingly granted him permission to propose to Charlotte. In spite of this concession, he refused to relinquish control of his daughter, and insisted that, throughout the engagement, the couple should be kept as far apart as possible. When, therefore, Leopold returned to his duties, Charlotte was sent to stay in her father's famous Pavilion in fashionable Brighton under the strict supervision of her grandmother and aunts. So compliant was she to this ruling that Leopold was finally permitted to visit her when the official announcement of the betrothal was published. Those who witnessed the reunion observed that the princess was totally in love and 'so happy…that she must please and flatter the object of her choice.'[20]

Leopold's happiness was tempered, however, by the fear that the 'moody' Prince Regent might change his mind and, for that reason, he was keen to ensure that the wedding would take place as soon as possible. Once again, he overcame his future father-in-law's objections, and succeeded in having the ceremony brought forwards to May 2nd that year. In the meantime, he was created a British citizen, and Parliament voted him an annuity of £50,000 as well as a purchasing Charlotte a wedding gift – Claremont House, a Palladian mansion in Surrey, sufficiently distant from London to enable the couple to be free of interference from Charlotte's family.

As was customary, the wedding took place in the evening, and, as Charlotte made her way from Buckingham Palace to Carlton House for the ceremony, the size of the crowds who had gathered along the route bore testimony to her popularity. Leopold, too, won the hearts of the people not least for the fact that he opted to wear a British uniform and for the part he was playing in Charlotte's liberation.

After the service, as guests gathered in the dining room for a reception, Charlotte and Leopold left for their honeymoon at Oatlands in Surrey – the recently rebuilt home of her uncle, the Duke of York. It was hardly the romantic idyll of which the young couple might have dreamed, since both felt ill on their wedding night, and the house was so filled with animals that the overwhelming stench increased their nausea[c].

Despite this unpromising start, and the Dutch Ambassador's description of the princess as 'an unruly boy in petticoats'[21], the newly-weds were ecstatic in each other's company, and, within a couple of days, Charlotte was effusively praising her 'perfect lover'. This admiration for her husband would continue to the end of her life, and all who visited Claremont were impressed by what was undoubtedly an unusually happy marriage.

"In this house," wrote Leopold's physician, Christian Stockmar, five months after the wedding, "reign harmony, peace, and love – in short, everything that can promote domestic happiness. My master is the best of all husbands in all the five quarters of the globe; and his wife bears him an amount of love, the greatness of which can only be compared with the English national debt."[22]

Even a year later when the honeymoon was all but forgotten, Stockmar was able to report that, 'The married life of this couple affords a rare picture of love and fidelity, and never fails to impress all spectators who have managed to preserve a particle of feeling.'[23]

"My domestic circumstances," Leopold wrote to a friend, "are the happiest that a man could desire, and my Charlotte is an amiable and glorious little woman. We have a mutual confidence and harmony which it would be very

---

[c] See Chapter 4

difficult for any evil-disposed person to disturb."[24]

Unimpressed by the gaudiness and bickering of the Prince Regent's court, Leopold and Charlotte lived quietly, enjoying simple domestic pleasures rather than frittering away the hours in gossip and small talk at society receptions. Older and more experienced than she was, Leopold was able to curb Charlotte's petulance simply by murmuring her name; and, for her part, Charlotte was happy to heed his advice in all matters relating to politics and the monarchy.

Convinced that, when Charlotte became Queen, she and Leopold would reign as equal partners, the country eagerly anticipated her accession; and. when it was rumoured that she was pregnant, politicians and the people looked forward enthusiastically to the birth of an heir. Sadly, their optimism faded when Charlotte suffered a miscarriage but hope soon revived when it was revealed that she was again expecting a child. This time, even greater care was taken in selecting a suitable physician to ensure that she would receive the best possible attention. To Leopold's regret, his own doctor, Christian Stockmar, declined the role on the grounds that, should complications arise, as a foreigner he would be blamed for any misfortune, but, he agreed to be present in the house at the time of Charlotte's confinement. The Princess herself chose Doctor Matthew Baillie, who also agreed to be on hand to assist whomever she and Leopold chose to engage as chief accoucheur. Initially, Charlotte intended to appoint her father's physician, Sir William Knighton, who had gained an excellent reputation attending aristocratic ladies, but, when she was seven months pregnant, a lady-in-waiting recommended Sir Richard Croft, physician to King George III, and the son-in-law of an eminent obstetrician who had written a highly-praised text book about childbirth.

Three weeks before the baby was due, Croft moved into Claremont House and immediately implemented a regime designed to weaken his patient's constitution in the belief that by so doing she would be prevented from over exerting herself. He ordered several blood-lettings and reduced her diet so dramatically that a typical meal consisted only of a slice of bread and butter washed down with a cup of weak tea. More helpfully, he ordered his royal patient to dispense with her corsets, explaining somewhat uncouthly that:

"A cow does not wear stays, so why should the Princess Charlotte?"[25]

Surprisingly, Charlotte appeared to thrive under this regime, remaining generally in good health and good spirits until seven o'clock in the evening of Monday 3rd November 1817, when she felt the first onset of labour. Croft was immediately summoned and, as he confirmed that all was going well, messages were sent to the various dignitaries who were required to attend a royal birth to authenticate the arrival of an heir. In the event, their haste proved unnecessary, for, throughout that night and the following day, as Charlotte alternately paced the rooms or lay on her bed, there was no evidence of progress in her labour. The tall, thin-faced accoucheur sought to ease her mounting despondency by explaining that the delay could be due to the possibility that she was carrying twins, but, as the hours ticked by and there was still no sign of an imminent birth, he realised that he was facing a terrible dilemma. Usually, if a confinement did not proceed as expected, the accoucheur had two options: the use of forceps, which had fallen out of fashion by the early 19th century, or the performing of a Caesarean section, which almost invariably resulted in the death of the mother.

Although, by the age of fifty-five, the experienced obstetrician was viewed by some as 'pompous, vain and self-opinionated' and by others as 'fidgety and good-natured', he was neither so arrogant nor so confident as to rely solely on his own judgement in a case of such national importance. It would have been helpful, it was later claimed, if either the Queen or the Prince Regent had been present to reassure him, but the former was in Bath and the latter in Suffolk, neither having thought it necessary to travel to Claremont. To make matters worse, none of the ladies of the household had ever had children or even witnessed a birth, and the only female attendant who could be of any support at all was Charlotte's nurse, Mrs Griffiths. Croft turned, therefore, to Baillie who agreed that a third opinion should be sought – that of the renowned botanist and fellow obstetrician, John Sims, who had produced various papers on complications in childbirth.

Late in the evening of Tuesday 4th November, Sims received Croft's message, and immediately began the sixteen-mile journey from London, arriving at two o'clock the following morning. Due to the lateness of the hour and his unwillingness to alarm the Princess, he did not examine the patient but listened to Croft's description of her symptoms and concluded that everything was progressing normally and the best solution was to wait and let nature take its course. At eight o'clock in the morning, although Sims had still not seen Charlotte, the three doctors signed an official bulletin stating that:

> "The Labour of Her Royal Highness the Princess Charlotte is going on very slowly, but we trust, favourably."[26]

On Croft's instructions, however, Charlotte had been denied any sustenance since her labour began on the Monday evening, and so, by Wednesday 5th November, she was utterly exhausted. That afternoon the doctors privately voiced their fears that the baby might already be dead, and when, after fifty uncomfortable hours, Charlotte finally gave birth to a remarkably large boy, their fears were proved to be well-founded. Although they concurred that the child had been dead for some time, all three set about trying to revive him, shaking him vigorously and rubbing his limbs until they were finally obliged to abandon their efforts and break the news to his mother.

On being told that her son was stillborn, Charlotte, weakened by excessive blood-lettings, semi-starvation and the trauma of the past three days, could only murmur that she grieved for England and for her husband. When, however, she realised that she was still bleeding, she summoned the strength to ask Sims if she, too, were dying. Unwilling to answer, he merely urged her to remain calm while he removed the placenta by hand, after which the haemorrhage subsided and he and Mrs Griffiths persuaded her to take a little gruel despite her difficulty in swallowing.

At ten o'clock, convinced that the worst was over, the doctors issued a statement, announcing the birth of a stillborn son and adding that, 'Her Royal Highness is doing extremely well.' The dignitaries returned to London, and Sims and Baillie retired to their beds while, contrary to later reports, Croft remained in attendance with Mrs Griffiths, who helped settle the Princess to sleep.

Accounts differ as to precisely what followed. Some reports claim that Mrs Griffiths removed herself to an adjacent room, while, Leopold, who had not left her side for three days, sat by Charlotte's bed as she slept. Others state that only Mrs Griffiths was present when Charlotte suddenly awoke, crying out that she had a dreadful pain in her chest and head, and difficulty breathing. Although her temperature was soaring, she felt cold, and her agony was so intense that the nurse summoned the doctors, who prescribed wine with opiates to ease her symptoms.

Throughout the entire process, Stockmar had been merely an observer but now Croft was so alarmed that he hurried to his room to wake him and ask him to explain to Leopold the seriousness of Charlotte's condition. Fifteen minutes later, Stockmar received an urgent message from Baillie, imploring him to come at once to the Princess' bedside.

> "She was," Stockmar recorded, "in a state of great suffering and disquiet from spasms in the chest and difficulty in breathing, tossed about incessantly from one side to the other…She stretched out her left hand eagerly to me, and pressed mine twice vehemently. I felt her pulse, which was very quick; the beats now full, now weak, now intermittent."[27]

Over the next fifteen minutes, Stockmar walked in and out of the room until he heard the death rattle from her throat, and she called out to him, 'Stocky! Stocky!' before lying back in exhaustion.

> "…but the rattle continued," he remembered. "She turned more than once over on her face, drew her legs up, and her hands grew cold. At two o'clock in the morning of November 6th, 1817 – about five hours after the birth of the child – she was no more."[28]

While Stockmar strove to comfort a broken-hearted Leopold, a message was sent to the Prince Regent, the Queen and various other members of the family, situated as far apart as Brussels and Hanover.

Immediately, those who could, raced to London, and when, at four in the morning, the Prince Regent arrived at Carlton House, one of his first actions was to write to Croft, thanking him for his skill and attention and concluding that he had no option but to submit to 'the will of heaven.' The following evening, he and his brother, the Duke of York, drank themselves senseless much to the disgust of their attendants.

This reaction contrasted sharply with the genuine grief of the public for whom Charlotte's untimely demise was a double tragedy.

"The death of the Princess Charlotte has filled the whole British Empire with grief, dismay, and mourning. It has effected what few events could produce – a unanimity of feeling; but, alas! it is the sad unanimity produced by an universal participation in the same irreparable calamity...At no period, perhaps, in the whole compass of our history, has the death of the presumptive heir (we may say heirs) to the throne, produced so poignant a sense of grief, so general a feeling of despondency."[29]

The loss of so young a princess was sorrow enough but, to compound the situation, Charlotte had come to symbolise the future stability of the country, and her passing had a profound effect on the mood of the entire populace. Across the land, places of amusement were closed and solemn church bells sounded every day from the moment of her death until her funeral.

"It really was," wrote Henry Brougham, "as though every household throughout Great Britain had lost a favourite child."[30]

In the meantime, unable to share the Prince Regent's resignation to the will of heaven, journalists and members of the public sought answers as to why the accoucheurs had not responded sooner to Charlotte's obvious physical distress; and in medical circles discussions were held about Croft's outlandish treatments and his failure to intervene as the labour progressed. It was generally agreed that Princess Charlotte had died due to the frailty of her constitution, caused by the frequent blood-lettings and her inadequate diet. More suspicious commentators hinted that Croft had poisoned her on the orders of someone in authority – the most obvious culprit being her unpopular father. Parliament was so concerned about the Prince Regent's reputation that initially it rejected calls for a post-mortem and full investigation into Charlotte's final hours for fear that rioting might ensure if the accoucheur, whom George had praised effusively, should be found to be at fault. As, however, the demands for an inquiry persisted, Parliament authorised an autopsy, which, to the annoyance of several medical authorities, reached no definite conclusions about the immediate cause of death.

Pamphleteers and armchair detectives were far from satisfied by the outcome and asked why the contents of the Princess's stomach and other organs had not been analysed, before reaching the conclusion that the process had been intended to protect the credibility of the doctors rather than to discover the truth about what had actually happened. Suspicions increased when, contrary to her husband's wishes, Charlotte's body was embalmed by Sir Everard Home and two assistants, who placed her internal organs in an urn, while an armed guard was placed around the Pall Mall premises of the undertakers, Messrs. France and Banting, to prevent the grieving public from seeing her body.

Following the embalming, Charlotte's coffin and that of her stillborn child were taken with due ceremony to Claremont and placed in a bedroom until the morning of the funeral when they were conveyed in a solemn procession to Windsor Castle. The service took place at eight o'clock in the evening of Tuesday 18th November, a dreary occasion made all the more gloomy by the darkness of the season and the black draperies covering much of the naïve and choir. Noticeably absent from the funeral and the interment in the Royal Vault was the Princess's father, who, according to some reports, was too overcome with grief to attend, while others explained his absence as being due to an old superstition that warned that kings – or regents – must avoid any proximity to the dead.

The country gradually came to terms with the loss but for Croft the weight of self-condemnation and public censure was too much to bear. For three months, unable to dismiss the thought that he was responsible for the tragedy, he lost all confidence in his own ability and became increasingly despondent until, while attending another patient in February 1818, he retired from the room, went downstairs and blew out his brains with a pistol.

Chapter 4 – 'She Will Yet be Queen of England'

George III– Queen Victoria's grandfather; King of the United Kingdom

Queen Charlotte – Queen Victoria's grandmother; wife of George III; Queen of the United Kingdom

George – Prince of Wales; Prince Regent; King George IV; Queen Victoria's paternal uncle

Caroline of Brunswick – Wife of George IV; Princess of Wales; Queen of the United Kingdom

Frederick – Duke of York; son of George III; Queen Victoria's paternal uncle

Frederica – Princess of Prussia; Duchess of York; wife of Frederick, Duke of York

William – Duke of Clarence; later King William IV; son of George III; Queen Victoria's paternal uncle

Adelaide – Princess of Saxe-Meiningen; Duchess of Clarence; later Queen Adelaide; wife of William IV

Edward – Duke of Kent; son of George III; Queen Victoria's father

Victoria – Princess of Saxe-Coburg Saalfeld; sister of Leopold of Saxe-Coburg Saalfeld; Duchess of Kent; wife of Edward, Duke of Kent; Queen Victoria's mother

Ernest Augustus – Duke of Cumberland; son of George III; Queen Victoria's paternal uncle

Frederica –Duchess of Mecklenburg-Strelitz; Duchess of Cumberland; wife of Ernest Augustus of Cumberland

Augustus – Duke of Sussex; son of George III; Queen Victoria's paternal uncle

Adolphus – Duke of Cambridge; son of George III; Queen Victoria's paternal uncle

Feodora – Princess of Leiningen; Queen Victoria's half-sister

In view of the fact that King George III had no fewer than fifteen children, it was remarkable Charlotte's death provoked such anxiety about the succession. Of the fifteen, however, the two youngest sons, Octavius and Alfred, had died before their fifth birthdays; and the youngest daughter, Amelia, had died a spinster in 1810 at the age of twenty-seven. Two other daughters, Augusta and Sophia, also remained single; and their three married sisters had produced no surviving children.

At the time of Charlotte's demise not one of her father's six surviving brothers had produced a legitimate heir, and, even in the highly unlikely event that the Prince Regent should effect a reconciliation with his wife, she was already in her fifty-first year, beyond the age of bearing a child.

Next in line to the throne was Frederick, Duke of York, who, in 1791, had married Frederica of Prussia – the somewhat eccentric eldest daughter of King Frederick William II. In the days following their wedding, journalists optimistically reported that this was a genuine love-match but, within three years, the couple had separated and the increasingly unconventional Frederica had established her own household at Oatlands Park in Surrey, which she filled with eighteen dogs and numerous flocks of birds. The couple had no children, and, while it was rumoured that Frederica, who liked to stay up all night being read to, found the prospect of sleeping with her husband repugnant, Frederick told one of his mistresses that he would rather slit his own throat than be compelled to live with his wife at Oatlands. Although separated, the couple never obtained a divorce but their marriage officially ended in 1827 when Frederick died of dropsy.

The next eldest brother, William, Duke of Clarence, had fathered no fewer than ten children during his twenty-year liaison with one of the most famous actresses of the age, Dorothea Jordan. The 'Fitzclarences' were openly acknowledged as William's offspring but, although they were largely raised at court, their illegitimacy barred them from the succession.

The King's fourth son, Edward, Duke of Kent, also had a long-term mistress – Julie St. Laurent, the charming and intelligent wife of a French baron, whom he had first met in Geneva. Following the baron's death, Julie and Edward lived openly together and it was widely rumoured that they had secretly married in a Roman Catholic ceremony. In his letters to his brothers, friends and ministers, Edward frequently added messages from Julie, suggesting that she was largely accepted in his social circle, as she travelled with him to his various postings, including an extended sojourn in Canada where he worked to promote free education, earning the gratitude of the Canadians, who renamed St John's Island in his honour.

As his elder brothers showed little inclination to find suitable brides, the fifth son, Ernest Augustus, Duke of Cumberland, appeared to be the most obvious candidate to father a legitimate heir. In 1815, he had married his cousin, Princess Frederica of Mecklenburg-Strelitz, but within three years of the wedding she had given birth to two still born daughters but had yet to produce a surviving child.

In 1793, the sixth son, Augustus, Duke of Sussex, had secretly married the Earl of Dunmore's daughter, Lady Augusta Murray, who bore him two children – a daughter and a son. Since, however, he had not obtained the King's permission to marry, the union contravened the Royal Marriages Act and was therefore deemed invalid and was officially annulled in 1794. The couple continued their relationship for a further seven years, after which Augustus contented himself with mistresses until 1830 when, again in contravention of the Royal Marriages Act, he married Lady Celia Underwood, who would later be created Duchess of Inverness by Queen Victoria.

The youngest of George III's surviving sons, Adolphus, Duke of Cambridge, was a twenty-four-year-old bachelor at the time of his niece's death, so it remained to be seen whether he, too, would settle with a mistress, or would contract a legal marriage and produce an heir to the throne.

Charlotte's death had significantly altered the position of her uncles, several of whom realised that the situation could work to their advantage as any one of them could produce the long-for heir. Moreover, since most had incurred substantial debts, the prospect of an increased annuity from Parliament was too great a temptation to resist. With unseemly haste, they abandoned their long-term mistresses and embarked on a frantic race to find appropriate brides.

Even before Charlotte's death, the Duke of Clarence's financial straits had placed such a strain on his relationship with Dorothea Jordan that his passion for the actress had waned. His efforts to woo more respectable women had been largely unsuccessful but now, at the age of fifty-two, he sent his younger brother, the Duke of Cambridge, on a fruitless quest through the German courts in search of a fecund princess who might be willing to accept his marriage proposal. In the meantime, his mother suggested that Princess Adelaide, the twenty-five-year-old daughter of the late Duke George of Saxe-Meiningen, was available, so, although he had only met her on one previous occasion, he forwarded a proposal, which she immediately accepted and prepared to travel to England for a summer wedding.

William, though, was quickly disillusioned when he learned that Parliament was not prepared to grant him a higher annuity than that of his younger brothers and so marriage would be less profitable than he had imagined. For a while, he ungallantly left his fiancée in some doubt as to whether the wedding would ever take place, while Parliament, weary of bailing out impoverished princes, refused to yield to his threat to break off his engagement. When his spokesman informed the House of Lords of a figure that would be more pleasing to him, a certain Lord King jumped to his feet to announce that:

> "The question is not what it might please the Duke of Clarence to take, but what it might please the people to give him!"[31]

Accepting defeat, William agreed to be married as planned but the wrangling had so increased his unpopularity that the ministers refused to prepare a reception for Adelaide's arrival in England. No cheering crowds gathered to welcome her to the country and, when she reached London's Grillon Hotel, she discovered that neither her fiancé nor any member of his family was waiting to receive her. Instead she was forced to rely solely on the kindness of the hotel's proprietor until the Prince Regent deigned to pay her a visit later that evening; but, when William eventually made an appearance, she displayed no signs of disgruntlement, and the couple appeared to strike up an immediate rapport.

On 11th July – to save expense – a double wedding ceremony was held in the old Kew Palace, as William and Adelaide were married alongside his younger brother, fifty-year-old Edward, Duke of Kent, and a thirty-one-year-old widow, Victoria of Saxe-Coburg-Saalfeld.

In spite of their age difference and William's reputation as a ladies' man, the marriage was to prove remarkably happy. Adelaide cleverly organised her husband's accounts and made his home so comfortable that he no longer felt the need to seek romantic diversions elsewhere. Due to the cost of living in England, soon after the wedding the couple moved to Hanover where life was considerably cheaper, and their obvious happiness and mutual affection gave rise to the hope that it would not be long before they secured the succession. Sadly, though, in March 1819, Adelaide contracted pleurisy and gave birth to a premature daughter who survived for only a few hours. When she was discovered to be pregnant for a second time, William decided that the child should be born in England, but the journey proved too arduous for Adelaide, who miscarried in Calais just six months after the death of her baby daughter. A year later, there was cause for optimism when, on December 10th, a second daughter, Elizabeth, was born. Mindful of the loss of her elder siblings, Elizabeth's parents took every precaution to protect their baby and to ensure that she would be raised in a healthy and happy environment but, in spite of their efforts, she contracted a gastro-intestinal disorder and died at the age of only three months in March 1821.

Although throughout the next decade there were regular reports that Adelaide was pregnant again, William was quick to dismiss the rumours and resigned himself to the fact that they would never have children. It would, therefore, fall to one of his brothers to father a future monarch, and already, by the time of little Elizabeth's death, three healthy babies had taken their place in the line of succession.

George III's fourth son, Edward, Duke of Kent, had enjoyed a rather chequered military and political career. His successes in Canada, and his skill and courage as a military commander in the West Indies had been tarnished by the fact that he had also provoked a mutiny by his harsh treatment of the troops while he served as Governor of Gibraltar. Due to his penchant for gambling, he had accrued so many debts that by 1818 he, like his elder brothers, saw a respectable marriage as the only solution to his financial crisis. His motives were not entirely selfish for, after more than a quarter of a century with his beloved mistress, Julie St Laurent, he had begun to contemplate his own mortality and was distressed by the thought that, in the event of his death, Julie would be left with no substantial inheritance or income. Privately, he began to consider the prospect of marrying any one of several European princesses, and Charlotte's death added greater urgency to his quest.

Following his niece's funeral, he repaired to Claremont to comfort the grieving widower, Leopold, who reintroduced him to his sister, a thirty-one-year old widow, Victoria of Leiningen (née Saxe-Coburg Saalfeld), whom he had met briefly for the first time two years earlier. Pretty and intelligent, Victoria's many qualities made a deep impression on the Duke, who was told that since the death of her husband, Prince Karl of Leiningen, she had been diligently raising her daughter, Feodora, and skilfully carrying out her duties as Regent for her young son, Karl.

Baron Stockmar, Leopold's mentor and physician, knew Victoria well and rated her very highly, not only as his master's sister but as a person in her own right.

"She was of middle height," he recorded, "stout and full, yet of good build, with beautiful brown hair and eyes, and, in addition, of remarkable youthful freshness; naturally cheerful and friendly; altogether a lovely and charming appearance. She was also fond of fine clothes, dressing well and tastefully. Nature had endowed her with warm feelings, and her natural dispositions were altogether on the side of truth, love, and friendship; of unselfishness, compassion, nay even magnanimity itself."[32]

In early 1818, with Leopold's encouragement, Edward visited Victoria at her home in Amorbach, Bavaria, and, within days of his arrival, he proposed and was duly accepted. Broken-hearted Julie resigned herself to the inevitable and, after accepting a reasonable pension, withdrew to a convent in Paris, emerging some years later to marry an Italian nobleman.

The betrothal was viewed so favourably by the British Parliament that when Edward asked for £2000 per annum for his bride's 'pin money' in addition to his own increased income, his request met with few objections. This increase, however, barely resolved his pecuniary difficulties and, when the couple were married in England in the joint ceremony with the Clarences, Edward was obliged to use the funds granted to him for the liquidation of his debts to meet the cost of the far from lavish celebrations.

The Kents' married life began in such reduced circumstances that, after a brief honeymoon at Claremont, they returned to Amorbach where all who met them commented on their obvious happiness and mutual affection. When, however, Victoria was discovered to be pregnant, Edward recalled a gypsy prophecy that he would one day father a great monarch, and decided that they must return to England for the birth.

> "The interesting situation of the Duchess causes me hourly anxiety," he wrote to a friend, "and you, who so well know my views and feelings, can well appreciate how eagerly desirous I am to hasten our departure for Old England...My wish is that [the birth] may take place on the 3rd of June, as that is the birthday of my revered father, and that the child, too, like him, may be Briton-born."[33]

Rooms were prepared for couple in Kensington Palace and, partly to allay the cost of a coachman and partly due to his desire to protect his wife and unborn child, Edward insisted on driving the coach for most of the overland journey. The couple arrived safely in London in mid-April 1819, and five weeks later – ten days sooner than Edward had hoped – a healthy baby girl was born. The following month, she was christened in the Cupola Room of Kensington Palace, where, after much hesitation and interference from the Prince Regent, she was given the names Alexandrina Victoria, although throughout her early childhood she would be known simply as 'Drina', and later 'Victoria'.

Edward's love for his daughter was matched only by his pride at the prospect of the fulfilment of the gypsy's prophecy.

"Look at her well!" he boldly announced. "She will yet be Queen of England."[34]

Few, at the time, believed his assertion since the Duchess of Clarence could yet bear a child, and the baby Victoria was only fourth in line to the throne. Nonetheless, Edward's confidence irked his brothers, particularly the Duke of Cumberland, whose own son, born just three days after Victoria, came lower in the line of succession than a 'mere girl'.

"My little girl," wrote the Duke of Kent, "...[is] strong and healthy; *too healthy,* I fear, for some members of my family, by whom she is regarded as an intruder."[35]

Unfortunately, as his daughter thrived, Edward's health was about to take a sudden turn for the worse, leaving him little time to enjoy the new-found pleasures of fatherhood. In the winter of 1819-1820, he took his small family to Sidmouth in Devon, where the cost of living was cheaper than in London, and where the sea air was more conducive to wellbeing than was the smog of the capital. The weather was particularly damp and inclement that winter, and, after walking along the beach in the rain, Edward contracted a fatal pneumonia, dying on 23rd January 1820.

His wife, the Duchess of Kent was left in a particularly unenviable position, for not only had she lost a devoted husband but she now found herself a stranger in a foreign land with an eight-month-old baby to raise single-handedly. Her brothers-in-law were far from supportive and, when King George III died a few days after her husband, the former Prince Regent – now King George IV – treated her with such disdain that it was widely believed that she would return to Amorbach or her native Coburg. The new King frequently threatened to take her daughter from her, and, to compound her problems, the Duke had left her with a mass of debts and no visible means of repaying them.

In view of baby Victoria's position in the line of succession, however, the Duchess decided to remain in England, occupying the few rooms which the new King had reluctantly allotted to her in Kensington Palace, and relying heavily on her brother, Prince Leopold, for financial assistance. Friendless and desperate, she turned for help to her late husband's equerry, John Conroy – an ambitious and self-seeking man, who instantly took charge of the household and of Victoria's upbringing.

Assuming that the little princess would accede to the throne before she reached her majority, Conroy anticipated the necessity of a regency and, since the Duchess of Kent was the most likely candidate for the role of regent, he set out to control both mother and daughter in the hope that, by ruling them, he would in effect rule the country. In order to ensure Victoria's complete subservience, he isolated her from her peers and from her late father's family, instituting what was known as the 'Kensington System' to prevent her from being swayed by any outside influence. With only her dogs and dolls for company, every aspect of her life was monitored and controlled to the point where she was not permitted to ascend or descend a staircase unattended and, even into her nineteenth year, she slept in her mother's bedroom. For a while, she found solace in the company of her beloved stepsister, Feodora, who was fifteen years her senior and more like a kindly aunt than a playmate, but, before Victoria's ninth birthday, she had departed for Germany to marry a Prince of Hohenlohe-Langenburg.

Unsurprisingly, Victoria relished any opportunity to spend time with children of her own age, which made visits from her extended family, events to be cherished. Throughout her lonely and repressed childhood, therefore, she developed a deep and lasting affection for her cousins, whom she viewed as surrogate siblings to whom she would remain devoted to the end of her life.

Chapter 5 – 'My Poor Blind Cousin'

George IV – Prince Regent, then King of the United Kingdom; Queen Victoria's paternal uncle.

Ernest Augustus – Duke of Cumberland; Queen Victoria's paternal uncle

William – Duke of Clarence, later King William IV; Queen Victoria's paternal uncle

Frederica – Princess of Mecklenburg-Strelitz; Duchess of Cumberland; wife of Ernest Augustus

Queen Charlotte – Wife of King George III; Queen Victoria's paternal grandmother

Adolphus – Duke of Cambridge; Queen Victoria's paternal uncle

George of Cumberland – Son of Ernest Augustus; Queen Victoria's cousin

George of Cambridge – Son of Adolphis; Queen Victoria's cousin

With the exception, perhaps, of King George IV, none of Victoria's uncles was as unpopular as her father's younger brother, Ernest Augustus, Duke of Cumberland. Coarse in conversation, battle-scarred and blind in one eye, Ernest's rough behaviour and unprepossessing features gave him the appearance of a stereotypical villain. 'A tall, powerful man with a hideous face,' as one German visitor observed, his expressions often reflected a cruel streak in his nature, which, according to the Duke of Wellington, led him to take pleasure in creating discord and to find enjoyment in other people's discomfort.

"Ernest is not a bad fellow," said his brother, the Duke of Clarence, "but if you have a corn he's sure to tread upon it.'[36]

By the mid-1820s, he had been accused of a myriad of crimes, ranging from fraud and bribery to incest, rape and murder. The wives of several prominent politicians claimed to have been victims of his unwelcome advances, and he was even said to have fathered a child by his own younger sister, Sophia. So unpopular was he that when, in the spring of 1810, he fell victim to a violent attack from his valet, rumours abounded that his assailant had either been acting in self-defence or was driven to such drastic measures by his master's cruelty.

The attacker, Joseph Sellis, had crept into the Duke's room while he slept, and struck him so fiercely with a sabre that, had the blade not caught on the bed-hangings, he almost certainly would have been killed. Sellis continued to strike him to the point where, according to his surgeon, his 'scalp and skull [were] completely divided, so that the pulsation of the arteries of the brain were distinguished.'

Public sympathy, however, centred on the assailant who, having fled the scene, was later found dead in his own apartment, having slit his throat with a razor. Various explanations were put forward for Sellis' behaviour, some claiming that the Duke had been having an affair with the valet himself or his page, and he had attacked the former when he threatened him with blackmail. Others suggested that Sellis had lost his reason on discovering the Duke in bed with his wife, while the less salacious Colonel Willis suspected that he had been provoked by 'the taunts and sarcasms that the Duke was constantly, in his violent coarse manner, lavishing on Sellis' religion, who was Catholic.'[37]

The defamatory tales persisted for over two decades but it was not until 1832, when a pamphleteer named Joseph Phillips openly accused him of murder, that Ernest responded by suing Phillips for libel. The pamphleteer was found guilty as charged and sentenced to six months imprisonment but,

"…still, in the face of all this, such were the prejudices of the people, such their detestation of the duke, that, though the verdict in the libel case was so distinctly in his favour, the feeling, I believe, of nine-tenths of the lower class and of the great majority of His Royal Highness's political enemies was that of the man in the old adage who 'complied against his will,' they, as he, were 'of the same opinion still.'"[38]

Ernest had acquired numerous enemies in every area of his life. Many politicians despised him for his strong opposition to Catholic emancipation, his corruption, and his outspokenness, which had prompted the Duke of Wellington's temporary withdrawal from politics. Scandal followed scandal, and in 1813, he was forced into temporary exile after illegally trying to influence the outcome of the Weymouth election. His brief banishment from Britain, however, proved to be more of a blessing than a punishment, for it was not only less expensive to live on the Continent, but also, while staying in Germany, he met and fell in love with his twice-married cousin, Frederica of Mecklenburg-Strelitz – 'a lady of whose gallantries and passions Berlin had many piquant stories to tell.'[39]

Frederica's reputation was hardly any more salubrious than that of her suitor. When she was only eighteen years old, her first husband had died of diphtheria and, soon afterwards, she accepted a proposal from Ernest's younger brother, Adolphus, Duke of Cambridge. Within weeks of the betrothal, however, she began an affair with a Prussian officer, Prince Frederick William of Solms-Braunfels, who, on discovering that she was pregnant, offered to marry her. Jilting her English fiancé, she accepted Prince Frederick William's proposal before giving birth to a daughter who survived for only eight months. The couple went to have seven more children, three of whom did not survive infancy, but relations between them rapidly deteriorated. When, due to ill health exacerbated by excessive drinking, Prince Frederick William lost his commission and his income, his family urged Frederica to seek a divorce. Initially, she refused to do so until Ernest Augustus arrived in Berlin, and, despite his unattractive appearance, she welcomed his amorous advances. Her complaisant husband was willing to grant her a divorce but when he died unexpectedly before arrangements had been finalised, it was widely and erroneously rumoured that she had deliberately poisoned him in order to marry Ernest.

The wedding took place in Berlin on May 29th 1815, and, in spite of the gossip, Ernest's elder brothers welcomed Frederica into the family. His sisters, still smarting from her treatment of Adolphus, were far less accommodating; and Queen Charlotte so disliked her new daughter-in-law that she allowed a letter to be leaked to the press, stating that Frederica should never be allowed to set foot in England. When Ernest ignored his mother's protestations, and announced that he and his bride would travel to London for a second ceremony in Kew Palace, the Queen spoke openly of her disdain for Frederica and suggested that the true reason for Ernest's return was to persuade the Prince Regent to allow him to replace his brother, the Duke of Cambridge as Governor of Hanover.

In response to the Queen's slanders, Frederica's brother, the young Duke of Mecklenburg-Strelitz, sent her a letter, the tone of which was, she claimed, so insulting that she refused to divulge its contents to anyone.

> "The notion among this worthy family seems to be," wrote Henry Brougham, "that the youth never would have written such a letter as it must

have been, had he not been backed by the Duke of Cumberland, and that the letter must have been sure of the prince's support; so this has put oil on the flame."[40]

The Queen's antipathy towards Frederica intensified as the years went by, and when she fell ill in June 1818, it was claimed that her illness was caused by:

> "...information which she received of the Duchesses of Cumberland and Cambridge[d] having met and embraced. This meeting took place as if by accident, but really by appointment, in Kew Gardens; and the Duke of Cambridge himself informed the Queen of it. She was in such a rage that the spasm was brought on, and she was very near dying."[41e]

Having won the support of King George IV, however, Ernest remained in England for three years, living in Kew and St. James' Palace from where he continued to irk many of his relations. Even later, when he had settled in Germany, his frequent visits to London proved an unwelcome inconvenience to his family, as when his elder brother and erstwhile supporter, the Duke of Clarence, succeeded as King William IV, he found Ernest's behaviour so ungracious and disruptive that he confessed to having 'a very bad opinion of the Duke of Cumberland and wished that he would live out of the country.'[42]

Surprisingly, though, in view of his reputation, Ernest was a loving husband and a devoted father to the children of Frederica's previous marriages[f]. His

---

[d] See Chapter 6

[e] Queen Charlotte recovered from this illness but died five months later, by which time her husband, George III's condition had deteriorated to the point where he was completely unaware that she had passed on.

domestic joy was complete when, following the birth of a stillborn daughter, a son was born on 27th May 1819. Six weeks later, the baby was christened George in a ceremony presided over by Jane Austen's elder brother, Henry – a clergyman attached to the British Embassy in Berlin.

According to journalists, George was 'a fine healthy looking boy' but his childhood was soon to be marred by an illness which left him blind in one eye – a condition that might have been inherited from his father. A few years later, his problems were severely exacerbated due to an accident that occurred while he was playing with his cousin, George of Cambridge[g]. Accounts vary as to exactly what happened – some stating he was throwing a heavy purse into the air when the tassel caught his 'good' eye; others suggesting that he was struck by a curtain weight or a watch chain – but all concur that the resulting damage to his iris impaired his vision so severely that surgery was deemed necessary. Unfortunately, during the operation, the surgeon's hand slipped, severing the optic nerve and leaving him completely and permanently blind. For his father's more superstitious critics, George's affliction confirmed an old rumour that the mother of the valet, Sellis, had accused Ernest Augustus of murdering her son and, as he had escaped justice, she had put a curse upon his descendants.

Although his blindness marred his otherwise handsome appearance, George's parents refused to treat him as an invalid and insisted that he should learn to adapt to his disability. A footman stood behind him at dinner to cut his food, and an attendant was always on

---

[f] Frederica's eldest son, Frederick, was the same Prince Frederick of Prussia with whom Princess Charlotte had been in love shortly before her marriage to Prince Leopold.
[g] See Chapter 6

hand to act as his guide, but his education continued as before, the only alteration being that rather than reading his lessons himself, his tutor now read them to him. His father paid a good deal of attention to the appointment of his attendants, selecting a 'spooney-looking cove in barnacles' for a German master, whose accent, combined with that of his Cockney nursery maid left George with a rather strange manner of speaking. One morning, while a member of the household was fishing, George passed by and asked politely:

"Gut morning, my dears; how goes it to you? 'Ave you den alridy catched vun trout?"[43]

Remarkably, in spite of his blindness, George continued his riding lessons and became a competent horseman, whose fearlessness in the saddle was often disconcerting for his companions. When, while visiting England in 1853, for example, he accompanied his cousin, Victoria, to a military review, she reported that her enjoyment of the event was spoiled:

"...by the nervousness which I was in at having my poor blind cousin on horseback next to me. It is a sad sight, and one which keeps me in a constant state of anxiety, as one is afraid of saying or doing anything which may pain or distress him, or of his meeting with any accident."[44]

Nonetheless, she had to concede that her fears were largely unfounded, since:

"...he manages it wonderfully well, hardly ever makes a mistake, and manages so well at dinner. He is very cheerful, kind, and civil, and would be very good looking if it were not for his poor eyes. He likes to go everywhere and do everything like anybody else, and speaks of things as if he saw them."[45]

What George lacked in one sense, he compensated for in another, developing such a highly-tuned ear that music became his greatest passion. His parents encouraged his interest, appointing the renowned pianist, Louise Dulcken – who also taught Queen Victoria – to teach him the piano; and he went on to compose many of his own pieces, including chorales, oratorios and a complete symphony. Later, he would write a book – *Ideas and Reflections on the Properties of Music* – in which he described the depths of his feeling for the subject.

> "With ardent love," he wrote, "I have striven from early youth to make music my own. It has become to me a companion and comforter throughout life; it has become more and more invaluable to me. The more I learned to comprehend and appreciate its boundless exuberance of ideas...the more intimately its poetry was woven into my whole being."[46]

His ambitious father, meanwhile, never lost sight of the fact that, in the event of Victoria's death, George stood to inherit the British throne, and, in 1826, he asked his brother, King George IV, to persuade Parliament to increase his annuity to provide for his seven-year-old son's education. The King, drawing attention to the requirements of both George and Victoria, duly contacted the Chancellor of the Exchequer, telling him to press the case, since both children had 'attained an age at which it is proper that adequate provision should be made for their honourable support and education.'[47] Initially, the House of Commons was divided on the matter. Several ministers argued that Ernest was not to be trusted and might well use the money to 'pay debts contracted abroad, or to pay annuities which he had granted at home.'[48] The motion was, therefore, defeated by a majority of fifty-eight votes, but over the next few days further arguments ensued until it was eventually agreed that the stipend would be increased on condition that George should live in England. For the next few years, therefore, he divided his time between London and Hanover, endearing himself to the British even more than he had to the Hanoverians. Lady Lyttelton, who had initially thought that he had 'a conceited and disagreeable look', soon altered her opinion, considering him:

> "...the most interesting creature I ever saw, never did I exert more not to show what I felt at our first meeting, for to see that lovely creature led about is not to be told – his good humour, his sweet way of expressing himself, his gratitude for every kindness is not to be expressed – but he certainly sees nothing, such a real dear as he is, it is enough to break one's heart."[49]

In England, as a grandson of King George III, he was viewed as an English prince, but George himself was quick to dispel this idea, 'No, I am German.'

His allegiance to Germany did not prevent British journalists from speculating about his future career, and, before he was ten years old, reports appeared in the press that he was about to be betrothed to his cousin, Princess Victoria. While *The Times* protested against the idea of arranged marriages of children, the rumours spread across Europe, and when one London journalist reported that Victoria had been promised to a French prince, his counterparts in Paris stated that this could not be true since she was already affianced to George of Cumberland.

Ernest Augustus was quick to give credence to the story and to instil in his son an awareness that only Victoria stood between him and the throne. In response

George teased his cousin mercilessly, reminding her of the fate of Marie Antoinette and Mary, Queen of Scots; and with, perhaps, a hint of envy, he mocked her failure to grasp certain lessons with the retort, 'A pretty sort of Queen you will make!'[50]

Such jibes reduced the young princess to tears but her affection for her 'poor blind cousin' never waned. She had, though, little inclination to marry him, and their meetings became increasingly infrequent due to her mother's dislike of his father and the British court in general. Aware of the distance between them, journalists soon began to report that Victoria had passed over George of Cumberland in favour of another Cousin George – the only son of her uncle, Adolphus, Duke of Cambridge.

Chapter 6 – 'God Knows How Attached I Am To This Country'

Adolphus – Duke of Cambridge; Queen Victoria's paternal uncle

Augusta of Hesse-Kassel – Duchess of Cambridge; wife of Adolphus

> Children of Adolphus and Augusta (Queen Victoria's Cambridge cousins):
> George
> Augusta
> Mary Adelaide

'Tall and finely formed, with a fair complexion and regular features,'[51] Adolphus, Duke of Cambridge, had a distinguished military and civil career, inspiring such loyalty and respect that in 1816 his brother, then the Prince Regent, appointed him as the Viceroy of Hanover[h]. His diligence and diplomacy combined with his courage in battle soon earned him the affection and admiration of the Hanoverians; and in England, too, he was viewed as morally and intellectually superior to his brothers.

> "His manners and address are most prepossessing," wrote Sir James Biddell. "He inspires at first sight confidence and respect, which at every successive interview are increased. To judge of him by the common rules of good breeding and elegance, he fails in none.

[h] Since the Congress of Vienna in 1814, Hanover had been declared an independent Kingdom, ruled by the Head of the House of Guelph, who, at that time, happened to be Adolphus' father, King George III of Great Britain.

His air is fine and manly: he is perfectly well formed, and his countenance, especially when lighted up by a smile, is most pleasing."[52]

It was thanks to his reliability and familiarity with the German courts, that he had been asked to scour the Continent in search of a bride for his brother, the Duke of Clarence. Although he was unsuccessful in this endeavour, it was not for want of suggesting suitable candidates, including Augusta, a daughter of the Landgrave of Hesse-Kassel. No sooner had he made Augusta's acquaintance than he wrote to his brother extolling her many qualities in such effusive language that the amused Duke of Clarence suggested that, since he found her so attractive, he ought to marry her himself. Wasting no time, Adolphus proposed and, when Augusta – twenty-two years his junior – accepted him, he could hardly contain his joy. He was, he wrote, the happiest man on the globe, since:

> "...Every hour I feel that my esteem and attachment for my bride increases and she is really everything both as to heart, mind and Person that I could wish."[53]

The wedding took place in Kassel on 7th May 1818, and, as was the custom, a second ceremony was held in London some weeks later. Unlike the Duchess of Cumberland, Augusta – 'an agreeable woman, clever and well informed' whose conversation was 'more intelligent than is usual'[54] – received a warm welcome from her mother-in-law, Queen Charlotte, and the British people. So eager were the crowds to see her that, when she walked in the park, so many people pressed around her that she almost fainted in fear.

Following a brief honeymoon in England, Adolphus resumed his duties in Hanover, where he and Augusta divided their time between the Palace of Herrenhausen and Cambridge House. On March 26th

1819, Augusta gave birth to a son – yet another George – who, as the first legitimate grandson of George III, was viewed as a likely successor to the King. His moment of glory was remarkably brief, for Victoria's birth, just two days after his christening, reduced his status, and within a week he had descended still further down the line of succession thanks to the arrival of his cousin and namesake, George of Cumberland.

The son of a remarkably happy marriage, George enjoyed an idyllic childhood, living in the luxury provided by Adolphus' viceregal salary of £27,000 per year. In July 1822, a sister, Augusta, was born, and, as their parents insisted on having their children with them as often as possible, the family was often seen strolling happily along the avenue in front of their home, mixing freely with the local people. Outdoor activities were many and varied, as the children enjoyed sledging in the winter and boating in the spring; and, for George there were the usual hunting expeditions so beloved by the upper classes of the day. Indoor entertainments were equally thrilling for little George and Augusta as their parents, renowned patrons of the arts, encouraged them to develop their musical and artistic abilities; and to participate in plays and tableaux vivants. Augusta, according to one member of the audience, 'acted her part capitally' and performed 'with an air and a grace which one seldom sees in so young a child.'[55] While George also enjoyed acting, his greatest passion was drawing, and, as his parents often took him to exhibitions, he not only acquired and an appreciation of the works of notable artists of the day, but also a desire to foster his own innate talent. So successful was he in this endeavour that his cousin, Victoria, was delighted when he presented her with a book of his drawings for her birthday.

This happy domesticity was not, however, without its dramatic and anxious moments, as when George contracted a potentially fatal strain of scarlet fever. He appeared to be over the worst when his condition suddenly deteriorated, and his doctors, fearing he was dying, urgently sent a message to his father who was at dinner. Rising at once from the table with his glass of Steinberg wine in his hand, the Duke flew to his son's bedside and forced him to drink. George immediately began to revive and, although he remained frail for several months, he eventually made such a complete recovery that, from then onwards, his birthday was toasted each year with a glass of the life-saving Steinberg.

This, though, was not George's only, nor his most terrifying, brush with death. One morning, to his horror he awoke to find one of his assistant tutors, Mr Welsh, kneeling by his bed crying out that during the night a voice had commanded him to kill his royal pupil. Fortunately, a valet heard the commotion and succeeded in restraining Welsh, who was subsequently declared insane and sent to a 'lunatic asylum'.

Happily, Welsh's replacement, John Ryle Wood, was of a far more balanced character and struck up such a rapport with his pupil that, when the eleven-year-old prince was sent to continue his education in England, the Duke asked the tutor to accompany him.

The timing of the move was significant for, just two months earlier, George IV had died and the new King William IV and the childless Queen Adelaide were eager to welcome their nephew into their home and to oversee his upbringing. Knowing that the kindly Queen would care for her son, brought small consolation to George's distraught mother, who found the prospect of being separated from her 'angel boy' so unbearable that she decided in advance to make their goodbyes as brief as possible. As George set out for England, she accompanied him only as far as Mayence, leaving him to continue the journey with his father and Wood. Hardly had she left him, though, than she began the first of her daily letters to him, assuring him of her love and her longing to see him again.

> "Be always very open and confiding towards the Queen," she urged. "Tell her everything, and all that you wish, very openly and frankly. With the King be respectful but not shy and nervous, which makes you appear so quiet and formal. When you write to me, do so quite alone, as your heart dictates…God protect you!"[56]

George, too, felt the pain of separation from his family, making every reunion traumatic due to the prospect of another parting. Thanks, though, to the generosity of the King and Queen, he quickly adapted to life in England, travelling with the court between London and Brighton, and seldom finding himself short of playmates. Groups of Eton schoolboys were invited to join his games, as were the children of the surgeon, Sir Everard Home, but his most regular companion was his cousin and namesake, George of Cumberland. Growing up together in Hanover, the two boys had become good friends and had first travelled to England together at the age of two, to be presented to their uncle, George IV. Both loved the rough and tumble of boisterous games, which left them so dirty and ragged that Lady Lyttelton fondly described them as the 'two urchin princes'[57]. There were occasional meetings, too, with Cousin Victoria; and, when King William arranged a ball for her fourteenth birthday, and George was chosen to lead her into the ballroom, rumours immediately circulated about their imminent betrothal.

Apart from providing him with enjoyable recreations, the King and Queen paid careful attention to George's education. Wood reported that he chattered too much during his lessons and, although he continued to make good progress in French and art, he had a lackadaisical attitude towards Latin and Greek. Rather than resenting such criticism, George chastised himself mercilessly, filling his diaries with references to his shortcomings, followed by firm resolutions to improve his behaviour.

Surprisingly, in view of his later career, the greatest hurdle he sought to overcome was his timidity while riding and particularly when facing jumps. This, said Wood, caused his parents much anxiety, to which George insolently retorted, 'That is my look out,' resulting in his being banished to his room for breakfast. When, though, he saw a little girl cantering on one of the Queen's large horses, he was ashamed to see that she rode so fearlessly while he was plagued by nerves, and, scolding himself for his cowardice, resolved to overcome his fears. Through sheer determination, he became a competent horseman and, while still a child, he mastered driving a four-in-hand.

Notwithstanding his self-deprecation and scruples, he was a cheerful and charming boy, whom visitors described as 'very polite, extremely manly, civil and obliging.'[58] All in all, it was widely agreed that:

> "...he does so well in England that those that love him must own the King and Queen's education is perfect for him."[59]

His love of England did not prevent occasional bouts of homesickness or dim his happiness at being reunited with his family. He was deeply grateful for his mother's determination to brave regular attacks of seasickness in order to visit him; and he appreciated the efforts to which she went to arrange parties to welcome him home for the holidays.

One particularly memorable holiday occurred in the winter of 1833-1834, when for the first time he met his new baby sister, Mary Adelaide, who had been born in November. In January, George's tutor christened the 'beautiful baby' in a ceremony during which guests were impressed by the behaviour of the Cambridge children. Mary, it was said, bore a striking resemblance to her elder brother, who was 'much improved in every way', while, her sister, Augusta, 'looked very well in white with blue ribbons, and behaved very well.'[60]

When the celebrations were over, George returned to England, much to his mother's chagrin, for each separation from him caused her immense heartache. It was disconcerting, too, for her to realise that, unlike his Cumberland cousin, he viewed himself as more English than German. A tour of the entire country increased his love for all things British, and, even later in life as he embarked upon many travels, he could hardly contain his joy at being in 'old England' again.

In 1835, as his education neared its completion, his parents visited him to witness his admission to the prestigious Order of the Garter. Again, he dreaded the prospect of their departure, but already an even greater sadness was preying on his mind. Soon, he would return permanently to Hanover, and, to make matters worse, he would be separated from the tutor who had been at his side for the past eight years. He prayed that his stay in Germany would be brief and he would soon been free to return to England, for, as he wrote, 'God knows how attached I am to this country and to its inhabitants.'[61] His only consolation was the thought of:

> "...seeing my parents and sisters, which is, of course, always a source of great pleasure to me, for they are all goodness to me, and I should be

very ungrateful if I were not to return theirs with mutual affection."[62]

When, however, in July 1836, he finally returned to Hanover, his sadness was quickly alleviated by the appointment of a military governor and the commencement of a period of military training. As was the custom for princes in Germany, he had, at the age of nine, been commissioned as a colonel in the Hanoverian Regiment of Guards, but now he began his duties in earnest. Throwing himself eagerly into his career, he recorded that one of the happiest days of his life was when he first mounted a guard on the viceregal palace and saw the pride in the eyes of his sisters and parents.

He had barely been involved in active duties for a month, however, when his prayers for a speedy return to England were answered. In June 1837, word arrived that his beloved uncle, King William IV, had died and his eighteen-year-old Cousin Victoria had ascended the throne.

Chapter 7 – 'Out And Out The Nicest Cousins We Have'

Augusta (Reuss of Ebersdorf) – Queen Victoria's maternal grandmother
Franz Frederick – Duke of Saxe-Coburg Saalfeld; Queen Victoria's maternal grandfather
Sophie – Daughter of Frederick Franz; Queen Victoria's maternal aunt
Emmanuel Mensdorff-Pouilly – Sophie's husband

The cousins on Queen Victoria's mother's side of her family might have lacked the distinction of being the grandchildren of a King, but, although they were descended from the less prestigious dynasty of the Dukes Saxe-Coburg Saalfeld, the Coburgers would make such influential marriages that the German Chancellor, Otto von Bismarck, scathingly referred to the duchy as the stud farm of Europe.

Much of their success was due to the ambition of Queen Victoria's grandmother, Countess Augusta Reuss of Ebersdorf – 'a most remarkable woman,' in the Queen's opinion 'with a most powerful, energetic, almost masculine mind, accompanied with great tenderness of heart, and extreme love for nature'[63]. In June 1777, Augusta had married Franz Frederick Anton, the widowed fifth Duke of Saxe-Coburg Saalfeld. An amiable, artistic and cultured man, Franz Frederick had fought in the Napoleonic Wars and, following several defeats, he lived to see the dissolution of the Holy Roman Empire, dying four months later in December 1806, at the age of fifty-six. His lack of economic adroitness combined with the devastations of war had left the duchy virtually bankrupt and in danger of being subsumed into Napoleon's empire. His pious and intelligent widow, however, was not prepared to see her children's inheritance destroyed, and immediately took upon herself her late husband's responsibilities with such gusto and courage that she earned the greatest respect and admiration of the people of Coburg.

The couple's eldest child, Sophie, combined the finest qualities of both of her parents. From her mother, she had inherited physical beauty, a strong will and a love of learning; and from her father, an appreciation of art and literature, which inspired her to become an author in her own right. Romantic by nature, she declared that she would only marry for love, and had rejected several eligible suitors when, at the age of twenty-four, she visited Schloss Fantasie, the Bavarian summer residence of the Duchess of Württemberg. The castle had become a refuge for many French aristocrats fleeing the revolutions, among them the Mensdorff-Pouilly family, who had escaped from France twelve years earlier.

As soon as they came of age, Emmanuel Mensdorff-Pouilly and his elder brother, Albert, had put themselves in the service of the Austrian Emperor in the war against Napoleon, and, following Albert's death in battle in 1799, Emmanuel served with such distinction that he quickly earned promotions and was awarded the prestigious Military Order of Maria Theresa.

Enamoured of the dashing young soldier, Sophie persuaded her parents to overlook their difference in rank and grant them permission to marry. The wedding took place in Coburg in 1804, and, eighteen months later, at the height of the Napoleonic Wars, their eldest son, Hugo, was born. As the French army was rapidly approaching, Sophie fled with the baby to Saalfeld, but, on discovering that they were no safer there, she hurried back to Coburg.

Following Napoleon's ultimate defeat, life became more peaceful for the young family and, over the course of seven years, a further five sons were born, one of whom, Alfred, died before his third birthday. The surviving sons – Hugo, Alfonse, Alexander, Leopold and Arthur – were raised with few pretensions and spent many happy hours playing with their Coburg cousins and the sons of their father's fellow officers. Sophie was particularly keen to provide them with a good education and appointed a young and inspirational tutor, Christoph Florschütz, who recognised the importance of play in early childhood and made their lessons more of a pleasure than a chore. A talented story-teller, he made use of picture books to develop his pupils' imaginations, and, as they grew older, he harnessed their physical strength in rigorous outdoor pursuits, including long walks, creative games and a variety of sporting activities[i]. While all the boys responded well to his teaching, Alfonse gained the reputation of a particularly gifted scholar.

Their father's continued active service in the Austrian army also enabled the boys to come into contact with people of different cultures. They travelled with him through his various postings in Austria and Czechoslovakia until they settled in Mayence, where he was appointed Vice-Governor. There, there were endless opportunities for adventures in the city's Roman ruins and the seventeenth century fortress; and, as always, the chance to mix with the local people and the sons of soldiers. Predictably, as they grew older,

---

[i] Florschütz so impressed Sophie that she would go on to recommend him as a tutor to her nephews, Ernest and Albert of Saxe-Coburg Gotha.

they followed their father into the Austrian army, where Alexander's diligence earned him rapid promotions.

In England, meanwhile, as the Duchess of Kent discouraged visits from her late husband's Hanoverian relations, she was eager to introduce her daughter, Victoria, to her Coburg cousins. Eagerly the Princess anticipated making the acquaintance of 'dear Uncle Mensdorff and dear Aunt Sophie' and, when the family finally visited England, the adolescent Victoria was enthralled by the handsome and unassuming brothers. She could hardly find sufficient superlatives to describe their charm and good manners, and was especially enamoured of Alexander, whose features were so striking that even the Prime Minister, Lord Melbourne, commented on the beauty of his hair and eyes, while Victoria herself was especially struck by his eyebrows!

The happy family was not, though, without its share of sorrows. When Leopold died unexpectedly at the age of seventeen, his mother was so devastated that her own health began to decline and, by the age of fifty-four, she was unable to walk unaided. In 1835, three years after Leopold's death, Emmanuel and Sophie planned to visit eighteen-year-old Arthur, who was stationed with his garrison in Bohemia. In view of his wife's increasing frailty, Emmanuel tried to dissuade her from making the journey but, dismissing his concerns, she insisted on adhering to their plans. On arriving in the village of Tuschimitz, the couple found themselves housed in a ramshackle cottage with few amenities, and Sophie, in considerable pain, developed a fever and was confined to bed. By the evening of 8th July, the worst appeared to be over, and, when Emmanuel looked in on her in the early hours of the following morning, he was relieved to see that she was sleeping soundly. Soon afterwards, though, a maid entered her room and, discovering that she was not breathing, realised that Emmanuel had mistaken death for sleep.

Her body was taken back to the family home in Bohemia, and the thousands who gathered for her funeral bore testimony to the popularity of the Mensdorff-Pouilly family throughout the region.

Shared sorrow brought her family closer together, and the bond that had always existed between Emmanuel and his sons became even stronger.

"It is quite beautiful," observed their cousin, Victoria, "to see the love the father has for his sons, and vice versa – and the affection the four brothers have for one another. This is so rarely seen that it does one's heart good to witness it."[64]

The Duchess of Kent, while grieving for the loss of her sister, sought to shower her nephews with the maternal affection that they had lost. They repaid her kindness with devotion and, although their meetings were rare, their regular correspondence convinced the young Victoria that they were 'out and out the nicest cousins we have.'[65]

Disregarding the conventions of the day, Sophie had found happiness with a man whom she loved, but, had the plans of the Russian Empress, Catherine the Great, come to fruition, her life would have been very different.

Nine years before Sophie married Emmanuel, the Empress had invited her and her two younger sisters, Antoinette and Juliane, to Russia in the hope that her sixteen-year-old grandson would choose a wife from among them. At fifteen-years-old Sophie was the most obvious candidate, but Grand Duke Konstantin Pavlovich passed over her and Antoinette in favour of their fourteen-year-old sister, Juliane.

Not daring to defy the Empress by rejecting Konstantin's proposal, Julianne returned to Coburg to begin a course of religious instructions to prepare her to convert to Orthodoxy – a prerequisite of Russian Grand Duchesses of the era. In early 1796, she was received into the Orthodox Church and given the name Anna Feodorovna before marrying the Grand Duke on 26th February.

The young couple barely knew one another and, although Konstantin claimed that he 'admired' Juliane 'greatly', he was far more concerned with his mistresses and his military career than with his wife. Moreover, as Juliane soon learned, her husband's reputation for intelligence and kindness was tarnished by his notoriously violent temper. On one occasion, for example, while he was inspecting the troops, he spotted in the distance an officer whose jacket was not buttoned to the neck. Summoning him over, the Grand Duke demanded an explanation for his failure to wear his uniform correctly. The officer replied that he was not on duty and the unbearable heat had compelled him to loosen his collar. Konstantin, incensed by his response, struck him violently in the face in front of the entire brigade, causing him such humiliation that, later that evening, the officer took his own life, explaining that he could not live with such disgrace.

Konstantin's temper was not his only failing. The Empress, who had taken full responsibility for his upbringing, was impressed by his linguistic skills, his enjoyable conversation and pleasing personality, but even she was forced to admit that he was petulant and impulsive, and when he 'heard of any splendid action he was filled with the desire to go and do likewise; his enthusiasm is very quickly aroused'[66] but he invariably lacked the perseverance to carry his projects through to fruition.

Life with a volatile husband was made all the more difficult for Juliane by the constant squabbling among members of the Imperial Family and the icy atmosphere of her home, Gatchina where, according to her mother, everything was:

"...stiff and silent in the old Prussian manner...The officers of the Grand Duke's entourage are like figures cut out of an old scrapbook."[67]

Nine months after the wedding, the Empress died and was succeeded by Konstantin's unpredictable father, Tsar Paul I. In spite of her loneliness and longing for her home, Juliane made a favourable impression on the new Tsar's Court and, more particularly, on her brother-in-law, Grand Duke Alexander[j], and his wife, the German-born Grand Duchess Elizaveta. Unfortunately, her friendship with the couple only exacerbated the strain on her marriage, as Konstantin felt that Alexander and Elizaveta always took her side against his own. In response, he controlled all her movements, even confining her to her quarters for days at a time and forbidding her from entering any room in which Alexander was present.

Far from accepting her situation meekly, Juliane stood up to her overbearing husband and when, three years after the wedding, she fell ill following a violent argument, she hurried home to Coburg in the hope that her mother would help her to obtain a divorce. She was quickly disillusioned when the Duchess, fearful for the family's reputation, urged her to return to Russia to make peace with Konstantin. After taking a cure in Carlsbad, Julianne yielded to her mother's wishes but over the next few months, relations between the couple

---

[j] Alexander succeeded as Tsar in 1801, following the murder of his father, Paul I.

deteriorated further, until, on the night of March 23rd 1801, the Tsar was murdered by a group of conspirators, and Juliane took advantage of the ensuing chaos to escape again to Coburg.

This time her mother accepted that the marriage was merely a distressing charade, and agreed to help her to begin divorce proceedings. The process, however, was longer and far more complicated than she had envisaged, since Konstantin refused to co-operate with her wishes. Resigning herself to the fact that the marriage might never be dissolved, she took comfort in the arms of a lover, a divorced nobleman, Jules Gabriel Emile de Seigneux, by whom, in 1808, she bore son.

Within two years, the affair with de Seigneux came to an end, but it did not take long for Juliane to find a new paramour – Rudolf von Schiferli, a Swiss surgeon and professor, whom she had appointed as her chief steward. In 1812, she gave birth to a second illegitimate child – a daughter named Louise Hilda Agnes – but, for the sake of appearance, the little girl was adopted by a wealthy family in France. Juliane settled with her lover in Berne, where, in 1814, she acquired a romantic mansion, Elfenau, and devoted herself to charitable works and tending the extensive gardens.

Konstantin, however, had never lost hope that she would eventually return to Russia, and in 1814, he travelled to Elfenau with her brother, Leopold, in the hope of effecting a reconciliation. Julianne received them graciously but adamantly refused to be swayed, and in 1820, Konstantin, finding solace in the arms of Jane, Countess of Grudzinska, finally granted her the divorce that she craved. The settlement enabled the Grand Duke to marry the Countess, who was duly granted the title, Princess of Lowicz, but Juliane's freedom came at a cost, since she was treated as a social outcast and, according to her brother, she 'felt painfully…the neglect to which she was subjected for many years afterward.'[68]

Juliane outlived her daughter, her lover and most of her immediate family, and spent the final years of her life isolated at Elfenau, where, on 5th August 1860, she suffered a stroke and died ten days later, a few weeks short of her seventy-ninth birthday. The tragedy of her life, wrote Leopold, was that 'with an amiable husband, generous-hearted as she was, she would have been an excellent wife'. If, Leopold continued, Konstantin had chosen her elder sister, everything would have been very different, for Antoinette 'would have suited that position wonderfully well.'[69]

As it was, Antoinette also spent much of her married life in Russia, though her marriage was virtually as disastrous as that of her sister.

In 1776, Princess Sophia Dorothea, a daughter of the Duke of Württemberg, became the second wife of Konstantin's father, the future Tsar Paul I. Despite Paul's notoriously difficult temperament, the marriage was happy, as Sophia Dorothea – then known as Maria Feodorovna – adored her husband, assuring him that 'all my life will I devote to you and give you constant proofs of my attachment and of the love with which my heart is beating for you.'[70] Paul was equally enamoured of his bride, whom he considered well-educated, intelligent, pretty, graceful and, all in all, 'just as nice as I expected.'[71]

At the time of their wedding, Sophia Dorothea's younger brother, Alexander, was only two years old but he soon developed a passion for her adopted country and, in 1798, at the age of twenty-seven, after serving in the armies of Württemberg and Austria, he transferred to the Imperial Russian Army as a General in the Riga Cuirassiers. The same year, he married nineteen-year-old Antoinette – 'a clever, amiable' woman, 'possessed of a great *esprit de conduite*'[72] – who settled with him in Russia.

Alexander was an able diplomat and military leader and, when his nephew, Alexander I, acceded to the throne, he devoted himself to his service, receiving rapid promotions as a reward. Alexander's eldest brother, Frederick, meanwhile, succeeded his late father as Duke, and was rewarded by Russia's enemy, Napoleon, for his services to France[k] by being created King of Württemberg. Following his coronation, Frederick promptly bestowed the title of Dukes and Duchesses upon all his younger siblings – an act which held little meaning for the self-assured Alexander who informed a military governor that:

> "...a Russian General-in-chief does not think himself inferior in any respect to a King of the Confederation, since it only depends on the Emperor Alexander to elevate me to that dignity, if he thinks fit; and then I shall be king like any other."[73]

This pomposity was but one aspect of Alexander's character that irked his wife, who increasingly distanced herself from him. Three years after the wedding she gave birth to a daughter, Marie; and year later to a son, who survived for only a few months, by which time Alexandra and Antoinette were living virtually separate lives. When in 1802, she was rumoured to be pregnant for a third time, gossips insisted that the father was a local clergyman. With occasional reconciliations, over the next eight years,

---

[k] In 1816, Frederick defected and joined the allies in their campaigns against the French

three legitimate sons were born – Alexander, Ernest and Frederick William – the youngest of whom died at the age of five in 1815.

As children of an unhappy marriage, the Württembergs were deprived of the broad academic education of their Mensdorff cousins, but spent much of their time in outdoor pursuits at which the boys excelled. Their mother's untimely death at the age of only forty-four in 1824, brought them further under their father's influence, and Alexander and Ernest followed him into military careers. They had, though, inherited Antoinette's good looks and regal stature, and when, in 1833, they visited England, they made a very favourable impression on their cousin, Victoria. Their kindly attention, and her obvious enjoyment of their company led to the inevitable rumours that she was about to be betrothed to one of the brothers – an idea that was encouraged by the Duchess of Kent, who particularly favoured Ernest, notwithstanding the fact that he was already in love with a Princess of Baden.

Entranced by their swashbuckling stories of campaigns in Turkey and Russia, Victoria so enjoyed their company that she dreaded their departure, and no sooner had she bid them goodbye that she wrote plaintively:

> "We shall miss them at breakfast, at luncheon, at dinner, riding, sailing, driving, walking, in fact everywhere!"[74]

Her sorrow was compounded when, within hours of their leaving Kensington Palace, she received the news that their father, who had been ill for some time, had died during their absence.

Having formed such a high opinion of her dashing and courageous cousins, Victoria was deeply disillusioned when rumours began to reach her that, like many wealthy, young officers, they regularly engaged in bouts of drinking, gambling and womanising. She had, she felt, been deceived by their amiable appearance, and within three years of their visit, she could only sigh that they were living very *bad* lives. Of all her cousins, the Württemberg brothers became her most infrequent visitors, and her correspondence with them was extremely limited compared to that with many of her other relations. Their sister, Marie, however, would soon gain a special place in her heart, as the beloved stepmother of her cousin and soon-to-be consort, Prince Albert of Saxe-Coburg-Gotha.

Chapter 8 – 'So Close A Bond Between Brothers.'

Ernest I – Duke of Saxe-Coburg Saalfeld/Saxe-Coburg-Gotha; Queen Victoria's maternal uncle

Augusta – Dowager Duchess of Saxe-Coburg Saalfeld; Queen Victoria's maternal grandmother; mother of Duke Ernest I

Louise of Saxe-Altenburg – Duchess of Saxe-Coburg; first wife of Ernest I; Prince Albert's mother

> Sons of Ernest I and Louise:
>
> Ernest II – Elder son of Ernest I; later Duke of Saxe-Coburg-Gotha; Queen Victoria's cousin
>
> Albert – Younger son of Ernest I; Queen Victoria's cousin

Arthur Mensdorff – youngest son of Sophie of Saxe-Coburg Saalfeld; Queen Victoria's cousin

Marie of Württemberg – Daughter of Antoinette of Saxe-Coburg Saalfeld; second wife of Ernest I of Saxe-Coburg-Gotha; Queen Victoria's cousin

On the death of his father in 1806, Ernest of Saxe-Coburg-Saalfeld inherited a duchy in chaos due to the ravages of war and the late Duke's economic incompetence. French soldiers occupied Coburg, and for twelve months, Ernest could not even enter his homeland but remained in exile in Konigsberg until the Russians signed a treaty with Napoleon, and Ernest's sister, Juliane, succeeded in persuading the Tsar to restore the duchy to him. Returning home in 1807, he discovered with horror the conditions in which his sixty-thousand subjects were living, as livestock had vanished from the countryside; industry was almost non-existent; and even the ruling family was left in such dire financial circumstances that his brother-in-law, Grand Duke Konstantin, mocked,

"He rules over six peasants and two village surgeons."[75]

In spite of his youth, Ernest quickly set about restoring Coburg's fortunes, working so diligently that he earned the respect and affection of his people; and when, in 1826, the Duchy of Gotha was added to his tenure, he impressed his now one-hundred-thousand subjects by his:

> "…his extreme humanity and kindness and by
> the unwearied solicitude with which he watched
> over the interests of his country."[76]

His private life was far less reputable, as his enjoyment of feasts, parties and the company of dubious women led to his court being viewed as one of the most immoral in Europe – a notion that gained greater credence in 1823 with the publication of a book of memoirs by a young French actress named Pauline Panam. Mlle Panam claimed that, while visiting Paris with his brother, Leopold, the Duke had seduced her when she was only fourteen-years-old. When she subsequently discovered that she was pregnant, he had promised to obtain for her a position of lady-in-waiting to his mother, but as the Duchess Augusta refused to entertain her, he introduced her instead to his sisters, Sophie and Juliane in the hope that they would provide her with comfortable employment. Mlle Panam, however, was not to be discarded lightly, and, news of the affair travelled so quickly that plans for Ernest to marry Grand Duchess Anna Pavlovna – a daughter of Tsar Paul I – were abandoned due to the subsequent scandal.

Ernest's mother, meanwhile, was determined that he should make an advantageous marriage to prosper Coburg's fortunes and, when sixteen-year-old

Princess Louise of Saxe-Altenburg – 'an exquisite, charming lady, with blond locks and blue eyes'[77] – became the sole heiress of profitable estates in Gotha, she urged her thirty-three-year-old son to propose. Louise's mother had died when she was only a few days old, and her father, who had a penchant for dressing in women's clothes and going by the name of Emilie, had remarried the intelligent and kindly Karoline of Hesse-Kassel, who became a devoted stepmother to Louise, and would later play an important role in her children's upbringing.

The wedding took place in 1817, and within two years, Louise had given birth to two sons, Ernest and Albert. Childlike herself, she lavished all her affection on them, playing their games and writing long descriptions of their progress and appearance. Ernest, she said, was tall for his age, with large black eyes that were always full of mischief; but Albert, was 'as lovely as an angel,' and simply:

> "...splendid – of extraordinary beauty. He has large blue eyes, a little mouth, a delicate nose, and dimples on each cheek. He is tall and lively and always merry."[78]

It was a view shared by many visitors to Coburg, one of whom, while still a child, spent an afternoon playing with the 'the brown Hereditary-Prince Ernst, four years old...and the altogether lovely, blond-locked Prince Albert, whose whole figure savoured of the angelic.'[79]

Their grandmother, Dowager Duchess Augusta, was far less effusive in her praise, for, although she had originally described Albert as the 'pendant to his pretty cousin, Victoria', when he was fourteen months old she wrote that he 'runs about like a weasel. He is teething, and as cross as a little badger from impatience and liveliness. He is not pretty now, except his beautiful black eyes.'[80]

In character and temperament the brothers could hardly have been more different, as Ernest, robust and impervious to criticism had inherited many of his father's traits; while Albert, who bore a striking resemblance to his mother, was sensitive, frequently laid low by minor illnesses, and prone to tearful tantrums and fits of rage. The disparities, however, merely strengthened the bond between the boys, who, throughout their childhood and adolescence were inseparable.

"We shared every joy and sorrow together," wrote Ernest. "...so close a bond between brothers is not often to be met with."[81]

With a loving mother, an indulgent father, a myriad of affectionate relations, and a kindly nanny to oversee the nursery, the boys enjoyed an idyllic childhood in the family's beautiful summer residence of the Rosenau. The playrooms were filled with wooden toys, model forts and numerous picture books; and outdoors, there were trees to climb, dens to build, lakes to swim, gardens to plant, and expansive grounds in which to practise fencing, boxing and athletics. Their feisty grandmother, who took a keen maternal interest in their progress, frequently urged them to take plenty of a fresh air and exercise for the sake of their health and to burn off the energy of their often unruly and over-boisterous behaviour.

On birthdays and holidays, local schoolboys joined them for picnics and games; and their father's numerous relations regularly visited. On one such occasion, in honour of the Duke's birthday, Ernest and Albert greeted their beloved Uncle Leopold with great ceremony, much to the delight of their maternal step-grandmother. It was, she wrote:

"...a most pleasant sight, that of these happy young people playing on the large meadow, and jumping about like grasshoppers. Ernest and Albert went in full armour to meet a procession of knights and hunters...Ernest stammered forth a short address (for his comrades confused him), in which he thanked his kind uncle for having come across the sea to spend the feast with them, and begged his favour for Albert, his comrades, and himself."[82]

Sadly, though, the domestic idyll was soon to be shattered, for marriage had done nothing to dampen the Duke's enthusiasm for amorous adventures. Even in the year of his wedding, one of his mistresses bore him a daughter, who would later marry her cousin, the illegitimate son of Ernest's sister, Juliane; and in 1819 – the year that Prince Albert was born – a servant girl named Margarethe Braun, gave birth to his son, who was also named Ernest Albert.

Aware of her husband's infidelities, Louise took lovers of her own, and when, in 1824, the Duke discovered that she had begun a liaison with his stable master, Alexander von Hanstein, he seized the opportunity to effect a permanent separation. Louise was ordered from the house and forbidden from seeing her children again – a particularly cruel fate for so devoted a mother. On hearing that she had been banished, the people of Coburg rose up in protest, marching towards the palace and damaging the property of some of the Duke's closest acquaintances. Ernest withdrew to Vienna but, unwilling to risk forfeiting Louise's inheritance, he refused to grant her a divorce that would enable her to marry von Hanstein. Left with no alternative, Louise attempted to force his hand by living such a scandalous life that he would feel obliged to distance himself from her.

"The duchess," wrote one minister, "has assuredly been playing wild pranks with lovers, nor has she tried to hide them. She asserts a defiant freedom in her manners, saying and doing with innocently-saucy frankness what others conceal; and with it all she is loveable to a seductive degree."[83]

Eventually Ernest yielded, and Louise married von Hanstein but there was to be no happy ending for the couple. Ostracised by society, and desperately missing her sons, she developed cancer and died in great pain at the age of only thirty. Before her death she made a strange will, bequeathing a large annuity to her second husband on condition that he would never spend a night away from her body. Von Hanstein, therefore, had her coffin transported with him on all his travels, until one day, shortly after the Duke's death, he discovered it had been stolen. Her son, Ernest, had found the unseemly business so distasteful that, following his accession to the dukedom, he arranged for his mother's body to be taken and buried with due ceremony in Coburg[1].

Although at the time of Louise's death, her sons had not seen her for seven years, the news was deeply distressing for them. Many years later, Albert was shocked on discovering the details of her final illness, and it was particularly shocking for him to realise that, in the words of his step-grandmother:

"The thought that the children had forgotten her, distressed her very much. She wished to know if they ever spoke of her. I answered her that they were far too good to forget her; that they did not know of her sufferings as it would grieve the good children too much."[84]

---

[1] Ernest also ensured that Von Hanstein did not lose his annuity.

Louise's life and death left Albert with a horror of infidelity, but neither he nor Ernest blamed their father for what had happened, and, in the absence of their mother, they became even more devoted to him. Simultaneously strict and indulgent, the Duke did his utmost to provide the boys with an excellent education and such a happy childhood that, according to Ernest, 'a more beautiful bond between a father and his sons it would be difficult to find.'[85]

At the recommendation of his sister, Sophie, he appointed the Mensdorffs' enlightened tutor, Christoph Florschütz, under whose guidance the young princes progressed with ease through the schoolroom. Florschütz, enjoyed the company of his pupils as much as they enjoyed his, and he was particularly impressed by Albert's diligence and his unfailing concern for others.

> "Of the many virtues which distinguished the Prince," he wrote, "two deserve special mention; for they were conspicuous even in his boyhood, winning for him the love and respect of all...One was his eager desire to do good and to assist others; the other, the grateful feeling, which never allowed him to forget an act of kindness, however trifling, to himself."[86]

Although Albert was naturally studious and sensitive, he and Ernest were also known for their sense of humour and their love of practical jokes, as when Albert filled the pockets of a visiting lady with cheese, only to discover she had taken her revenge by placing a live frog in his bed. On another occasion while visiting the theatre, the boys threw stink bombs into the orchestra pit, earning a swift rebuke from their highly amused father. Never, however, did they allow their jokes to descend into cruelty, for, as a regular companion, their cousin Arthur Mensdorff recorded,

Ernest was naturally kind and Albert 'was never severe or ill-natured, the general kindness of his disposition preventing him from pushing a joke, however he might enjoy it, so as to hurt anyone's feelings.'[87]

Growing up in the beautiful Thuringian countryside, both boys had a love of nature and the outdoors, where they boxed, staged mock battles, had swimming lessons, and, as one companion recorded, 'we are a cheerful and noisy company. We have had a boat built to suit us, which bears our several flags and in which we row ourselves.'[88]

Like many of their relatives, Queen Victoria's Coburg cousins, were constantly surrounded by animals and were particularly devoted to their dogs. On one occasion, while they had been out for a day in the country, the weather became inclement and, it being too dark to return home, they sought refuge at a local lodging house. When the proprietress refused to allow them to take their dogs to their room, Ernest arrogantly insisted that, as a future Duke of Saxe-Coburg, he could do whatever he wished. The more tactful Albert corrected him gently, reminding him that they were guests in the woman's house and must therefore accept her rules. He was not, though, willing allow his dogs to stay outdoors, and eventually persuaded her to allow them to sleep in the warm kitchen.

Their father, meanwhile, had long been contemplating taking a second wife but his reputation as a philanderer proved a major obstacle to several available princesses. By the age of thirty-three, however, his niece, Marie of Württemberg, was still single and when, in 1832, the Duke proposed, she, somewhat desperately, accepted him. That winter, as she left her home in Bohemia, Albert and Ernest rode out to accompany her back to Coburg for the wedding. Although she was their cousin, henceforward they dutifully addressed her as 'mama' and showed her the affection which her husband failed to give. True to form, the Duke was no more faithful to his second wife than he had been to his first, and the lonely Marie resigned herself to a loveless marriage, as she quietly committed herself to her duties as the Duchess of Saxe-Coburg Gotha.

Chapter 9 – 'A Want of Education & Knowledge of the World'

Ferdinand – Prince of Saxe-Coburg-Saalfeld; Queen Victoria's maternal uncle

Antonia Kohary – Wife of Ferdinand of Saxe-Coburg-Saalfeld

> Children of Ferdinand and Antonia:
> Ferdinand
> Augustus 'Gusti'
> Victoire
> Leopold

Leopold – Prince of Saxe-Coburg Saalfeld; later King of the Belgians; husband of Charlotte of Wales; Queen Victoria's maternal uncle

Louise d'Orléans – Daughter of King Louis-Philippe of France; second wife of Leopold of the Belgians

> Children of Leopold and Louise:
> Louis-Philippe
> Leopold – Duke of Brabant
> Philippe – Count of Flanders
> Charlotte

Dashing and handsome, with an impressive military record in the Austrian army, Ferdinand of Saxe-Coburg-Saalfeld was second only to his brother, Leopold, as Queen Victoria's favourite uncle. In appearance he bore a strong resemblance to Ernest, but there their similarities ended for, while the latter used his charm and good looks to further his amorous exploits, the former was utterly devoted to his Hungarian wife, Maria Antonia Kohary.

The marriage, which took place in 1815, was so advantageous to the impoverished Coburgs that it was widely believed that Ferdinand's mother had engineered the match in order to gain access to Antonia's fortune. The rumours were given greater credence when Ferdinand agreed to abandon his Lutheran faith to convert to his bride's Catholicism – a deed which led to much condemnation from many devout German Protestants, who believed that the prince had sacrificed his sacred duty on the altar of Mammon.

Antonia was certainly immensely wealthy, for, as the sole heiress to her father's vast estates in Austria, Hungary and Slovakia, she had a fortune of approximately one-hundred-and-fifty-million pounds in twenty-first century values. The Koharys also stood to gain from the match, for, in spite of their wealth, they lacked significant aristocratic status until the engagement when the Austrian Emperor elevated Antonia's father from the relatively lowly title of Count to that of Prince.

In reality, however, this was a genuine love match, as, from the moment that the twenty-one-year-old prince set eyes on the eighteen-year-old heiress, he was in love, while she was drawn to his charm, good-looks and kindness, regardless of a Russian General's description of him as 'defective in intellect [with]…a handsome, regular face, with a thinly contracted nose, in which intellect alone is wanting.'[89]

Eleven months after the wedding, a son, also named Ferdinand, was born, to be joined two years later by a brother, Augustus ('Gusti'), followed by Victoire in 1822, and Leopold in 1824. In spite of their mother's vast wealth and their father's proximity to the Austrian Emperor, the Kohary[m] children were raised in relative simplicity and shielded from the intrigues of society at

---

[m] In 1826, when Antonia came into her inheritance, Ferdinand added 'Kohary' to the family name of Saxe-Coburg.

large. Even their cousin, Queen Victoria, was amazed by their sheltered upbringing, referring always to Victoire as a 'dear child'; and, commenting that as Ferdinand neared his twentieth birthday, he remained 'very new to the world.' Ferdinand himself was aware of his lack of experiences, confessing later that he was very much ashamed of his 'want of education and knowledge of the world'[90].

This self-condemnation was not entirely justified, however, for, in spite of their unassuming manner, their innate reticence and their father's alleged lack of intellect, Queen Victoria was impressed by their intelligence, believing that Gusti was 'extremely quiet and silent' because, in reality, there was 'a great deal in him.'[91] When he visited England, she observed, he spent a good deal of time unobtrusively studying the objects in the rooms and reading the newspapers, while his elder brother was 'by far more forward for his age in his mind...They have both learnt, and know, a great deal, and are both very orderly and tidy.'[92]

Apart from receiving an extensive academic education from a trusted tutor named Dietz, their father's continued service in the Austrian army, gave the children the opportunity to experience different cultures. Their childhood was spent in the courts of Vienna, Berlin and Coburg, as well as on the family estates in Slovakia, allowing them to master several languages fluently.

When they visited England, the young Victoria could hardly find sufficient language to praise the attributes which she found most appealing – particularly their good looks, kindness and thoughtful attention to her. She was moved, too, by the kindly manner in which their father treated them, and the way in which they showed him respect and obedience.

In fact, so effusive was she in her descriptions of them that 'Uncle Leopold', who was busily trying to engineer a match between Victoria and Albert of Saxe-Coburg-Gotha, made a point of comparing him favourably to his Kohary cousins.

Were it not for the fact that Roman Catholics were barred from marrying into the British Royal Family, either one of the elder boys might have proved a strong contender for Victoria's hand; and, it was thanks partly to her affection for them that she would later become so zealous in defending the rights of her Catholic subjects. When a wave of 'anti-papist' sentiments swept the country, she wrote to her aunt that she could not 'bear to hear the violent abuse of the Catholic religion, which is so painful and cruel towards the many good and innocent Roman Catholics.'[93]

Not everyone, though, shared Victoria's high opinion of the brothers. When they visited their cousins in the Rosenau, Ernest of Saxe-Coburg-Gotha found their reticence irksome, and considered Ferdinand 'sharp', cold and guilty of a 'want of feeling.'[94] Another companion, Prince Chlodwig of Hohenlohe-Schillingsfürst, thought Gusti 'tedious'; while Lady Lyttelton found his obsession with bear-hunting so dull and distasteful that, after one conversation with him on that subject, she felt moved to comment:

> "How unlike an English youth! He had just been distressed by a letter from Hungary, telling him of the death of his favourite nightingale, and the loss of his little tiny lap-dog."[95]

Later, though, she altered her opinion when Gusti and his younger brother came to her assistance when she returned home from a long carriage drive to find no groom in sight to tend the horses.

> "Without our calling anyone, the two Princes, Augustus and Leopold, perceived our state, and

98

you should have seen with what grace they sprang from their horses, rushed to our carriage, opened the door, let down the steps, and helped us out in a single Augenblick, and then such pretty bows and speeches! I wonder what Englishmen would have thought of such a thing!"[96]

Like Ernest and Albert of Saxe-Coburg-Gotha, the brothers were so attached to one another that when, in the spring of 1836, Ferdinand was about to leave for Portugal, Gusti found the prospect of separation almost too much to bear. In the weeks leading up to Ferdinand's departure, his brother became increasingly despondent and, when the day came for him to set sail, Gusti returned home alone with his eyes swollen with tears.

For Ferdinand, though, the separation marked the beginning of a great adventure which would see him rise from the relatively lowly position of the son of a Hungarian noblewoman to titular King of Portugal. This elevation was largely due to the machinations of his Uncle Leopold, who was simultaneously seeking to secure a lofty position for Albert of Saxe-Coburg; and, but for a timely turn of events, might also have raised Ferdinand's brother, to the position of King of the Belgians.

Although the death of Princess Charlotte had deprived her widower, Leopold, of the influence he hoped to gain in Britain, within little more than a decade, he had been offered the choice of two alternative thrones. His first opportunity arose in 1829 when an international conference concluded that Greece, freed from Ottoman domination, should be granted full independence and the establishment of a monarchy. When Leopold was offered the crown, he received the backing of France and Russia, and in Britain only two voices were raised in opposition: those of Ernest Augustus of Cumberland, who had taken a dislike to the Coburgs; and Leopold's sister, the Duchess of Kent, who dreaded his leaving her alone in England. Ultimately, after much soul-searching, he declined the offer on the grounds that the country was likely to face many more political upheavals, and the monarch would find himself in a very precarious position. Later, he came to regret his decision and, when the crown had been given to the ineffective and 'detestable' Otto of Bavaria, he wrote ruefully to a friend:

> "I fancy that I could have done much good there. Indeed, although I know well the disadvantages, I often have a sort of home-sickness for it."[97]

His only consolation, as he told his niece, Victoria, was that his decision had enabled him to remain closer to her. Nonetheless, he continued to maintain a strong interest in the region and, when Otto was finally overthrown, he considered proposing his nephew, Ernest of Saxe-Coburg-Gotha, as his replacement.

With twelve months of refusing the Greek crown, Leopold was again approached with the offer of becoming King of another newly-independent nation. Since the Congress of Vienna in 1815, Belgium – then known as the Southern Netherlands – had been entirely absorbed into the Kingdom of Holland. In theory, the idea appeared practicable but in reality it soon became clear that the predominantly Roman Catholic Belgians had little in common with the Protestant Dutch, who, according to one commentator, 'treated the Belgian provinces not much better than the territory of a conquered nation.'[98]

For over a decade tensions mounted until July 1830 when revolution erupted in Paris, inspiring the Belgians to follow suit and demand their independence. In August, riots broke out on the streets of Brussels and, within a short time, the Dutch troops had been driven from the capital. By October, a provisional government had been established, leading to another international conference in London where, after much wrangling, it was agreed that Belgium should be declared a permanently neutral and independent country.

Ostensibly, the Belgians were free to choose their own king, but from the start foreign powers tried to influence the process, leading to a good deal of international wrangling. Supported by several members of the new provisional government, the French King, Louis Philippe, proposed his sixteen-year-old son, the Duke of Nemours, which immediately prompted vehement opposition from the British Foreign Secretary, Palmerston, who feared that this was a cunning French plan to annex the new kingdom. Louis Philippe withdrew his son's name from the candidacy but he was not in the least impressed by Palmerston's alternative suggestion – Leopold of Saxe-Coburg Saalfeld, whom he viewed as an English puppet. In an attempt to satisfy both parties, Alexander Gendebien, a member of the Belgian provisional government, suggested that Leopold should marry the French King's daughter – an idea which Louis Philippe rejected, explaining that, although Leopold was 'a handsome fellow, a perfect gentleman, very well informed, very well educated…there are family objections, prejudices perhaps, which are in the way of the projected union.'[99]

Sebastiani, the French Foreign Minister, went even further, warning Gendebien that, 'If Leopold puts one foot into Belgium, we shall fire cannon balls at him.'[100]

101

Once again, Leopold feared the instability of the throne and when, in the spring of 1831, a Belgian delegation arrived at Marlborough House to present him with the crown, his initial reaction was to refuse their offer. Over the next few days, the delegates assured him that he was the first choice of the Belgian people; and, what was more, they promised that they would fully support his vision for the future of the country and its monarchy. After much detailed discussion, Leopold finally yielded to their entreaties and, by early summer, he was preparing to leave for Brussels.

On 21st July, he made his triumphal entry into the capital where, amid great rejoicing, he was crowned in a lavish ceremony in the Place Royale.

> "Gentlemen," he announced, "I only accepted the crown you offered me with a view of fulfilling a task as honourable as it is useful, that of being called to consolidate the institutions and maintain the independence of a noble people. My heart knows no other ambition than that of rendering you happy."[101]

The speech endeared him to his new subjects, and his popularity increased throughout his reign due to his tireless efforts to work for the good of his adopted country. At the same time, he won the respect of the British by renouncing the £50,000 annuity which he had been granted on his marriage to Princess Charlotte; and he earned the support of the French, whose help he summoned when, within weeks of his coronation, the Dutch launched an unsuccessful invasion. To consolidate his relations with France and to satisfy his Catholic subjects, he finally persuaded Louis Philippe to allow him to marry his twenty-year-old daughter, Louise of Orléans, by promising to raise their children as Roman Catholics and to allow Louise to make frequent visits to her parents.

The Belgian people were delighted by his choice of a bride, and as one eye-witness noted:

"The nation was literally transported with joy at seeing their Queen, who was introducing the Catholic religion into the dynasty. Her complexion was white and rosy, and her figure bore a family likeness to the two houses of which she was the issue. She had the features of the Bourbons, whilst her blonde hair and her general deportment reminded me of the Archduchesses."[102]

Leopold's Coburg nephews also adored her; and his niece, Victoria, became one of her closest friends since they were, according to Albert of Saxe-Coburg-Gotha, 'so exactly on the same footing, that a bond of friendship was formed between them spontaneously; and it was a friendship of which Victoria could rightly be proud.'[103]

For Louise, though, marriage to a virtual stranger thirty years older than herself was a duty rather than a delight and she never felt able to reciprocate the affection which he apparently felt for her. Fulfilling her marital duties was more of a chore than a pleasure, but she shared her husband's delight when, in 1833, a son, Louis Philippe, was born. The baby, whom they fondly nicknamed Babochon, thrived for the first few weeks of his life but, before he was six months old, he had developed a series of illnesses and by April 1834 he was diagnosed as suffering from a serious inflammation of the lungs and mucus membranes. The efforts of the English physician, Dr Clarke, were of little avail and he died on May 16th 1834, two months before his first birthday. His parents were inconsolable, and, although she had never met him, Victoria could hardly contain her sorrow at the death of her 'beautiful' little cousin.

Babochon's death left the King without a successor and he was on the point of naming his Roman Catholic nephew and namesake, Leopold of Saxe-Coburg Kohary, as his heir when, in April 1835, a second son – also named Leopold – was born. Two years later, the dynasty was secured by the birth of a third son, Philippe, to be followed in 1840 by a daughter, Charlotte, named after her father's first wife, the Princess of Wales.

Growing up in the beautiful environs of the Royal Palace of Laeken in the outskirts of Brussels, the children enjoyed playing in the extensive parks and acquiring the necessary accomplishments of their station. When Leopold was five-years-old, his father created him Duke of Brabant, and conferred on his brother, Philippe, the title of Count of Flanders. In spite of these illustrious titles, the children were raised in relative simplicity, thanks largely to their father's renowned parsimoniousness. Unlike their Kohary cousins, they often felt deprived of their parents' attention, as the King had little time for his children, and the unhappy Queen displayed a singular lack of affection, openly criticising little Leopold's large beak-like nose which, she said, disfigured his whole appearance.

On more than one occasion, the Queen wrote firm notes to her eldest son, warning him against the laziness with which he approached his lessons. The King also had firm ideas about his boys' education, writing to their tutor that:

> "It is absolutely necessary that the children, especially Leopold, should manifest concentration, even in small details of ordinary life. As the children are very observant and

notice everything that is said in their presence, one must be very prudent, and things they ought not to know should not be mentioned in their presence."[104]

Even when the young Duke of Brabant mastered four languages fluently, and displayed a particular interest in architecture, natural sciences and botany, he failed to impress his father, who askance at his cold-heartedness and the merciless way he bullied his younger brother, referred to him scathingly as 'the little tyrant.'

Alongside their academic teachers, the princes were appointed a military tutor to instruct them in martial arts and physical education. Used to fast horses, they were fearless riders and, in 1848, thirteen-year-old Leopold's spirit of adventure almost led to disaster. He had set out alone on a large stallion which suddenly bolted, and, were it not for the swift action of a stable boy who bravely seized the bridle, the prince might well have been thrown to his death. Leopold never forgot the groom's heroism and, to the end of his life, ensured that he always had a good position in his service.

Quieter and more reserved than his brother, Philippe shared many of his mother's characteristics, particularly her profound religious sentiments, her dislike of attention and a lack of interest in politics. His sister, Charlotte, however, showed such political acumen that her father enjoyed lengthy discussions with her and commented on more than one occasion that it was a pity that she was not a boy.

She was, wrote one witness, 'capable of mastering with extraordinary quickness whatever she had read...displaying a stern industry and a point of abstract attention which was much assisted by an excellent memory."[105]

Although, of all three children, Charlotte alone enjoyed a bond of affection with her father, she had few playmates of her own age and, as much of her childhood was spent in the company of pious older women, she gained an air of maturity beyond her years. Like her cousin, Victoria, she compensated for the lack of friends, by creating imaginary worlds for her collection of dolls, but some of her happiest hours were spent playing with Queen Victoria's children, and during her visits to England she became 'the admiration of everyone', capable of winning hearts by her cheerful self-possession.

Chapter 10 – 'To Live as a Child of God'

Ernest Augustus – Duke of Cumberland; later King of Hanover; Queen Victoria's paternal uncle
    Son of Ernest Augustus:
    George

Adolphus – Duke of Cambridge; Queen Victoria's paternal uncle
    Children of Adolphus:
    George
    Augusta
    Mary

When, on 21st June 1837, eighteen-year-old Victoria ascended the throne, few could have predicted that the young and inexperienced Queen would reign for the next sixty-two years or that she would give her name to one of the most progressive eras in British history. For her extended family, though, it was clear from the moment of her accession that dramatic changes were afoot, particularly for the Cambridge and Cumberland cousins.

For a quarter of a century, the Kings of Britain had also ruled Hanover but, as Salic Law precluded females from the throne, the Kingdom passed to Victoria's uncle, Ernest Augustus, Duke of Cumberland. The rumours that had plagued him for most of his adult life, escalated on his niece's accession, as it was widely believed that he would not be content with Hanover alone and had already planned a coup to wrest the crown from the 'mere girl', Victoria. So persistent were the stories that the Duke of Wellington advised him to leave the country as soon as possible, adding that he should take care not to be pelted by the crowds on his departure.

Ernest Augustus set out at once to take possession of his new kingdom, but, while the Hanoverians were happy that at last they would have a resident monarch, his reputation had preceded him and he had barely arrived in the country when he almost provoked a revolution. Stating that he had played no part in the formation of the moderate constitution which his brother had established four years earlier, he ordered its suspension on the grounds that it did not serve the people. His purpose, he claimed, was to rescue Hanover from the 'menace of reform', and, when ministers objected, he dissolved parliament in clear demonstration that he intended to rule as an autocrat.

These high-handed actions 'caused great odium to be attached to his name by all Liberals, both English and Continental'; and feelings ran so high in England that politicians argued that he should be struck from the British succession. Impervious to criticism, though, Ernest maintained the suspension and, four months later, went so far as to abolish the constitution altogether.

As the kingdom appeared to be on the brink of revolt, the new King calmly and confidently pointed out the potential repercussions in the event of his enforced abdication. His son, George, was next-in-line to the throne but his blindness had already raised many questions about his ability to rule; and, if George were passed over, the throne would go either to his uncle, the Duke of Sussex, whose marriage to a commoner would jeopardise the succession; or to the Duke of Cambridge, who, despite his immense popularity in the kingdom, was staunchly loyal to his brother and would not countenance usurping his authority.

Ultimately, therefore, Ernest triumphed and, as the threat of revolution waned, he prepared to undertake 'one of the hardest tasks that man ever did, namely, to stay revolutionary principles, and to maintain strictly monarchical ones.'[106]

Despite these inauspicious beginnings, his strength of character and commitment to his duties soon won him the confidence and affection of the people. Throughout the fourteen years of his reign, Hanover prospered as he encouraged the construction of railways to improve trade and communications; and supported rapid industrialisation, which led to the building of new towns, where 'large shopfronts were daily extended; plate-glass windows, a sure proof of prosperity, were everywhere introduced: whereas, in the old time, nothing of the sort had been seen.'[107]

Without veering from his monarchical principles, he introduced many popular reforms some of which curbed the powers of the aristocracy in favour of workers and businessmen; and culturally, too, he improved the quality of life for the ordinary people, by arranging funding for theatres, galleries and opera companies to bring the arts to the masses[n].

Victoria's accession wrought changes, too, in the life of her uncle, Adolphus, Duke of Cambridge, who, for almost a quarter of a century had acted as the Viceroy of Hanover. With Ernest Augustus' arrival, the post became obsolete, and the Duke was forced to return with his family to England.

> "The kingdom of Hanover is separated from the Crown of Great Britain," wrote his son, George, "and my father is therefore removed from the Government of that country, where he has lived for these 24 years, and where we have all been born. Alas! Our connection with it is now

---

[n] See Chapter 15

suddenly broken off: for though we are still, and by God's blessing ever shall remain Princes of Hanover, yet we shall live for the most part in this country."[108]

Arriving home, the Cambridges settled briefly in Piccadilly, before moving to Cambridge Cottage in Kew – a 'very bad' house, in George's opinion, despite its 'cheerful' situation and proximity to London. Kew, at the time, was little more than a village but it boasted a long connection to the Royal Family. At the height of his insanity, George III had been incarcerated there; and his mother had begun work on the famous gardens, which subsequent generations of princes would develop The Dukes of Kent and Clarence had once occupied Cambridge House; and the Duke of Cumberland also had a property in the village, where, following his accession as King of Hanover, he continued to stay there whenever he was in England.

In spite of their son's apprehensions, the Duke and Duchess of Cambridge settled happily into their new life, enjoying walks in the park, participating in charity work and mixing freely with the local people. To outsiders, the Duchess often appeared cold and unfriendly but, as her letters to son reveal, her aloofness concealed a deep and abiding love for her family. Her more approachable husband was renowned for his affability and the charming and affectionate way he related to his children, particularly his youngest child, Mary, who utterly adored him.

The move from Hanover to England had been particularly traumatic for Mary, as most of her playmates remained behind and, as her sister, Augusta was nine years her senior, and her brother, George, had been posted to Gibraltar, initially she felt deeply the loss of her former companions. Like Queen Victoria and Charlotte of Belgium, she found comfort in her large collection of dolls, to which she became so attached that, even when she grew beyond adolescence, she was often seen in public carrying one in her arms.

Unlike her cousin, Victoria, however, Mary was not deprived of young company for long, as her parents invited their friends' children to Cambridge Cottage, which echoed with childish laughter as the little girls excitedly threw themselves into noisy games of chase and hide-and-seek. Unwaveringly loyal, Mary inspired great affection in people of all ages, as her striking blue eyes and long lashes enhanced the natural beauty of her face, which was almost always illuminated by a bright, benevolent smile. She was also known for her delicate hands and long tapered fingers with which she played beautifully on the piano, and which enabled her to become a talented needlewoman. Even in later life, when her immense weight became her most obvious feature, she retained her graceful hands and her ever-winning smile, and continued to inspire such affection that it was generally agreed that she was the most popular member of the entire Royal Family.

As a child, her smiles were brightest in the company of her father, and few treats brought her greater pleasure than her daily walks with him to feed the ducks in the park. Lenient to the point of indulgence, the Duke rarely corrected her, even when she hid from her governess to avoid tedious lessons. Invariably, it would be left to her father to find her, but, when he did so, he merely smiled and urged her to hurry back to the schoolroom. In spite of this clemency, the Duke and Duchess took their daughters' education very seriously. When Augusta developed a passion for history, they were quick to accommodate her interest by buying her books on the subject for her birthdays. For Mary, they appointed a kindly governess, Miss Draper, known affectionately to her pupil as Draperchen. After two years, though, she was replaced by the stricter Miss Howard, who responded more firmly to her pupil's lackadaisical behaviour by imposing a punishment, which both Mary and her father considered excessive. For failing to remain attentive in class, she was forced to forgo her afternoon walk with the Duke so that she could spend the time catching up with her studies. As much put out by this as his daughter was, the Duke raised several objections but later, on reflection, confessed that the governess' actions were correct and humbly assured her that in future he would support her disciplinary methods.

The Duke's leniency was balanced by the firmness of the Duchess, who, determined to instil in her daughter a sense of responsibility, spent time every Saturday morning reviewing her progress throughout the previous week, and, if she had done well, she was permitted to invite friends for a walk and afternoon tea; if not, she must write them an apology, explaining that she could not entertain them that day, since she was 'in disgrace'.

Both the Duke and Duchess were devoutly religious and took care to impart their Christian values to their children. Much thought went into appointing religious instructors; and daily prayers were routine for the whole family. The Duke's own faith was combined with an outspoken honesty, which often provoked much amusement among clerics and churchgoers. When, for example, a local parson preached a homily on the evils of swearing, the Duke called out in agreement,

'A damned good sermon!'

On another occasion, as the same cleric read the Gospel account of the tax collector, Zacchaeus, promising to give half his wealth to the poor, the Duke rose to his feet in protest, insisting that half was far too much, and a tenth would be more appropriate. Again, as a certain vicar prayed for rain in a time of drought, the Duke was heard to murmur that the prayer would not be answered until the wind had changed; and, while visiting the Duke of Devonshire at Chatsworth, he suddenly disrupted family prayers by announcing at the top of his voice:

"A damned good custom, this!"

When Mary was nine years old, her father appointed his own private chaplain, Reverend William Harrison, as her religious instructor. Under his guidance, she began the practice of reading passages from the bible each morning, and, as he frequently preached at the Foundling Hospital, she came to recognise the necessity of living her faith by involving herself in various charitable activities. Harrison prepared her for her confirmation; and helped her, too, to cope with the first great sorrow of her life – the death of her beloved father.

Towards the end of June 1850, the Duke had begun to suffer from stomach pains and, as he grew progressively weaker, his doctors, unsure of the cause of his illness, prescribed stimulants which provided temporary relief from his symptoms. On the evening of the 27th, Queen Victoria visited him at Cambridge House but the occasion, which might otherwise have brought him comfort, ultimately served only to exacerbate his condition. The meeting had been most cordial but, as the Queen's carriage pulled out of the courtyard, a would-be assassin, Robert Pate, lurched forwards and struck her head with the heavy brass end of his cane. Momentarily stunned, she nonetheless managed to assure the crowds that she was unharmed as they pounced upon her assailant and led him away to justice. The Duke was so shocked when he heard what had happened that, over the next few days, he fluctuated between apparent recovery and imminent death. On several occasions, Reverend Harrison was summoned to pray with him until, by early evening on July 8th, he rallied and it appeared that the worst was over.

Suddenly, however, shortly before ten o'clock, while George and Mary were dining downstairs and the Duchess had briefly left the room, 'he opened his eyes wide, uttered a faint exclamation and fell back lifeless without a struggle.' By the time his wife and children returned to his room he was dead.

> "Alas!" wrote George, "Not one of us was in the room at the moment, though we none of us left him for more than half an hour at a time to enable him to sleep. He had spoken to my Mother but a few minutes before his death, and his head and intellect were to the last as clear as possible."[109]

His one consolation was the thought that his father had not suffered greatly in his final moments; while Mary resignedly looked forward to an ultimate reunion in heaven.

> "As we sat by his death-bed," she wrote, "and watched his fine countenance, lighted up with a placid, happy expression, unlike the one of suffering which had rested upon it for the last days, all fear of death seemed to have passed away, and we felt that he was now thoroughly happy, and that it would be selfishness to wish him back again amongst us."[110]

Augusta, who by then was married°, had set off to London as soon as she heard that her father was ill, but arrived five hours too late to bid him goodbye. Heartbroken as they were, she and Mary sought to

---

° See Chapter 19

comfort their mother, whose fortitude and dignity in the midst of her grief won the affection and respect of all who came into contact with her.

The death of her father marked the beginning of the end of Mary's childhood, for, four months later as she celebrated her seventeenth birthday, she began preparing for a confirmation – an event which served the dual purpose of making a formal commitment to the Church of England, and going through a rite of passage from adolescence to adulthood. The importance and enormous significance of the occasion, suddenly dawned on Mary when a date was set for the ceremony shortly before Christmas.

"Am I prepared for it?" she wrote anxiously to Harrison. "This is a very serious consideration, and the happiness or misery of my future life depends on the answer I am able to give; but if I fervently pray to God to bless my very humble endeavours to become a Christian, and live as a child of God, I trust I shall be able one day to answer truly and sincerely in the affirmative."[111]

For the next few weeks her anxieties persisted while Harrison, urging her to trust in God, endeavoured to assure her that all was well. At last, on 19th December, she arrived at the small church in Kew to be confirmed by the Bishop of Gloucester in a ceremony attended by Queen Victoria as well as her own immediate family. George, who took the role of her father, recorded that she answered the Bishop's questions with clarity and confidence, and, when the service was over, she wrote to a friend that she now felt so much more mature that she was fully prepared to embark on her life as an adult. The youngest of Queen Victoria's paternal cousins had come of age.

Part II – The Machinations of Uncle Leopold

Chapter 11 – 'The Call of Ambition & Family Traditions'

Ferdinand of Saxe-Coburg-Kohary – Son of Ferdinand of Saxe-Coburg-Saalfeld; titular King of Portugal; Queen Victoria's cousin
Maria II de la Gloria – Queen of Portugal; wife of Ferdinand of Saxe-Coburg-Kohary

While the young Victoria had been growing up in the seclusion of Kensington Palace, another future Queen, just a few weeks her senior, had been living a remarkably eventful life in Brazil and Portugal. By her sixteenth birthday in 1835, Maria II de la Gloria had been widowed and ousted from her throne before being reinstated three years before Victoria's accession.

In 1826, when Maria was seven-years-old, her grandfather, King Joao VI of Portugal died, but his rightful heir – Maria's father, Pedro – was absent from the country, having been proclaimed Emperor of Brazil two years earlier. Absent, too, was Pedro's younger brother, Miguel, who had been exiled following a series of attempted coups in which he hoped to seize the throne in order to implement his own reactionary policies. King Joao's death, therefore, led to a period of uncertainty, as, although Pedro was the rightful heir, few Portuguese favoured a union with Brazil, and Miguel's many supporters were urging him to return and declare himself King.

In an effort to resolve the situation, Pedro, abdicated the Portuguese throne in favour of his daughter, Maria, and sought to appease his brother by appointing him regent. Having been assured that he would be able to marry his niece, the Queen, as soon as she came of age, Miguel ostensibly accepted the terms and returned from his exile in 1827. As calm appeared to have been restored, Maria visited England, where she first made the acquaintance of ten-year-old Princess Victoria.

"Our little Princess," wrote Lord Greville, "is a short, plain-looking child, not nearly so good-looking as the Portuguese."

The following year, however, Miguel reneged on his agreements and organised a coup which forced the child-Queen to seek refuge in Austria and England. While there, she again met Victoria, who thought her 'very kind, very tall for her age' and possessed of 'a beautiful figure.' The precariousness of her position, however, soon took a physical toll on Maria, and when Victoria met her again in 1833, she had gained so much weight that Victoria noted, 'she is grown very tall but also very stout.'[112]

Her father, meanwhile, abdicated the throne of Brazil in favour of his son, and, returning to Portugal in 1834, succeeded in overthrowing Miguel and restoring the crown to Maria, for whom he would act as regent until she reached her majority. Six months later, at her father's behest, she married the young Prince Auguste of Leuchtenberg – a former contender for the throne of Belgium. The marriage was short-lived as, two months after the wedding, Auguste returned sweating from a shooting excursion, and threw off his coat despite the chill of the season. Within a short time, he developed pneumonia and was hastily given the Last Rites, before expiring on March 28th 1835 at the age of only twenty-four. Seven months later, Maria's father also died, and the fifteen-year-old Queen was deemed old enough to rule in her own right.

Few statesmen at the time considered a woman capable to carrying out her duties alone, and, since the death of Auguste, discussions had been held all over Europe about finding the Portuguese Queen a suitable consort. As various candidates were suggested, King Leopold of Belgium wasted no time in proposing his nephew – Victoria's cousin, Ferdinand of Saxe-Coburg Kohary.

At the time, Ferdinand was living a sheltered life, pursuing his interests in art and music, with little interest in politics. He had no desire to be uprooted from his carefree existence, and his father was equally reluctant to see him saddled with the weight of responsibility that would accompany his lofty position as the husband of the Queen of Portugal. Regardless of their personal feelings, King Leopold instructed his physician and advisor, Baron Stockmar, to press Ferdinand's case with Count Lavradio, the Portuguese envoy to England, pointing out that, as a Roman Catholic, just three years older than Maria, he had all the necessary attributes of an ideal consort. At the same time, aware that a Portuguese marriage would enhance the status of his family and extend his own influence in Europe, Leopold used all his charm to pressurise his nephew into accepting his wishes, leaving the unfortunate Ferdinand torn between his own inclinations and his sense of duty.

"What," wrote the King's minister, General Goblet, "were his first emotions when the overtures of the Portuguese government invaded the peace of his Hungarian home? The idleness and timidity of youth in conflict with the call of ambition and family traditions must have resulted in painful and intimate struggles, of which the hearth of the Koharys has preserved the secret. But, beyond doubt, King Leopold had to put forth all his authority to overcome the modest repugnance of his august nephew."[113]

Ultimately, under pressure from his uncle, Ferdinand yielded, and his father returned from Hungary to Coburg, to meet with Stockmar and Lavradio to negotiate the details of the marriage contract. After much discussion it was agreed that the nineteen-year-old prince would be granted an annuity from the Portuguese government, which would be doubled in the event of the birth of a son, at which time, too, under the Portuguese constitution, he would be given the title of King throughout his wife's lifetime. Ferdinand himself had only one request – that he should be created Commander-in-Chief of the army – a demand with which the Portuguese only reluctantly complied before he and Maria were married by proxy on 1st January 1836.

> "I cannot say how happy I am," wrote Ferdinand's cousin, Victoria, "to become thus related to the Queen of Portugal, who has always been so kind to me and for whom I have always had a great affection. She is warm-hearted, honest and affectionate, and when she talks, is very pleasing...She is far from plain too; she has an exquisite complexion, a good nose and fine hair."[114]

Two months passed before Ferdinand set out to meet his bride for the first time and, as the day of his departure approached, he developed a bad cold – possibly a reaction to his anxiety about his future. Uncle Leopold sought to ease his fears by inviting him to Brussels, where he went to great lengths to introduce him to Portuguese domestic politics, thus making himself indispensable to his anxious nephew. His advised Ferdinand to remain silent at first throughout all political meetings until he had had time to acquaint himself with the characters and opinions of the various ministers. In the long run, he suggested, Ferdinand could arrange a complete reorganisation of the country, using as a model his own endeavours in Belgium. Advice came from England, too, as the Foreign Secretary, Palmerston, jokingly suggesting that the tall prince should stoop as he walked among the Portuguese people, who were generally smaller than he was, and he would create the impression of appearing to be keen to listen to all they were saying.

To ensure that his counsel would be heeded, King Leopold arranged for his own agent, Sylvain van de Weyer – a diplomat who had played a major part in the creation of the Belgian constitution – to accompany Ferdinand as an advisor along with the young prince's former tutor, Dietz, who would exercise a paternal influence over him for the first few years of his marriage. By the time that his nephew left Brussels, the King was convinced that he was well-prepared for the daunting task that lay ahead of him.

> "The stay here has done Fernando a great deal of good," he told Victoria, "and it cannot be denied that he is quite another person. It has given me some trouble, but I have written down for him everything which he ought to know about the organisation of a government in general, and what will be necessary in specifics to carry on successfully the Government in Portugal."[115]

Following the sojourn in Brussels, Ferdinand and his brother, Gusti, travelled on to England where Victoria was so impressed by Ferdinand's intelligence and perspicacity that she, too, was convinced of his future success. He was, she wrote to her uncle, 'full of courage, spirits, and goodwill'[116] and, despite the wrench of leaving his family, he set out cheerfully for Lisbon aboard a British gunboat.

As the ship docked on the banks of the Tagus River, the Prince received a warm reception from the crowds, making his arrival in Lisbon all the more disconcerting. There, the crowds were silent and the atmosphere was hostile, as many Portuguese viewed him as a British tool. Filled with the arrogance of youth, he did not help his own cause when, in his first address to the army, he adhered to Dietz' advice and upbraided the troops for their insubordination, stressing that he intended to exert a firmer discipline in the future. Seasoned veterans were aghast at such a display from an inexperienced soldier, and he soon created further animosity among the aristocracy by paying them little attention and refusing to allow them to sit in his presence.

His bride – 'a psychological conundrum', according to Ernest of Saxe-Coburg-Gotha – was equally dismissive of those of lower rank, never speaking to strangers and 'wasting but few words on the courtiers'[117].

Rather than discouraging this aloofness, Dietz constantly reminded Ferdinand of his exalted position, while van Weyer repeated King Leopold's sentiments that courage and firmness were his strongest weapons. As he relied so completely on these advisors, their presence provoked increasing resentment among the Portuguese, and, within five months of his arrival in the country, a popular uprising demanded the overthrow of the government and restrictions on the power of the monarchy.

Pessimistically prophesying a descent into total revolution, van Weyer urged Ferdinand to take up his position as Commander-in-Chief and lead his army against the rebels. Ferdinand prepared to do so, only to discover that the troops had already deserted. In a panic, he was on the point of following his advisors' counsel and fleeing with his wife to the British naval vessels that happened to be anchored in the harbour, when Maria wisely stepped in and tearfully agreed to establish a liberal and constitutional government. To her regret, this would limit the power of the monarchy; and, to Ferdinand's annoyance, it deprived him of his commandership of the army, but Maria had shown political acumen that was lacking in her husband, justifying his cousin, Ernest of Saxe-Coburg-Gotha's description of her as 'a thoroughly clever woman.' While visiting the couple some years later, Ernest reported that:

> "I have never heard a mistaken or illogical opinion from her lips, nor any flat or hasty remark, and that means a great deal...Everything which Donna Maria says is apposite, and generally accompanied by a keen display of wit. She hears and notices everything, and, as Ferdinand often assures me, can comprehend the most difficult matter at a glance...I have often noticed with pleasure how much interest she takes in everything, and how little she is inclined to be prejudiced."[118].

Meanwhile, fearing that the uprising would provide an ideal opportunity for Maria's uncle, Miguel, to return and seize power, van Weyer wrote to King Leopold, begging him to rally his troops in support of his nephew and the Queen. Leopold immediately requested the assistance of Britain and France but, when both declined to help, he approached the British Foreign Secretary, Palmerston, and asked for the loan of the British fleet to transport his own troops to Portugal. Again, Palmerston refused but, over the next few weeks, as Ferdinand and Maria retired to their palace in Belem where they planned to revoke the recently-accepted constitution, British ships appeared in the Tagus River, ready to evacuate the Royal Family if necessary.

The British presence served only to exacerbate a difficult situation, strengthening the belief that Ferdinand was merely a foreign puppet, and, as the attempted counter-revolution failed, his unpopularity reached its nadir. When he appeared in the street, he was pelted by stones and buckets of waste; and on one occasion as he was out riding, bystanders, pretending not to recognise him, claimed he was a madman and needed to be returned to an asylum. Gradually, calm was restored but, over the next few years, the country continued to be plagued by changes of government and political upheavals.

Eager to keep abreast of events, Queen Victoria asked her cousin, Alexander Mensdorff, to take a sabbatical from the Austrian army to visit Portugal and assess the state of affairs. Although Ferdinand was delighted to see his kinsman, the Portuguese ministers viewed Alexander as an English spy and resented his presence in the country. He was, though, able to make several important observations, including the fact that many of Ferdinand's errors were the fault of his advisor, Dietz, under whose influence he behaved like an autocrat. Eventually, under the weight of intense criticism, Dietz was forced to leave the country – much to the annoyance of Ernest of Saxe-Coburg-Gotha, who viewed him as a scapegoat for the interfering British.

> "Dietz had hardly a single enemy amongst the Portuguese politicians of all opinions," he later wrote, "…His removal from Queen Maria's Court was solely the work of the English Cabinet, which was not a little surprised that, after he was gone, things in Portugal became not better, but worse."[119]

Ferdinand had, however, learned from his early mistakes and, with maturity and experience, he gradually lost the brashness of youth. When Ernest visited him some years later, he confessed to being ashamed of his former faults and told his cousin 'how great a difference he feels within himself, compared with the state of mind in which he came here.'[120]

If, however, his political life had been fraught with difficulties, his marriage was proving to be surprisingly happy. From their first meeting, he and Maria had become very fond of one another, and when, within a year of the wedding, she became pregnant, she gladly handed over all of her duties to her husband. Maria was an 'exemplary wife and mother' who lived 'only for her [rapidly growing] family'. In September 1837, a son, Pedro, was born, and over the next fifteen years, she gave birth to ten more children, only six of whom survived beyond infancy.

With the birth of an heir, Ferdinand became the titular King of Portugal and devoted much of his time to promoting arts and culture throughout the country. Maria, too, was keen to improve health care and education for the masses, winning herself the epithet 'Dona Maria the Educator.' As devout Roman Catholics, they both took an interest in the restoration of churches and monasteries which had been left in ruins since religious orders were suppressed in 1834, and Ferdinand acquired the sixteenth century Monastery of Our Lady of Pena, which he transformed into a summer residence for the Royal Family.

Chapter 12 – 'Something of an English Look'

Leopold I – King of the Belgians; Queen Victoria's maternal uncle

Alexander of Württemberg – Son of Queen Victoria's aunt, Antoinette of Saxe-Coburg-Saalfeld
Marie Christine – Princess of Orléans; a daughter of King Louise Philippe of France; wife of Alexander.
> Son of Alexander and Marie Christine:
> Philippe

Albert – Prince of Saxe-Coburg-Gotha; son of Duke Ernest I; maternal cousin of Queen Victoria; later Prince Consort of Victoria
Ernest – Prince of Saxe-Coburg-Gotha; Albert's elder brother; later Duke Ernest II

Duchess of Kent – Queen Victoria's mother

Not content with having raised one nephew to a position of power, King Leopold of the Belgians spent much of the 1830s busily arranging alliances for other members of his extended family.

In 1837, he was instrumental in bringing about the marriage of his sister-in-law, Marie Christine of Orléans, and Alexander of Württemberg – the son of his sister, Antoinette. Since Alexander was not a Roman Catholic, many members of the French clergy objected to the match, and the Archbishop of Paris refused to allow the wedding to take place in a cathedral. A compromise was reached when Alexander agreed to raise his children in his wife's faith, and a ceremony was organised in a tiny chapel in Versailles, four months after Queen Victoria's accession.

The marriage was a triumph for Uncle Leopold, who was well aware that, since Alexander was descended from a relatively lowly German dynasty, his prospects of marrying the French King's daughter would, under other circumstances, have been extremely remote. For the young groom, though, this was a love-match as he and his bride were devoted to one another. A renowned sculptress and artist, Marie Christine was known for 'the vivacity and the zest with which she entered into all amusements;'[121] and, as one commentator wrote, her 'rare qualities were the charm and admiration of all around her.'[122]

With a beautiful wife whom he loved deeply, Alexander was prepared to forfeit the 'bad life' which had so shocked his cousin, Queen Victoria. Tragically, though, within a year of the wedding, Marie Christine was diagnosed with consumption, and, after giving birth to a son, Philippe, in July 1838, she was advised to travel to Italy, in the hope that the warmer climate might aid her recovery. During a four month stay in Genoa, her health gradually deteriorated and, by the time that she moved to Pisa in December, she knew that she was dying. While she spent her final weeks praying for her husband's conversion to Catholicism, her brother, the Duc de Nemours hurried to her side. In a letter to his parents, he described her last moments, as she realised that the end was nigh.

> "Mama! my parents, my brothers, my sisters," she exclaimed, "my friends...Alexandre, I ask you to become a Catholic. My God! My God! forgive me, I have sinned. See the power of religion! See the strength that it gives! The little too; do it. Alexander; become a Catholic; swear to me, you will raise our son in this religion...swear to me..."

At seven-thirty in the evening of January 2nd 1839, as her sufferings were so intense that she could barely speak, she took the religious medal that she always wore around her neck and handed it to her husband, begging him to wear it, until at last, shortly after eight o'clock, her breathing ceased.

"Alexander and his poor son!" gasped the Duc de Nemours. "I am torn to pieces for them."[123]

Perhaps fearing that it would damage the image of the monarch if it were known that a member of the Royal Family had died of consumption, the King of France made no official announcement of his daughter's death and did not order his court into mourning, so it was left to Alexander's family to publish the details of what had happened. As the grieving widower returned to Paris with his infant son, the Duc de Nemours remained to organise a Mass for his sister in Pisa, before accompanying her body back to her homeland, where respectful crowds lined the route to her interment at the Chapel Royal in Dreux.

King Leopold, meanwhile, was absorbed in his plans to bring about an even more prestigious match – that of his nephew, Albert of Saxe-Coburg-Gotha, and his niece, the young Queen Victoria. According to some accounts, the plan had been concocted by King Leopold's mother within days of Albert's birth, and when he was still a small child, his nurse had told him that one day he would marry the Queen of England.

Whether or not the story is true, when Albert was sixteen years old, his uncle set about preliminary investigations into whether or not the young prince was suited to the role of consort. The ubiquitous Stockmar was sent to Coburg to assess his character and temperament, and, after only the briefest of meetings, he was able to report that Albert had a dignified manner and, in time, would probably grow into a most attractive young man. More significantly, he added, 'It may prove, too, a lucky circumstance that even now he has something of an English look.'[124]

As with Ferdinand of Saxe-Coburg-Kohary, Albert's wishes were of little importance, since, according to Stockmar, all that was required of him was a willingness to 'sacrifice mere pleasure to real usefulness.'[125]

Although it was not yet time to broach the subject of marriage directly, Stockmar advised King Leopold that it would be helpful to introduce the cousins to one another. Drawing Victoria's mother, the Duchess of Kent, into the plot, the King suggested that she should invite Albert and his brother, Ernest, to stay for a month at Kensington Palace in time for Victoria's seventeenth birthday celebrations in 1836. Albert – officially at least – was not to be told of the purpose of the visit, but the King could not resist confiding his hopes in Victoria.

True to form, the lonely princess was overjoyed to meet her German relations, and gushed with enthusiastic descriptions of their charms. They had even superseded her Kohary cousins in her estimation as she confided to her journal:

> "Dearly as I love Ferdinand, and also good Augustus, I love Ernest and Albert more than them, oh yes, much more. Augustus was like a good, affectionate child, quite unacquainted with the world, phlegmatic, and talking but very little; but dearest Ernest and dearest Albert are so grown-up in their manners, so gentle, so kind, so amiable, so agreeable, so very sensible and reasonable, and so really and truly good and kind-hearted."[126]

Albert, she noted, was the cleverer and more pensive of the two, but he was also full of wit and fun, and, most endearingly of all, he shared her love of dogs and paid a good deal of attention to her beloved spaniel, Dash.

For his part, although he was fond of his cousin and was grateful for the warm welcome he received from King William IV and Queen Adelaide, Albert was far less enthusiastic about his stay in England. The damp weather affected his health; the late hours exhausted him; and, having contracted a 'bilious fever', he was relieved when the holiday was over.

In spite of Albert's reservations, Uncle Leopold felt that the visit had been such a success that he invited Albert and Ernest to further their education in Belgium so that he could groom the former for his intended role. Stockmar fully supported the plan, since Brussels, in his view, would provide the princes with 'the best opportunity for making acquaintance with really great society, with politics, and life as it is.'[127]

The brothers were given a small but comfortable house, sufficiently secluded to allow them to reside in relative obscurity, but close enough to the city to give them easy access to galleries and museums. Albert thrived in the studious atmosphere created for him by some of the most eminent scholars and scientists in Belgium, and made use of every moment in Brussels to broaden his education. With Uncle Leopold's encouragement, he continued to exchange letters with Cousin Victoria, but their platonic missives contained little suggestion of a budding romance.

After ten months in Brussels, the brothers progressed to the University of Bonn, where, again, Albert flourished in the academic surroundings. Throwing himself enthusiastically into his studies, he nonetheless found time to pursue his passion for art and to enjoy a carefree existence with his fellow students.

"Prince Albert," wrote one of his companions, " possessed a lively sense of the ridiculous as well as a great talent for mimicking and it could scarcely fail but that the immediate subjects for the exercise of this talent should be his own attendants, and the professors, who, while absorbed in their lectures, exhibited some striking peculiarities and odd manners. Prince Albert could take these off inimitably and by his good memory was able to produce whole sentences out of their lectures to the general amusement of the company."[128]

All too soon, though, the carefree days drew to an end, and, as Ernest prepared to embark on a course of military training in Dresden, Albert's spirits sank as he returned to Coburg. Mirroring Gusti's sentiments when Ferdinand left for Portugal, Albert wrote to his stepmother that the prospect of being separated from Ernest haunted him like a nightmare, and, after his departure, he wrote dejectedly:

"Now I am quite alone. Ernst is far off and I am left behind; still surrounded by so many things that keep up the illusion that he is in the next room."[129]

Meanwhile, in England, King William had died and Victoria had ascended the throne, prompting a dutiful letter from Albert, expressing his hope that she would enjoy a 'happy, long and glorious' reign.

Although the young Queen graciously accepted his good wishes, her dramatic change in status left her little inclination to consider him as a potential groom. Finally liberated from her mother and John Conroy, she had no intention of sacrificing her new-found freedom to a husband, and, what was more, she had become infatuated by a most unlikely figure – her Prime Minister, the aging roué, Lord Melbourne.

Rumours were rife that the eighteen-year-old sovereign spent every possible moment in Melbourne's company, often disappearing with him on riding expeditions for up to six hours a day; and when he was voted out of office, she treated his successor, Robert Peel, with such contempt that he found it impossible to form a government, and Melbourne was duly returned to power. While Victoria rejoiced at her triumph, the public, who had greeted her accession with such high expectations, was far from amused by such a petulant and unconstitutional display, and when she appeared in at the Windsor Races, she was greeted with jeers and calls of 'Mrs Melbourne.'

Stockmar, who had been sent to England to advise her and monitor her progress, was equally unimpressed by her behaviour and wrote to his master in Belgium:

> "The late events in England distress me. How could they let the Queen make such mistakes to the injury of the monarchy?"[130]

Though mildly perturbed by this turn of events, King Leopold was not unduly concerned, knowing that Melbourne was nothing more than a fleeting infatuation, and confident that his protégé, Albert – now languishing in Coburg – would eventually win the Queen's heart.

To further his plans, the King decided that Albert must spend time in sophisticated company to enable him to become more of a man of the world. He arranged, therefore, a tour of Switzerland and Italy for Albert, under the ever-watchful eye of Baron Stockmar. In Italy, 'intoxicated' by the beauty of Renaissance art, Florentine architecture and the Tuscan countryside, Albert gradually recovered from the trauma of parting with Ernest, and accepted Stockmar's suggestion that he should return to England to pursue his cousin once more.

While King Leopold was confident that this time his suit would be successful, Stockmar had many reservations about his ability to impress the passionate Victoria. He lacked, said the Baron, the ability to engage in small talk or flirtations and, while men enjoyed his company, he was 'a little too 'empressé''with women, 'too indifferent and too reserved.'[131]

His fears, however, were groundless. When, tanned by the Italian sun, Albert arrived in England in the autumn of 1839, Victoria no longer saw him as a likeable cousin, but rather as a strikingly handsome young man, exuding charisma and confidence. From the moment that she set eyes on him, she gasped in wonder at his appearance.

"At half-past seven," she wrote in her journal, "I went to the top of the staircase to receive my two dear cousins, Ernest and Albert, whom I found grown, changed, and embellished. It was with some emotion that I beheld Albert, who is *beautiful*."[132]

In the days that followed, she breathlessly recorded in detail every moment she spent in his company.

Somewhat surprised to learn of her genuine feelings for him, Albert confessed that he was at a loss to understand why he should inspire such affection. At the same time, too, though, he could not deny his own developing attraction to her, and when, sooner than expected, she proposed, he accepted without hesitation. That evening, he wrote that it had been the happiest day of his life; while Victoria wrote to Stockmar:

"Albert has completely won my heart...and I feel certain that he will make me very happy."[133]

On his return to Coburg, Albert sent his fiancée passionate letters, expressing his eager anticipation of the wedding; and, when his aunt, the Duchess of Kent, wrote to tell him that his 'poor little bride' was so lonely without him that she was 'sitting alone her room, silent and sad,'[134] he replied that the thought had touched him deeply, and 'oh that I might fly to her side to cheer her!'[135]

Not everyone, though, shared Victoria and Albert's excitement. The Queen's uncle, King Ernest Augustus of Hanover, so despised the Coburgs that he encouraged a number of xenophobic Members of Parliament to create as many difficulties for Albert as possible. In Parliament, they squabbled over his allowance; and leaked slanders to journalists about the *foreigner,* who they falsely claimed had secretly converted to Catholicism. Even the Duke of Cambridge, who had been one of the first to wish Victoria joy on her engagement, raised strong objections when she announced that her husband should come immediately after her in the order of precedence; and the aristocracy mocked him because: .

> "...he did not dress in quite the orthodox English fashion;...he did not sit on horseback in the orthodox English way;...he did not shake hands in the orthodox English manner etc. etc. all this even those...who knew and esteemed him could not quite get over. One heard them say, "He is an excellent, clever, able fellow but look at the cut of his coat, or look at the way he shakes hands.""[136]

More alarmingly still, Victoria's former governess, Louise Lehzen, also took exception to the Prince. Fearing that he would usurp her position as the

Queen's closest confidante, she made it clear that she had no intention of loosening her hold over Victoria, but would make mischief for anyone who attempted to come between her and her illustrious pupil.

Albert stoically bore the slurs in silence, and took comfort from the cheering crowds who gathered to greet him at Dover when he returned to England for his wedding. The five hours crossing had been particularly rough, and, although he had not yet recovered from sea-sickness, he managed to respond to the warmth of the welcome and to adhere to his plan to visit Canterbury en route to Windsor Castle, where the Queen was eagerly anticipating their reunion.

The wedding took place in the Chapel Royal of St James' Palace on the afternoon of February 12th 1840, and was attended by several of Victoria's uncles from both sides of her family. The Duke of Sussex, it was noticed, found the ceremony particularly moving, while one of the late King William's illegitimate sons sobbed loudly in the gallery when the couple spoke their vows. The Duke of Cambridge, though, was, according to one of the bridesmaids:

> "...decidedly gay, making very audible remarks from time to time...After it was over we all filed out of the chapel in the same order, the Duke of Cambridge very gallantly handing the princesses down the steps with many audible civilities."[137]

Following a reception at Buckingham Palace, the bride and groom returned to Windsor Castle for a brief honeymoon; and, the following day, with uninhibited exhilaration, the Queen wrote to Melbourne of her 'gratify and bewildering' wedding night, when Albert's:

> "...excessive love and affection gave me feelings of heavenly love and happiness. He

clasped me in his arms and we kissed each other again and again."

Enraptured as she was by Albert's physical charms, Victoria was not prepared to share with him her queenly authority. As she worked through her papers, her highly-intelligent husband was reduced to blotting her signature and standing idly outside the door while she discussed matters of state with her ministers. For all their mutual attraction and affection, it was obvious to them both that they barely knew one another, and it did not take long for their contrasting characters to clash.

Victoria, still revelling in her freedom, relished the social life of the capital where she could dance until dawn, but her more studious husband found the late nights exhausting; had no interest in the tittle-tattle of the ballroom; and felt oppressed by the unhealthy smog of London that contrasted so sharply with the pure air of his Thuringian home.

For the passionate Victoria, it was difficult to comprehend Albert's self-restraint, for, unlike her, he did not easily show his feelings, but withdrew to his rooms in silence when she ranted and raged. In her frustration, she flew into tantrums, hammering on his door and ordering him to allow her in, but still he failed to respond, denying her access to him until she had calmed down.

Victoria was not the only one who had difficulty in grasping the complexities of Albert's character. Even his brother, who knew him better than anyone, considered him a 'psychological enigma', in whom 'amiability went hand in hand with critical severity.'[138]

"The greatest warmth and self-sacrificing love would sometimes change to painful coldness," Ernest recalled "...Yet, I never met with anyone, during my whole life, who had more feeling for mankind. Everything beautiful and noble...lived

138

in him. His constant thought was how to make people happy, and he could be as hard as possible to those same people."[139]

Confused and struggling to cope with so many dramatic changes in her life, Victoria clung to her familiar companion – the envious Louise Lehzen, who delighted in creating trouble between husband and wife. To Albert's despair, Victoria always sided with the governess, to the point where, three months after the wedding, he wrote:

"...the difficulty with filling my place with the proper dignity, is that I am only the husband, not the master, in my house."[140]

Initially, due to Lehzen's influence, the couple's problems increased with the birth of their first child, Vicky, in November 1841. The governess insisted on overseeing the nursery and, much to Albert's annoyance, 'the hag,' as he called her, kept the fire burning and the windows closed while she and the nurse sat gossiping and dangling his little daughter in their arms. No matter how forcefully Albert protested, Victoria refused to support him, and matters came to a head when the child became ill with what Lehzen dismissed as merely a childish ailment. Convinced that there was something seriously wrong with Vicky, Albert railed against 'the crazy, stupid, common intriguer with a lust for power', and warned Victoria that if their baby died, it would be on her conscience.

Stockmar, now assuming the role of marriage-guidance counsellor, agreed that the Queen was too deeply under Lehzen's sway, and failed to place sufficient confidence in her husband.

"The Queen is influenced more than she is aware of by the Baroness," he wrote to her erstwhile idol, Lord Melbourne. "In consequence of that influence, she is not so ingenuous as she was two years ago. I do not think that the withholding of her confidence does proceed wholly from indolence, though it may partly arise, as the Prince suggests, from the entire confidence which she reposes in her present Ministers, making her inattentive to the plans and measures proposed, and thinking it unnecessary entirely to comprehend them; she is of necessity unable to impart their views and projects to him who ought to be her friend and counsellor."[141]

Melbourne attempted to use his influence to persuade her to pay more attention to Albert, but it was not until Stockmar threatened to withdraw all his support from her, that she finally agreed to pension off Lehzen and send her back to her native Germany.

From the moment of Lehzen's departure, Victoria came to rely totally on her 'beloved angel, Albert,' with whom, over the next fifteen years, she produced eight more children. With each pregnancy her dependence upon him increased and her admiration for his political acumen knew no bounds. She trusted his judgement so implicitly that not a single official paper passed through her hands without his having first read it; and it was often left to him to dictate a reply. He met regularly with ministers, wrote numerous letters to Parliament and advised the Queen on virtually every domestic issue and foreign policy. Within their own home, too, it was he who made all the plans for their children – supervising their education and arranging happy and useful recreations. He was, said the Queen, the head of the household, and her only regret was that her ministers refused to grant him the title of King.

Chapter 13 – A Man 'Who Always Wants a Part to Play'

Ernest I – Duke of Saxe-Coburg-Gotha; Prince Albert's father; Queen Victoria's father-in-law & maternal uncle
Ernest II – Duke of Saxe-Coburg-Gotha; Prince Albert's elder brother; Queen Victoria's cousin
Albert – Prince of Saxe-Coburg-Gotha; Queen Victoria's consort & cousin
Alexandrine – Princess of Baden; wife of Ernest II of Saxe-Coburg-Gotha
Alfred – Duke of Edinburgh; second son of Queen Victoria & Prince Albert

King Leopold of the Belgians – Queen Victoria's maternal uncle

Leopold – Prince of Saxe-Coburg-Kohary; Queen Victoria's cousin
Ferdinand –Prince of Saxe-Coburg-Kohary; Titular King of Portugal; Leopold's elder brother; Queen Victoria's cousin

Isabella II – Queen of Spain
Luisa Fernanda – Infanta of Spain; sister of Isabella II
Maria Christina – Mother of Isabella II

In manners and morals no two brothers could have been more dissimilar than Princes Ernest and Albert of Saxe-Coburg Gotha. While the latter was constantly extolled as a model of virtue and angel of purity, the former had followed their father's example in a voracious pursuit of pretty women. Even by the time that he embarked on his military career in the service of the King of Saxony, he had contracted venereal disease, which marred his handsome features, leaving him 'thin...hollow-cheeked and pale' and lacking in beauty. Two years later, when he fathered an illegitimate daughter, Hélène[p], by a certain Miss Steinfplug, Albert naively believed that the only means of stopping his philandering was for him to find a respectable bride as soon as he was certain that his illness was cured.

With typical foresight, Uncle Leopold had already begun searching for a future Duchess of Coburg, and his first thought was his sister-in-law, Clementine of Orléans – the youngest daughter of King Louis Philippe of France. When King Leopold broached the subject with Ernest, he gallantly replied that any man would be honoured to be married to Clementine, but, to his regret, their religious differences created virtually insurmountable problems. Considering that his uncles Leopold and Ferdinand, and his cousin, Augustus of Württemberg had happily married Roman Catholics, this sudden devotion to his Lutheran faith, seems to be more of an excuse than a matter of principle.

Undeterred, Uncle Leopold soon produced an alternative candidate – Adelgunde, the sixteen-year-old daughter of King Ludwig of Bavaria, and younger sister of 'the detestable Otto' of Greece. Once again, though, religious differences put paid to the plan, as the predominantly Roman Catholic Bavarians had little desire to welcome a Lutheran prince, who adamantly refused to raise his children in their faith.

Ernest's father was also busily trying to secure him a bride, believing that the sooner he married, the

---

[p] Ernest did not provide for his illegitimate daughter and, later, Hélène was left in such dire straits that it fell to Queen Victoria's eldest daughter, Vicky, to rescue her from poverty.

sooner he would settle in Coburg to prepare for his future role as Duke. By chance, within months of the birth of Ernest's illegitimate daughter, Prince William of Prussia, a younger brother of King Frederick William III, happened to pay the Duke a visit at his summer residence in Gotha. Accompanying him was his pretty daughter, sixteen-year-old Marie, and, before the visit was over, the two fathers had reached an agreement that their offspring would be betrothed.

Although no official announcement was made, Ernest was happy with the arrangement and, convinced that the affair had been settled, he looked forward to their wedding. In the winter of 1841, however, while he was stationed in Leipzig with the King of Saxony, he met an aide-de-camp who informed him that his intended bride had just announced her engagement to Crown Prince Maximilian of Bavaria. Unbeknown to Ernest, when Marie's parents looked more deeply into his background, they were shocked by his promiscuity and arranged a more profitable match. Marie would go on to become a popular Queen of Bavaria and the mother of the 'Swan King' – Leopold II, and his insane brother, Otto.

Insulted that he had not been informed of this change of plan, Ernest decided to deflect the shame of having been jilted by announcing his own betrothal as soon as possible. By chance, that very day, Prince Karl Egon of Fürstenburg, a brother-in-law of the Grand Duke of Baden, arrived at the hotel where he was staying. During the evening, the two men played cards together and Ernest impulsively asked his companion whether he thought he might be considered a worthy contender for the hand of his niece, Alexandrine, the eldest daughter of the Grand Duke.

Prince Karl Egon assured Ernest that his suit would be well-received and that he could not find a lovelier bride. Like Ernest, Alexandrine had also been unceremoniously jilted by a fiancé – in her case, Tsar Alexander II of Russia, who had been on his way to visit her when he broke his journey in Darmstadt and suddenly decided to marry instead the daughter of the Grand Duke of Hesse.

Ernest returned to Dresden to solicit the support of Queen Marie of Saxony, who promised to speak to the Grand Duke on his behalf. She was clearly in no hurry to do so, as weeks passed before Ernest finally received the news for which he had been waiting – the Grand Duke and Grand Duchess of Baden would be happy to welcome him to their home in Karlsruhe in the New Year. Delighted, Ernest returned home to Coburg for Christmas, anticipating that his father would share his joy, but the Duke withheld his blessing, complaining that the whole affair had been 'badly managed' and the marriage would be of little benefit to the duchy.

In spite of this disappointment, in January 1842, Ernest set out for Baden where he received a warm reception from Alexandrine's parents. For all their hospitality, though, he was deeply perplexed by their apparent ignorance of the purpose of his visit, for, while they chattered away about all manner of subjects, they pointedly appeared to avoid any mention of their daughter. Eventually, unable to bear the suspense, Ernest interrupted the Grand Duchess to tell her that he wished to propose to Alexandrine. To his immense relief, she replied that she would be happy to welcome him into her family, but ultimately it was a matter for her daughter to decide.

Alexandrine was duly summoned and, after a moment's hesitation, Ernest found the courage to address her directly.

"As I looked at the Princess," he later recalled, "I was overcome by the conviction that hers was a nature to whom nothing but the most open character and the completest truth could be pleasing. So I said frankly that I had come to Karlsruhe for the purpose of asking her hand in marriage. 'Either,' I continued, 'tell me that you consent, and then I shall stay and we will learn to know one another better, or simply say the one word which your parents perhaps kept back out of anxiety and consideration for me. I shall in that case leave this house with the firm conviction that no one else will ever know anything of what has taken place to-day.'"[142]

Although she had only met him on one previous occasion, Alexandrine instantly accepted his proposal, prompting her overjoyed mother to express her opinion that marriages between strangers were generally more successful than those between acquaintances, which often led to mutual disappointment.

Elatedly, Ernest wrote to Uncle Leopold, describing Alexandrine as all he had ever wished for; and, so eager was he to be married that he arranged for the wedding to take place in May – just four months after he had proposed.

Noticeably absent from the ceremony were the groom's brother and sister-in-law, Prince Albert and Queen Victoria, who, despite being greatly relieved that Ernest had found a lovely wife, were prevented from travelling to Germany due to political unrest at home[q]. Instead they invited the couple to spend their honeymoon in England but, in view of the crisis, the

---

[q] Following the failure of Parliament to respond to the Chartists' demands for political reform, strikes were breaking out across Britain and there was a powerful feeling of impending disorder, rioting or even revolution.

newly-weds travelled instead to their new home – Schloss Kallenberg on the outskirts of Coburg, a wedding gift to them from Ernest's father.

By mid-summer, the political tensions had eased and Ernest took his new wife to England, where Queen Victoria was so delighted by 'sweet' Alexandrine that the two struck up an immediate friendship, which would continue to the end of Victoria's life.

The couple had been married for just eighteen months when, on the 29th January 1844, Ernest's father, the Duke of Saxe-Coburg Gotha, died quite suddenly at four o'clock in the morning, following a 'spasmodic internal infection.' A fortnight later, Ernest wrote to King Leopold of his deep sorrow at his father's death, and assuring him that he was readying himself to undertake his duties as the new Duke to the best of his ability. He was, he knew, guaranteed the support of his wife and his brother, who, devastated by the loss of his father, wrote to Baron Stockmar:

> "This shall not weaken my love for my widowed native land. I will help Ernest with heart and hand in the difficult task to which he is called...The good Alexandrine seems to me in the whole picture like the consoling angel."[143]

Alexandrine's devotion and tender ministrations were not sufficient to curb Ernest's philandering. Within two years of the wedding, he looked 'dreadfully ill', suggesting a recurrence of venereal disease. This did not prevent him from continuing his amorous adventures, and, in 1847, he began a brief affair with a renowned French opera singer, thrice-married Victoire Noel, who performed under the stage name Rosina Stoltz. In May 1848, Victoire gave birth to a son, Karl, and, although at the time it was said that the boy could have been fathered by any one of her many lovers, Ernest acknowledged him as his own. On his

146

seventeenth birthday, he gave him a knighthood, and, three years later, created him Baron von Stolzenau Ketschendorf.

Karl had not reached his fourth birthday, when Ernest began another liaison with a circus performer, Rosa von Lowenstern. This time, according to Count Paul Vassili, when his mistress became pregnant, Ernest arranged for her to marry his chamberlain before the child – a son, named Kamillo – was born. Henceforth this became his usual means of dealing with the mothers of his illegitimate children, many of whom he acknowledged as his own, although they were raised by various members of his suite.

Alexandrine endured his infidelities in silence, much to the annoyance of Queen Victoria, who told her eldest daughter that:

> "She is always left alone at home and Uncle E. only thinks of himself; it provokes me more than I can say."[144]

As the years went by, his affairs became even more blatant, as he moved two of his mistresses into his home – a situation which utterly appalled Queen Victoria but which Alexandrine accepted without complaint. More difficult for her to bear was her own childlessness, which made visits to England particularly painful. Watching the closeness of Victoria and Albert's ever-growing family, brought home to both her and Ernest the realisation of what they lacked. Reluctantly, Ernest agreed to make Albert's son, Alfred, his heir and from that moment on, he intended to have a say in the boy's upbringing. He asked that Alfred should continue his education in Germany – a demand which Alfred's parents refused on the grounds that he was also second-in-line to the British throne, but Albert assured his brother that he would ensure his son was well-acquainted with the politics and mores of the duchy.

Alfred's education was but one cause of a developing rift between Ernest and Albert, who had been growing apart ever since the latter's marriage. Not only was Albert horrified by Ernest's promiscuity and neglect of his wife, but also he was angered by his extravagance and failure to deal with the economic situation in Coburg, which resulted in his amassing so many debts that he was obliged to sell a part of his inheritance. Moreover, although he originally shared Albert's dream of a liberal and unified Germany, he gradually drifted towards the opposite end of the political spectrum, believing that it would benefit the duchy to support the more militaristic Prussians.

For his part, Ernest felt that Albert had become so English since his marriage that he failed to understand the needs of his native Coburg or the changing political situation in Germany as a whole.

> "My brother," he wrote, "was by no means inclined to consent to an energetic rule, such as I adopted… and in later years, he opposed the separation of state and family matters, which I had from the first looked upon as unavoidable, and still clung to the thought that the patriarchal rule, which in German States was still most decidedly shown in income and questions of domain, could be kept up."[145]

As early as 1845, a lady-in-waiting observed a coldness between the brothers when Ernest and Alexandrine prepared to return home following a holiday in England.

> "The parting of the Royalty was not so sorrowful as I expected; plenty of kissing, but no tears; and scandal even whispers that Ernest, in spite of all his love for his dear brother

Albert, found his sejour at Windsor 'un peu ennuyeux,' and therefore did not break his heart at going."[146]

The following year, the so-called 'Affair of the Spanish Marriages' provoked further disagreement between the brothers and drew their cousin, Leopold of Saxe-Coburg-Kohary, into the dispute.

From the moment that three-year-old Isabella II had ascended the Spanish throne in 1833, the question of her future consort had become a matter of international importance. King Louis Philippe of France hoped to secure her for one of his sons – a notion which Victoria and Albert appeared to support when they made a state visit to France in 1845. The British Government, however – and more particularly the Foreign Minister, Palmerston – opposed the idea on the grounds that it would increase French influence in the region and could potentially lead to the creation of a dual kingdom. Instead, Palmerston favoured King Leopold of the Belgian's proposed candidate – his nephew and Queen Victoria's cousin, Prince Leopold Saxe-Coburg-Kohary. The French, convinced that a Coburg prince would be controlled by Britain, raised such strong objections that Queen Victoria, keen to maintain good relations between Britain and France, assured Louis Philippe that she would not promote the match, and in return Louis Philippe withdrew his son's name from the list of potential consorts.

An alternative candidate was suggested – the devoutly religious and somewhat unattractive Count of Trapani. Isabella was no more drawn to Trapani than he was to her, since she and her younger sister were, according to the diarist Thomas Raikes, 'a most seedy, dowdy pair of infantas,'[147] and to make matters worse, the Queen was suffering from a skin complaint, which marred her less than alluring features.

Nonetheless, by 1846, Trapani was still considered to be the most likely consort, when Prince Leopold's father took him to visit his elder brother, King Ferdinand of Portugal. On their return journey, they ventured into Spain, which immediately raised French suspicions that this was a British ploy to bring Leopold and the Queen together. Queen Victoria, deeply offended by the allegation, assured Louis Philippe that this was far from the case – a fact supported by her brother-in-law, Ernest, who insisted that Leopold had not even visited Madrid, and, in view of the difficulties that his brother had faced in Portugal, neither he nor his father wanted a Spanish marriage.

Ernest himself, however, being 'one of the men who always want to have a part to play, and cannot wait until the turn of the wheel has again brought things round to a point where they can get their chance again,'[148] took it upon himself to travel to the Peninsular, ostensibly to visit his cousin, King Ferdinand. In Lisbon, while claiming impartiality, he made no secret of the fact that both he and the King of the Belgians considered Cousin Leopold the most suitable candidate for the Spanish Queen, and he let it known that he would happily to mediate in the matter.

To his delight, he soon received a letter from Isabella's mother, Maria Christina, who asked him to help her to promote Leopold's cause. She had, she claimed, tried to reconcile herself to the marriage of her daughter and the Count of Trapani but, as the King of the Belgians was well aware, she actually favoured an alliance with the Coburg prince, which would 'reconcile my daughter's happiness with that of the Spanish nation.'[149]

150

To satisfy the French, Maria Christina suggested that her younger daughter, Infanta Luisa Fernanda, should marry the Duc de Montpensier, the youngest son of King Louis Philippe; and she asked Ernest to obtain Queen Victoria's assurance that, should Leopold marry Isabella, Britain would respect her country's independence by refraining from interfering in Spanish politics.

Relishing his role as mediator, Ernest forwarded the letter to his brother, Albert, who received it with a combination of annoyance and embarrassment. Why, he wondered, had Ernest decided to meddle in a matter that did not concern him, particularly when Maria Christina's letter would strengthen the French belief that Queen Victoria was duplicitously promoting her cousin as consort. On Albert's advice, Queen Victoria, immediately sought to allay suspicion by forwarding the letter to Louis Philippe, and distancing herself from Ernest, whom Albert advised to cancel a planned visit to England on his way home from Spain.

"This gives us the appearance of faithlessness, intrigue, perfidiousness, etc., etc.," Albert wrote angrily to him, "and affords France just reason to complain. We have seen ourselves forced to wash our hands of the matter, and to explain to France that we are no parties to this step. This is naturally not believed, and your entirely inexplicable journey to Spain during Uncle Ferdinand's presence there, is a fact which makes appearances seem very much against us."[150]

Moreover, while agreeing that Leopold was by far the most suitable candidate, he doubted whether he would be willing to commit himself to marriage with a Queen of 'few small charms' in a country that was beset by political problems.

Others, meanwhile, were less convinced of Maria Christina's sincerity, believing that the letter was a ploy intended to embarrass Queen Victoria and to secure a stronger bond between Spain and France.

> "I met...yesterday," wrote Thomas Raikes, "a very clever and well-informed Spaniard, who is just arrived from Madrid, and who, among many other things, said we might rely upon it that she never meant this Coburg match at all, and that the proposal was only meant as a snare to us; and if we had listened to it, France would have taken advantage of our doing so, and laid to our charge the intrigues of which we now accuse her."[151]

The intrigues of which France was accused came to light four months after Ernest's visit, when it was suddenly announced that, under pressure from King Louis Philippe, Isabella was betrothed to her effeminate cousin, the Duke of Cadiz. More startlingly, on the very same day, Isabella's younger sister, Luisa Fernanda was engaged to be married to the French King's son, the Duke of Montpensier.

Queen Victoria was horrified that the young Queen had been forced against her will to accept such a 'wretch of a husband'[152]; and, what was more, it was clear that she had been deceived by Louis Philippe, who had failed to honour their agreement.

The affair resulted in a serious breach of relations between the French and British Royal Families, but within eighteen months, Queen Victoria would come to the aid of King Louis Philippe when he was ousted from the throne in the midst of a revolution.

Part III – Rumours of War & Revolution

Chapter 14 – 'In the Parisian Mob'

Louis Philippe – King of France
Amélie – Queen of France
Victoire – Princess of Saxe-Coburg-Kohary; Duchesse de Nemours; Queen Victoria's cousin
Louis, Duc de Nemours – Husband of Victoire; son of King Louise Philippe of France
Children of the Duc & Duchesse de Nemours:
Louis, Comte d'Eu
Ferdinand, Duc d'Alençon
Marguerite Adelaide

Louise – Queen of the Belgians; wife of King Leopold I; daughter of King Louis-Philippe of France

Gusti (Augustus) – Prince of Saxe-Coburg-Kohary; brother of Victoire; Queen Victoria's cousin
Clementine – Princess d'Orléans; daughter of King Louis Philippe of France; wife of Gusti
Children of Gusti & Clementine:
Philip
Ludwig Auguste
Clotilde
Amelie

Hélène – Widowed Duchesse d'Orléans
Comte de Paris – Helen's son; heir to his grandfather, King Louis Philippe

In the spring of 1840, Queen Victoria's cousin, Victoire of Saxe-Coburg-Kohary, married Louis, Duc de Nemours, the second son of King Louis Philippe and an erstwhile contender for the throne of Belgium. The couple had first met when Nemours was visiting his sister, the Queen of the Belgians, in Brussels, where they struck up an immediate rapport. Renowned for her beauty, piety and innocence, Victoire made an equally positive impression on Nemours' family, and, shortly before the wedding, Queen Amelie wrote cheerfully:

> "The dear, good child will be a delightful wife for Nemours and a pleasure and comfort to all of us."[153]

Graciously agreeing to wave the increased annuity which was normally accorded to the King's sons upon marriage, Nemours arranged for the wedding to take place in St. Cloud on 27th April. Several members of the congregation commented that Victoire's beauty exceeded their highest expectations, and, what was more, it was clear that she and the Duc were deeply in love.

Nemours, though, was a complex character who inspired admiration and affection in his friends but irritation and mistrust in his enemies. Devoutly religious, he had inherited his mother's piety but preferred to practise his good works in private and, according to his confessor, he 'spoke little of his profoundest feelings but he lived his faith to the full'[154]. His detractors, unaware of his charitable acts, would later accuse him of marital infidelity, but those closest to him claimed that this was an unfounded rumour created by republicans wishing to denigrate the Royal Family.

Whatever the truth of the stories, Victoire adored her husband, and when, a year after the wedding, he was posted with his regiment to Africa, his mother wrote him a letter stating that:

> "Sweet, dear Victoire only lives in Africa; whatever she says or does gives reference to you. She is indeed worthy of your love, and is an angel of piety."[155]

Until 1842, Nemours opted to play a somewhat unobtrusive public role, quietly supporting his elder brother and heir to the throne, the popular, Duc d'Orléans. That July, however, as Orléans set out to review the troops in Saint-Omer, the horses pulling his carriage bolted and he was thrown to the ground, fatally fracturing his skull.

His death prompted genuine mourning throughout the country, and the renowned poet, Alfred Musset, dedicated a poem to him:

> *"Pauvre prince! quel rêve à ses derniers instants!*
> *Une heure (qu'est-ce donc qu'une heure pour le Temps?),*
> *Une heure a détourné tout un siècle. Ô misère!*
> *Il partait, il allait au camp, presque à la guerre.*
> *Une heure lui restait ; il était fils et père :*
> *Il voulut embrasser sa mère et ses enfants."*

Nemours, who had been particularly close to his brother, was broken-hearted, and his grief came at a time when he found himself thrust into the limelight, which, until then, he had sought to avoid.

As the late Duc's son, the five-year-old Comte de Paris, was now the heir to the throne, the King appointed Nemours his regent in the event of his own early demise. The appointment was criticised by several ministers, who felt that his reticent manner and haughty appearance might alienate his nephew's future subjects, and therefore, according to the diarist, Thomas Raikes:

> "Marshal Soult…expostulated with him rather seriously on his retired habits and reserved manner, saying that he was now placed in a new position, which would require a very different line of conduct. The Duke replied that…now he himself felt the necessity of taking a more prominent part, and would act accordingly."[156]

Consequently, he and Victoire were compelled to become more involved in the social life of the capital, where they sought to restore the ancient etiquette and traditions of the Bourbons. Their insistence on adhering to customs which had become obsolete, heightened the public perception of Nemours as having too great a sense of his own importance and instilling the same self-centred values in his three children: Louis, Comte d'Eu; Ferdinand, Duc d'Alençon; and Marguerite Adelaide.

Due to his political and military duties, Nemours was frequently absent from his home, but Victoire found consolation in the company of her brother, Gusti, whose betrothal to Nemours' youngest sister, Clementine, was announced in February 1843.

While the announcement of Victoire's engagement had been general well-received in France, that of her brother was met with a combination of surprise and resentment. The aristocracy viewed Gusti as 'nothing more than a lieutenant[r] of Hussars'[157] whose dullness contrasted sharply with the vivacity of the ambitious and sparkling Clementine. Even his English cousin, Queen Victoria, who had always been very fond of him, considered him 'odd and inanimate' and found it hard to believe Clementine's assurances that she was truly in love.

Initially, Gusti intended to continue his service in the Austrian army, and the French Royal Family presumed that Clementine would move with him to Vienna. When, however, despite petitions from Queen Victoria and King Louis Philippe, the Austrian Emperor refused to grant him the title of Royal Highness, he resigned his commission and decided instead to settle

---

[r] He was, in fact, a Major in the Austrian 'King of Prussia's' Regiment.

with his bride in France, much to the disgust of many of his fellow officers, who were appalled by his arrogance.

> "[He] chose," recorded Thomas Raikes, "to be impertinent…to an Hungarian gentleman, a Comte Edmond Zichy…and got much the worst of it, He is a major in the Hussars here, and in consequence amenable to the common laws of society; everybody feels and says that Zichy was in the right."[158]

As the French court was still in mourning for the Duc d'Orléans, the wedding was a quiet affair, celebrated at eight-thirty in the morning at St. Cloud, with few royal guests beyond the immediate family, including Clementine's sister and brother in-law, the Queen and King of the Belgians. Thirteen months later, a son, Philip, was born, to be joined the following year by a brother, Ludwig Auguste, and two sisters Clotilde and Amelie in 1846 and 1848.

The family moved into a 'pleasant house' in Paris 'where there are often dinners and evening parties in the winter'[159]. Clementine, revelling in the role, was a charming hostess whose sparkling conversation impressed her many guests, but, at the same time, according to her future daughter-in-law, she dominated her husband and spoiled her children. Like the Nemours, they were raised with a strong sense of entitlement but their self-importance and that of their parents was about to be shattered by a terrifying revolution.

Since the revolution of 1789, France had gone through various political upheavals, from the First French Empire under Napoleon, through the Bourbon Restoration to the July Revolution of 1830, which saw King Louis Philippe ascend the throne. The passing of the British Reform Act led to demands for similar legislation to be enacted in France but, as the demands went largely unheeded, resentment festered across the country. In February 1848, a large crowd gathered in Paris, calling for immediate changes to the government and the removal of the Prime Minister, François Guizot. The military was called in to prevent the demonstration from escalating into a riot but, when a soldier accidentally discharged his musket, his fellow officers thought that an order must have been given to open fire, and began shooting indiscriminately into the crowd.

Fifty-one people were killed, and, in the ensuing chaos, an angry mob stormed towards the Tuileries where Louis Philippe, recalling the fate of his predecessor, Louis XVIII, took fright and abdicated in favour of his young grandson, the Comte de Paris. Donning a disguise, the King ordered the evacuation of the Royal Family and sent for carriages to transport him and his household to safety. Together with the Queen, Victoire, Clementine, Gusti, their children, and other members of the suite, he hurried across the courtyard to the place where the carriages should have been waiting, only to find that they had been seized by the mob, and a large number of troops had defected to the revolution. In the panic that followed, Nemours alone remained calm enough to search for alternative carriages, eventually finding three small broughams, each which was designed to carry only three people.

As the Queen fainted in fear, Louis Philippe caught her and lifted her onto a seat before hurriedly climbing into the brougham beside her. Gusti's children scrambled in after him, and Victoire's little son, the Duc d'Alençon, was pushed through the window onto his lap. When, though, the desperate Duchesse d'Orléans, mother of the Comte de Paris, asked what was to become of her and her children, the King harshly replied that the boy's youth and innocence would protect him.

"My dear Hélène," he said ungallantly, "the dynasty must be saved, and the crown preserved to your son. Remain here, then, for his sake. It is a sacrifice you owe your son."

As his carriage sped away, Victoire other members of the group scrambled into the remaining broughams, while Gusti and Clementine set off on foot through the crowds, making their way incognito to the railways station. Nemours, meanwhile, rallied the few remaining loyal troops to defend the Tuileries long enough to allow the fugitives to escape; then, taking charge of the little Comte de Paris, he appeared to vanish into oblivion.

The fate of those who had escaped in the broughams was equally uncertain, as the turmoil in the city made communication with the outside world virtually impossible. Within a few days, though, a few bedraggled refugees arrived in England, where an alarmed Lady Lyttelton observed:

> "They are all without clothes or money, and nobody knows what has become of those left behind. The Queen well, but sadly agitated...Think of the Duchess of Nemours! Lost! Missing! in the Parisian mob! They were all absolutely dragged out of their carriages, and the Duchess of Saxe-Coburg (the Princess Clementine) arrived in London in real rags, her only clothes torn half off, and she very nearly crushed to death in the mob."[160]

Nemours, meanwhile, had managed to pass unnoticed through the crowds, and, armed with an English passport, boarded a steamer. Remarkably, Clementine had happened to be on the same vessel with some of his children, one of whom heard his voice and instantly recognised him. On arriving safely in England, he discovered that his wife, Victoire, was still missing and a few days passed before Queen Victoria heard that she and the rest of their children had arrived safely in Jersey and would soon be making the crossing to England.

Queen Victoria immediately contacted the King of the Belgians to obtain his permission to house the fugitives at his Surrey home, Claremont, before gathering boxes of items to make their stay as comfortable as possible. It did not take long, though, for their presence to disrupt the orderly running of the household, as the young French princes' behaviour contrasted sharply with that of their English cousins. 'I hear that they are particularly naughty, riotous, disobedient and unmanageable,'[161] reported Lady Lyttelton when a dressmaker, sent to fit them with new clothes, was bitten and kicked until a nurse intervened and locked her assailants in a cupboard!

The children were not the only ones to cause their hosts consternation. A maid was caught stealing, and, much to the diligent Prince Albert's annoyance, Louis Philippe was so absorbed in self-pity that he made no effort to use his time wisely, nor even to unpack the boxes of gifts which Queen Victoria had sent. Even once they had settled in the country, their English attendants found their behaviour unsettling, particular those who were asked to accompany the French princes to a shoot. It was, wrote Lady Eleanor Stanley:

> '...a service of the utmost danger...particularly with the Duke of Nemours...They blaze away at any or everything, but...they don't hit the birds; there is a great joke against one of these French princes, that, in his excitement in looking after woodcocks, a blackbird getting up close to him,

he banged both barrels at it, missed, and was going to take his spare gun from the loader to try again, when he was stopped by seeing our Prince and all his gentlemen in fits."[162]

As Nemours struggled to regain possession of his private properties in France, Gusti and Clementine departed for their estates in Vienna and Coburg, where, according to Prince Chlodwig of Hohenlohe-Schillingsfürst, Gusti was 'as tedious as ever,' despite being married to such a 'clever, lively woman.'[163] They soon resumed their former lifestyle and, thirteen years later, at the age of forty-four, Clementine gave birth to a third son, Ferdinand, the future 'Tsar' of Bulgaria. Doting on 'her Benjamin', Clementine spoiled this 'child of her autumn days' to the point where, 'unable to regulate [his] undisputed mental gifts…she was weak as water where he was concerned.'[164]

A handsome boy with striking blue eyes, the spoiled young prince grew up with an almost fantastical ambition, and, according to several of his acquaintances, many frightening peculiarities. As he openly embraced atheism, his sister-in-law was convinced that he had committed himself to some satanic sect, which fuelled his desire to control everyone around him. Even his doting mother fell victim to his arrogance, as he often overruled her opinions and:

> "…to whom he would sometimes say, in his domineering manner, words that fortunately owing to her deafness she did not hear."[165]

Regardless of his behaviour, Clementine's loyalty to him never wavered, and, within a short time, she would be instrumental in gaining him a throne.

Back in England, the Nemours remained with the deposed King and Queen at Claremont, but the stress of the revolution had taken a severe toll on Louis Philippe, who died a broken man just two years later. Victoire settled happily in England, often spending time with her cousins, Queen Victoria and Prince Albert, who treasured her friendship deeply.

> "I have...dear Victoire to come and spend a night with me;" the Queen wrote to King Leopold on one occasion, "it does her always good, and we are just like sisters...She is a dear, noble, and still beautiful child."[166]

In October 1857, she gave birth to a daughter, Blanche, and, the following week, received a visit from Queen Victoria, who, despite being a little perturbed by her pallor, concurred with the rest of the family that she was recovering well from her confinement. Three days later, on 10th November, a maid was attending to her hair, when Victoire suddenly called out, 'Oh, mon Dieu!' and, before her husband could be summoned to the room, she had collapsed and died.

Distraught, Queen Victoria, convinced that her beloved cousin had died of some 'affection of the heart,' hurried back to Claremont where she found a tragic scene.

> "There was the broken-hearted, almost distracted widower – and her son – and lastly, there was in one room the lifeless, but oh! even in its ghostliness, most beautiful form of his young, lovely, and angelic wife, lying in her bed with her splendid hair covering her shoulders, and a heavenly expression of peace; and in the next room, the dear little pink infant sleeping in its cradle."[167]

Nemours remained at Claremont with his mother, until her death in 1866, after which he moved to Bushy House in South London, before returning to Paris several years later.

The French Revolution of 1848, had far reaching repercussions across much of the rest of the Continent, and its influence was felt in the quiet palaces of the King of the Belgians. His wife, a daughter of the deposed Louis Philippe, was severely affected by the death of her father, and, having already shown early symptoms of tuberculosis, her health spiralled into a rapid decline. In the hope of assisting her recovery, King Leopold arranged for her to be taken to Ostend but, just five months later, she died at the age of only thirty-eight.

> "We say and believe," wrote Baron Stockmar, "that men can be noble and good; of her we know with certainty that she was so. We saw in her daily a truthfulness, a faithful fulfilment of duty, which makes us believe in the possible, though but seldom evident, nobleness of the human heart."[168]

On a wider scale, events in Paris prompted similar uprisings in several European countries, and for a while, even Victoria's England was gripped by the fear of revolution.

Chapter 15 – 'Arming In All Directions'

George – Son of Queen Victoria's paternal uncle, Adolphus, Duke of Cambridge; later, Duke of Cambridge; Queen Victoria's cousin

Albert – Prince of Saxe-Coburg-Gotha; Queen Victoria's cousin & consort
Ernest – Duke of Saxe-Coburg-Gotha; Albert's elder brother; Queen Victoria's cousin

Ernest Augustus – King of Hanover; Queen Victoria's paternal uncle
George – Son of Ernest Augustus; Queen Victoria's cousin

Anticipating an armed uprising, Prince Albert fitted locks to the doors of his children's bedrooms and prepared escape routes from Buckingham Palace for the Queen and her family. His fears and those of several ministers were happily unfounded, as Queen Victoria's popularity played no small part in preventing 'a few little riots' from escalating into anything more serious.

Across the Irish Sea, however, the situation was far more precarious, as the serving soldier, George of Cambridge reported, 'Here we are also on the point of revolution.'[169]

The long-standing resentment against British rule in Ireland had been greatly exacerbated throughout the mid-1840s by a series of poor harvests and the destruction of the potato crop by 'the blight' – phytophthora infestans. As vast numbers of people depended upon potatoes for sustenance, the consequent famine resulted in mass emigration. Two million emigrants departed for Australia and the United States, and another three-quarters of a million settled in

England. Those who remained faced an appalling situation in which whole families died overnight of starvation, while others, weakened by hunger contracted fatal diseases, ultimately resulting in the deaths of approximately a million people.

> "Poverty," warned George, "and the numbers of the dead so increase there is scarce time to bury the latter, which must lead to terrible fever, if something is not soon done and measures taken to check this.'[170]

His gloomy predication was tragically accurate as epidemics swept across the country. In December 1846, seven-hundred people in one Dublin workhouse were suffering from dysentery; while the governor of a similar establishment wore:

> "The state of our poorhouse is awful; the average daily deaths in it, from fever alone, is eighteen; there are upwards of eleven hundred inmates in it, and of these six hundred are in typhus fever."[171]

The scale and effects of the famine inflamed anger at the English landlords who had charged such exorbitant rents that their tenants had been forced to rely solely on a diet of potatoes. Moreover, the callous attitude of certain British statesmen demonstrated a heartless lack of understanding of the extent of the suffering. The Treasury Secretary, Charles Trevelyan, for example, believed in the Malthusian theory of population control, and wrote that Ireland had been so over-populated that the remedy, which was 'altogether beyond the power of man', had been given by 'the direct stroke of an all-wise Providence in a manner as unexpected and as unthought of as it is likely to be effectual.'

George, who was more directly involved with the plight of the people, complained that insufficient help was being provided to alleviate the situation. He thought little of the efforts of a French cook named Soyer, who set up a soup kitchen and tried to show local people how to make healthy and inexpensive meals, as he felt that the cost of equipping and supplying the canteen could have been better spent, but he was even more disgusted that it was left to a Frenchman to 'make good the want of means of a Government.'[172]

Although he understood the people's grievances and desperation, he opposed the rising calls for a repeal of the Acts of Union, by which the United Kingdom of Britain and Ireland had been formalised; and he feared that growing support for Irish independence would quickly lead to rioting and violence.

One group demanding liberation was the Young Ireland Movement, which called for a bloodless revolution. Independent presses, funded by the group, published articles stating that the Irish owed no allegiance to Britain and expressing the widely held view that:

> "The present salvation and future security of this country require that the English Government should at once be abolished, and the English garrison of landlords instantly expelled."[173]

When further articles urged the people to arm themselves in their own defence, the Prime Minister, Lord Russell, drew attention to the fact that London had sent eight million pounds to alleviate Irish suffering, and a further four million had been voluntarily forwarded by English and Scottish donors. The rebels, on other hand, he said, had done nothing but stir dissent, and the only solution was the suspension of *habeas corpus,* which would enable the authorities to detain without trial any suspected conspirators.

Within days of the suspension, barricades appeared in the streets.

> "The people are arming in all directions," George reported. "Horrible pikes are made, rifles sold; altogether Dublin at present is as unpleasant as possible, and I shall be well pleased when it is well got over."[174]

The rebels might have had strong support for their cause, but the greater part of the Irish population opposed their methods, and, apart from a few skirmishes, their efforts to precipitate a revolution failed. Several of their leaders were captured and sentenced to transportation and, within a few months, a semblance of peace was restored. So confident was Queen Victoria that the violence was at an end, that in August 1849, she and Albert took their elder children to Ireland and were gratified by the warmth of the reception that they received. Although several unsuccessful attempts were made to petition the Queen to pardon the rebels, the crowds were generally welcoming, and many were impressed by the royal visitors' insistence on seeing Roman Catholic as well as Protestant charities in action.

> "Our Irish tour has gone off well, beyond all expectation," Prince Albert wrote on his return journey. "Of the enthusiasm that greeted us from all quarters you can form no conception; neither had we anywhere the smallest contretemps. The Catholic clergy are quite as loyal as the Anglican, the Presbyterians, and the Quakers."[175]

The following summer, George returned briefly to England to mourn his father, whose death had elevated him to the position of Duke of Cambridge. When the funeral was over, the Queen invited him to discuss with her his future prospects and those of his sisters; and, once he had secured annuities of £3000 each for Augusta and Mary, and his own income was raised to £12,000 a year, he returned to his post in Ireland and resumed his military duties.

While George had been warning of a potential uprising in Ireland, Ernest of Saxe-Coburg-Gotha was visiting his brother in England when he received word that revolution was rapidly spreading through Germany. Cutting short his visit, he returned home, visiting his uncle in Belgium en route, to discuss his ideas for introducing a new constitution. On his arrival in the duchy, he announced his plans to abolish press censorship and institute trial by jury, which initially seemed to satisfy his countrymen, the majority of whom received him warmly. Soon, though, he was told of insurrection in Coburg, from where a series of demands were put to him by the local burghers who assured him they wished only to maintain 'concord between Your Highness and your people' by obtaining:

> "...freedom of the Press, representation of the people in the German Confederacy, armament of the people and trials by jury which come to our knowledge in all parts of Germany, being convinced that the Fatherland can be secured from outside dangers, and rejuvenated internally by means of the adoption of these institutions."[176]

Ernest agreed to discuss the demands but the prospect of a full-scale revolution moved ever closer. In early April, prisons were stormed, workmen rioted and, as groups of insurgents attempted to persuade or bribe the army to mutiny, civil officials fled their posts and sought asylum in Gotha.

Ernest took swift and decisive action, providing extra armaments for his troops, calling out the Citizens'

Guard to remain on duty night and day until the unrest subsided, and setting out for Coburg to address the people directly. As news of his approach spread, a small but hostile crowd gathered to meet him in the town. Summoning a drunken innkeeper to open a function room, he invited the protestors and local workmen inside to discuss their grievances. Having heard their complaints, he urged them to allow the civil officials to continue their duties unimpeded, in return for which he promised to receive regular deputations to deal with any issues that the workers cared to raise. His efforts were successful, and, as the unrest gradually eased, he was relieved to realise he had weathered the crisis with his lands and title intact.

Once the immediate domestic issues were resolved, he focussed much of his attention on securing the independence of the duchy by aligning himself more closely with the powerful Prussians by offering them his support in their campaigns against the Danes over the disputed territories of Schleswig-Holstein.

In Hanover, meanwhile, King Ernest Augustus was equally successful in dealing with the revolution. At its height, insurgents gathered on the streets, smashing the windows of several prominent buildings and pelting with stones and other missiles the troops who were sent to contain them. In the surrounding German states, the military responded to such attacks with the utmost severity but in Hanover the officers retained their composure and, rather than retaliating, unflinchingly endured the blows without moving from their positions. Even when a small crowd reached the King's palace and called out a series of demands, the guards, who were summoned from the local barracks, saw only a peaceful demonstration and good-humouredly lowered their guns Once more, Ernest

Augustus responded shrewdly to the situation by ordering his Prime Minister to speak on his behalf, telling the mob that:

> "The King was quite willing to listen to any reasonable complaints, and to remedy, if possible, any proved grievances, but, if they made demands upon him which he did not think consistent with his honour to grant, he should immediately pack up his things, take the Crown Prince with him, be off to England, and leave them to their own devices; and, into whose clutches they would fall, they knew well."[177]

The Prime Minister concluded his address by stating that the King would wait twenty-four hours for a response, after which the protestors dispersed, returning soon afterwards to humbly request a meeting with him. The King listened intently to their arguments and, with remarkable grace, granted more reforms than they had requested, and later, when the revolutions had died down and other monarchs withdrew the concessions that had been made under duress, he insisted on abiding by his promises, telling his minister that:

> "He had pledged his royal word, and it was not his idea of justice or equity to retract that. What was done was done, and his ministers must act accordingly."[178]

Although he appeared to have mellowed with age, Ernest Augustus had lost none of his propensity for 'treading on corns' or taking a mischievous pleasure in the discomfort of his attendants. No one was spared from his acerbic humour, whether it be a lady attempting to impress him at a ball, or a faithful retainer who happened to adopt the wrong style of dress for a specific occasion. A stickler for tradition, his partial blindness did not prevent him from seeing any infringement of royal protocol, and he was quick to find an appropriate means of reprimanding any transgressor. On one occasion, for example, he remained at a ball until the early hours of the morning, by which time his aged Grand Marshall, who was expected to stay at his side, could hardly keep awake. Seeing that the majority of guests had already left, and the King was happily entertained by a posse of young women, the Grand Marshall crept away following the rendition of the National Anthem, which usually signified that the party was over. The King silently watched him make his surreptitious escape but, rather than calling him back at once, he allowed him plenty of time to return home and prepare for bed before sending an attendant to tell him that he wished to speak with him. Roused from sleep, the elderly gentleman struggled into his clothes and anxiously raced back to the ballroom, at which point the King merely smiled and bade him good night before calling for his carriage and returning to his palace.

For all his faults, Ernest Augustus shared none of his brothers' appetite for self-indulgence, but partook of only minimal alcohol and maintained an abstemious diet. Convinced that a combination of good food, exercise and rest was the most effective remedy for any ailment, he had little time for doctors who constantly prescribed medications. When he fell seriously ill, the physicians brought him daily concoctions, which they claimed were essential to effect a full recovery. The old King nodded as though to accept their prescriptions but, as soon as they had left the room, he ordered attendants to store the jars and bottles unopened in a cupboard. At length, as he regained his strength, the doctors proudly congratulated themselves on their success, at which point the King had the cupboard opened, saying:

"Yes, doctors, thank God [I am recovered]...but look there – count it up; don't you think, if I had drunk all that, I should have been dead long ago!"[179]

Inevitably, though, Ernest Augustus finally succumbed to the effects of age, and, in the autumn of 1851, he finally took to his bed where he drifted into semi-consciousness. On 17th November his chaplain was summoned to perform the Last Rites, and, that night he died peacefully in his sleep, surrounded by his children – his wife having predeceased him by ten years. On a cold snowy day, he was finally laid to rest in the family Mausoleum of Herrenhausen.

"Upon the demise of King Ernest," wrote his chaplain, "I believe a great man had fallen in Hanover."[180]

It was a view shared by many Hanoverians but by very few in England, where journalists reported that writing a eulogy was impossible since there was nothing good to say of him. Although she ordered the customary court mourning, Queen Victoria openly admitted that she could not pretend to feel sorrow at the death of an uncle whom she had never loved; and her lady-in-waiting was greatly amused at George of Cambridge's 'grief for Uncle Hanover being so much more mitigated than ours; he was in a spotted silk neckcloth and a light brown bear this morning, while we are still in sackcloth and ashes.'[181]

Queen Victoria did, however, look forward optimistically to the reign of his successor – her blind cousin, George – whom, she naively believed, would abandon his father's autocratic style of government in favour of a more constitutional monarchy[s].

---

[s] See Chapter 19

Chapter 16 – 'Unqualified Treachery & Brutality'

George – Duke of Cambridge; Queen Victoria's cousin
Augusta – Princess of Cambridge; Grand Duchess of
Mecklenburg-Strelitz; George's sister
Duchess of Cambridge – George's mother

Emmanuel Mensdorff-Pouilly – 'Uncle Mensdorff';
husband of Queen Victoria's maternal aunt, Sophie
Hugo Mensdorff – Queen Victoria's cousin; son of
Emmanuel and Sophie
Alfonse Mensdorff – Queen Victoria's cousin; son of
Emmanuel and Sophie
Alexander Mensdorff – Queen Victoria's cousin; son of
Emmanuel and Sophie

Following his service in Ireland, George, Duke of Cambridge, returned to London to take up a new position as Inspector of Cavalry. It was role which he approached with great enthusiasm and diligence as he sought to discover and implement the most up-to-date methods of training and military tactics. To further his knowledge, he studied the practices of other European armies and, in the late summer of 1852, made use of a visit to his sister, Augusta, in Mecklenburg, Germany, by returning home via Berlin to meet with King Frederick William IV in the hope that he might allow him to study the techniques of the Prussian Cavalry. The King was so impressed by his enthusiasm and manners that he invited him to attend the general manoeuvres the following year. George eagerly anticipated the experience but, as the day of his departure approached, the prospect of an imminent war in the Crimea compelled him to cancel his journey.

The complex causes of the Crimean War centred on the crumbling Ottoman Empire, the disintegration of which had encouraged several European powers to stake claims to different areas of the region. In 1853, Tsar Nicholas I began a campaign to gain control of the Dardanelles, which immediately raised British fears that, if the Russians proceeded towards Afghanistan, they might hinder access to India and damage Anglo-Turkish trade. The French, Austrians and Sardinians were equally alarmed, due to a long-standing dispute between the Roman Catholic Europeans and Orthodox Russians about access to the Holy Land, which, at the time was under Turkish control. It, therefore, suited the majority of the European powers to keep the Ottoman Empire intact, and they secretly encouraged the Turks to rise up and defend themselves against the Russian invaders. The Turks duly declared war on Russia, prompting the Tsar to order his fleet from its base at Sebastopol to sink the entire Turkish fleet at Sinope, with the loss of three thousand lives.

The attack was almost universally condemned, and journalists whipped up anti-Russian feelings by describing the Tsar as 'a brigand of the first water,' who had behaved with 'unqualified treachery and brutality'. *The Times* called on British people to prevent the tyrannical Tsar from dictating conditions in the Black Sea; the *Morning Chronicle* insisted that Britain had a duty to 'stop the aggressor with a blow'; and, as far away as Australia, one editor stated that 'the lamentable slaughter at Sinope puts to flight, at once and for ever, the idea of the possibility of the quarrel between Russia and Turkey being settled by any diplomatic arrangements.'

Although Queen Victoria hoped that war might be avoided, the army was being readied for action and

George was sent to France to liaise with the new Emperor, Napoleon III, prompting the press to ridicule him, suggesting that he was dallying in Paris for his own amusement. On his return home, he was given command of the Guards and Highland Brigades and, when Britain and France jointly declared war on Russia in March 1854, he was immediately posted to the Crimea.

Neither his rank nor his royal status prevented George from being placed in the thick of the fighting. He participated in the first significant engagement of the war – the Battle of Alma in September 1854, during which the joint British and French gained a resounding victory, and George's courage led to his being mentioned in dispatches.

> "His Royal Highness, the Duke of Cambridge," wrote his commanding officer, Lord Raglan, "brought his division into action in support of the light division with great ability, and had for the first time an opportunity of showing the enemy his devotion to Her Majesty, and to the profession of which he is so distinguished a member."[182]

Even amid the horrors of war, he was sympathetic to the sufferings of his wounded enemies. In a letter to his mother, he described an incident which took place soon after the battle, when the victorious British soldiers ascended a hill where they discovered a Russian General whose legs had been blown off. The Russian asked to see their commanding officer so that he might congratulate him on his victory. George hurried at once to the scene, and the General, not a little surprised by his youthful appearance, embraced him warmly and died in his arms.

In October, he led the 1st Division at Balaclava, witnessing the disastrous 'charge of the Light Brigade';

and, the following month, his horse was shot from under him during the Battle of Inkerman, resulting in reports appearing in the British press erroneously claiming that he had been seriously wounded. In fact, he suffered only bruising to his leg from his fall from the dying animal, and a graze to his hand as a bullet passed through the sleeve of his coat and shirt.

His concern for his men earned him such affection that they referred to him as 'our friend'; while his courage in battle earned their respect.

> "He was," said one officer, "indefatigable, rushing about to stimulate the resistance of the hard-pressed soldiers, and cheering them on wherever the enemy's ranks were thickest."[183]

Almost as horrific as the carnage of battle, was the realisation that more soldiers were being killed by disease than by enemy bullets. Cholera and typhoid were rife, wiping out whole brigades and rendering thousands of soldiers unfit for duty. Conditions for the wounded were appalling, as they lay lice-ridden in the rat-infested mud of makeshift hospital floors, but this did not prevent George from making regular visits to the casualties.

> "The Duke of Cambridge," a soldier recorded, "has several times called to enquire after the wounded, and made minute enquiries as to the nature of their injuries."[184]

Working in such close proximity to his men, it was inevitable that George, too, should eventually succumb to disease, and, following the Battle of Inkerman, he suffered a serious bout of diarrhoea. Plagued also by gout and recurrent fever, he was clearly too ill to continue his duties, and, in November, Lord Raglan ordered him to take a few days recuperation aboard the British naval frigate, *Retribution,* before resuming his duties.

The vessel was at anchor near Balaclava when, at about five o'clock one morning, the wind began to strengthen and, within three hours, had reached hurricane force. George, looking out from his cabin, saw other ships being dashed against the rocks while the Admiral of the *Retribution,* standing waist-deep in water, ordered his crew to throw rudder and guns overboard to lessen the load.

> "This was without exception the most fearful day of my life," George wrote in his diary. "…At two a thunderbolt fell and struck the ship, with a heavy shower of hail…Thus we lay all night hoping for the best, and a most fearful and awful twenty-four hours we spent, but God's mercy came to our rescue, and we were most providentially saved."[185]

As the episode exacerbated George's condition, Lord Raglan ordered him to Constantinople in the hope that a change of air might relieve his condition but, as November passed with little improvement, he asked permission to return home for the winter. Raglan arranged for him to appear before a Medical Board, after which he was sent to rest in Malta. By New Year, as Lady Eleanor Stanley reported, he was:

> "…still very poorly; it is intermittent, or Quotidian fever[t], coming on at a particular hour every day, and he cannot get up his strength. He wants to come home, I hear, but the Queen and Prince and Duchess of Cambridge want him to stop at Malta; the Duchess of Cambridge says if he comes home it will be another leave-taking when he goes back, and she thinks once going thro' that sort of thing is enough; besides she

---

[t] A form of malaria

says he ought to be there 'when Sevastopol tumbles down.'"[186]

Within a couple of weeks it was apparent that he was not fit to return to the Crimea and, at the end of the month, he returned home to a hero's welcome.

The war dragged on for a further twelve months, ultimately concluding with the signing of the Treaty of Paris in March 1856. George could rest easy for a while, but the peace agreements would lead to a separate conflict, in which two more of Queen Victoria's cousins would play an active role.

Since the death of their mother in 1835, the Duchess of Kent had maintained her regular correspondence with her Mensdorff nephews, as had Prince Albert, who had been one of their closest childhood companions. In October 1847, the Prince and the Duchess were shocked to hear that the eldest of the brothers, Hugo, had died quite suddenly following a short illness at the age of forty-one. The Duchess took comfort from the thought that his 'poor mother' had not lived to endure such sorrow, but Queen Victoria could think only of 'dear Uncle Mensdorff' who had been so proud of all four of his sons, and for whom Hugo's death was a devastating loss.

Within six months, the Queen's uncle faced the agonising prospect that one or even two more of his sons could be killed in the upheavals that followed the overthrow of King Louis Philippe in 1848. As revolutionary fervour spread through Europe, Hungarian and Italian separatists seized the ensuing chaos to demand independence from the Austro-Hungarian Empire; and, in March, the Kingdoms of Sardinia and the Two Sicilies gained the Pope's support to declare war on Austria.

180

As serving soldiers in the Austrian army, Alexander and Arthur Mensdorff accompanied the heir to the throne, the young Archduke Franz Josef, to Verona where both distinguished themselves on the battlefield. By the end of August, the Sardinians were defeated but the danger was far from over, for revolution had erupted in Vienna, and Alexander returned at once to suppress the uprising. Although his horse was shot from beneath him, he managed to escape unharmed and, by December, the worst of the violence had subsided, as the unfortunately disfigured and epileptic Emperor Ferdinand was forced to abdicate in favour of his nephew Archduke Franz Josef. The new Emperor did not forget the service which Alexander had rendered, and rewarded him by promoting him first to the rank of Colonel and, soon afterwards, to General.

While Alexander eagerly accepted the promotions, he was far less thrilled by the news that the Emperor wished to appoint him as the Austrian Minister to St Petersburg. Not only did he wish to remain in the country, but also feared that his liberal opinions would clash with the stand he would have to take as Austria's representative in Russia. His objections were swiftly dismissed by the Emperor, and he had no option but to accept the post, which turned out to be a difficult as he had expected. Soon after his arrival in St Petersburg he contracted typhoid and, for several weeks, remained in a critical condition; and, when he eventually recovered, he found himself so at odds with the official line that was expected of him, that he gave the impression of dithering, which so irked the Russians that he was soon dismissed from his position.

Returning to Vienna, he resumed his service in the Austrian army and, after being promoted to the rank of Field Marshal, he sound found himself in the midst of another conflict. The Sardinians, still smarting from their recent defeat by Austria, made use of the discussions at the conclusion of the Crimean War, to reiterate their demands for independence. Although they received little backing from Britain, the French Emperor, Napoleon III, was sympathetic to their cause and, in 1858, he signed a secret treaty promising them French support in event of an Austrian attack, in return for which France would receive Nice and Savoy. Bolstered by Napoleon's promises, the Sardinians staged a series of provocative manoeuvres along the Austrian border, inciting Franz Josef to issue a declaration of war.

Within weeks of the outbreak of hostilities in April 1859, forty-six-year-old Alexander led a cavalry division to Magenta in northern Italy, where his comrades were hastily fortifying every house in the town in preparation for an imminent attack. Although the French were outnumbered, the speed of their advance took the Austrians by surprise, and the bloody battle which followed was one of the most horrific that Alexander ever witnessed. The Austrians were defeated and the French were free to advance on Milan.[u].

Just under three weeks later, the Austrians were surprised for a second time when, by chance rather than design, on June 24th, they came face to face with Franco-Sardinian forces at Solferino. In sweltering heat, Alexander's cavalry charged into action, and, according to a Swiss observer:

> "The horses, more compassionate than their riders, seek in vain to step over the victims of this butchery, but their iron hoofs crush the dead and dying. With the neighing of the horses are

---

[u] The battle gave its name to the colour magenta, allegedly because it was the colour of the blood of the Austrian soldiers.

mingled blasphemies, cries of rage, shrieks of pain and despair. The artillery, at full speed, follows the cavalry which has cut a way through the corpses and the wounded lying in confusion on the ground. A jaw-bone of one of these last is torn away; the head of another is battered in; the breast of a third is crushed. Limbs are broken and bruised; the field is covered with human remains; the earth is soaked with blood."[187]

Although for nine hours the Austrians 'fought like lions', they were ultimately forced to retreat and the war was all but over[v]. But for the memories of the horror he had witnessed, Alexander had come through it unscathed and, shortly afterwards, was appointed to the more pacific role of Austrian Minister of Foreign Affairs.

---

[v] Shortly after the battle a Swiss businessman, Jean-Henri Dunant, toured the field and was so horrified by the lack of provision for the wounded that he created a society of volunteers to give impartial help in times of war. The society ultimately became the International Red Cross.

Chapter 17 – 'The People Are Frantic With Rage'

Karoline – Duchess of Saxe-Gotha; Prince Albert's step-grandmother

Duchess of Kent – Queen Victoria's mother; Prince Albert's aunt

Ernest – Duke of Saxe-Coburg Gotha; Prince Albert's brother

Marie – Duchess of Württemberg; Duchess of Saxe-Coburg-Gotha; Prince Albert's cousin & stepmother; Queen Victoria's cousin

King Leopold of the Belgians – Queen Victoria's maternal uncle

Philippe – Count of Flanders; King Leopold's son; Queen Victoria's cousin

Vicky – Queen Victoria's eldest daughter; Crown Princess of Prussia, later Empress Frederick

Alice – Queen Victoria's second daughter

Alexander Mensdorff – Queen Victoria's cousin

Thanks largely to the efforts of Prince Albert, Queen Victoria's once-fraught relationship with her mother became one of mutual affection and understanding. With the birth of her grandchildren, the Duchess of Kent played an increasingly important role in the Royal Family, often accompanying Victoria and Albert on their travels. Suites of rooms were provided for her in all the Queen's palaces, and she had also been given her own home – Frogmore House on the Windsor estate – where she frequently entertained the royal children.

Since his marriage, Albert had also maintained a strong attachment to his step-grandmother, Duchess Karoline, and to his stepmother and cousin, Marie (née Württemberg). In 1845, when he and the Queen visited

Germany, he made a point of ensuring that they had time to visit Duchess Karoline who was, by then, very deaf but so eager to see him again that, as soon as she knew that he was in the vicinity, she travelled the eight miles from Gotha to Reinhardtsbrunn to meet him before breakfast.

> "She was so happy to see us," wrote Queen Victoria, "and kissed me over and over again. Albert, who is the dearest being to her in the world, she was so enraptured to see again, and kissed so kindly. It did one's heart good to see her joy."[188]

When, three years later, Duchess Karoline died of pneumonia at the age of seventy-six, Albert was, according to the Queen, 'quite beaten down...and is so pale and sad it breaks my heart.'[189]

> "Alas!" he wrote to his stepmother, "the news you sent were heavy news indeed. The dear, good grandmama! She was an angel upon earth; and to us ever so good and loving."[190]

There was much, though, to take his mind of his grief, as his commitment to his adopted country had led him to dedicate himself wholeheartedly to the service of its people. Driving himself to the point of exhaustion, he played a major role in virtually every area of public life, from the intricacies of foreign affairs and internal politics, to the necessity of providing adequate clean water and hygienic housing for the poor. As the Daily News would later report:

> "Before more than a superficial attention had been paid by the higher classes to the necessity of improving the physical condition of those in the lowest position, he gave a powerful stimulus to improvement by the erection of a model cottage, at his own expense...He had been in quiet communication with sanitary reformers on

this topic [and] there is good authority for affirming that if the sanitary condition of agricultural labourers were as well attended to by proprietors throughout the country as on the estate of Her Majesty…the death-rate, even in that class…would be reduced by nearly one-half."

He spoke out on behalf of domestic servants; he encouraged education for the masses; brought art and culture to the public; and was eager to provide open spaces and gardens for the poor.

Within his own home, too, he drew up detailed plans for his children's education, and when, in 1858, his eldest daughter, Vicky, married the son of the heir to the throne of Prussia, he spent many evenings preparing her for her future role.

His efforts, though, had come at great personal cost, as stress and exhaustion took a severe toll on his already-fragile health. Even before his marriage, he had been afflicted by digestive disorders and fatigue and, by his late thirties, he had also developed rheumatism and a myriad of minor ailments. Since his early childhood, he had sought to conceal his emotions, which undoubtedly contributed to his the breakdown of his health, as it was noticeable that his symptoms were always worse in times of anxiety or grief. The wrench of parting with Vicky, for example, led to such a painful bout of rheumatism that his arm was virtually paralysed as he struggled to write to her:

"I am not of a demonstrative nature and therefore you can hardly know how dear you have been to me, and what a void you have left behind in my heart; yet not in my heart for there you assuredly will abide henceforth as you have always done, but in my daily life, which is evermore reminding my heart of your absence."[191]

The cold damp summer of 1860 exacerbated the pain in his joints, and the dreariness of the season was lightened only by the prospect of a holiday in his native Coburg that September. When, on his birthday in August, his stepmother, Marie, wrote to tell him how eagerly she anticipated his visit, particularly since her own health was rapidly failing, he replied that he was convinced that the weather was responsible for their ailments, and he optimistically suggested that a brighter autumn would restore her strength and his own.

In early September, he, Victoria and their second daughter, Alice, made the crossing to Antwerp where King Leopold of the Belgians joined them aboard the Royal Yacht *Victoria & Albert*. The King and his son, Philippe, Count of Flanders, planned to accompany them as far as Verviers – halfway between Liége and the German border – but the train had barely left the station a telegram arrived from Albert's brother, Ernest, warning that Marie was gravely ill and it would be better to postpone the visit. Since arrangements had already been made and the journey was underway, Victoria and Albert felt it was too late to abandon their plans and decided to continue, in the hope that Ernest was over-reacting and Marie had merely suffered temporary relapse.

At Schloss Friedenstein in Gotha, however, the sixty-one-year-old Dowager Duchess's condition was rapidly worsening. For months she had suffered from a series of infections and, as erysipelas led to toxaemia, she experienced such 'fearful sufferings' that her brother, Ernest of Württemberg, was relieved when she lapsed into unconsciousness until death brought her a 'merciful release' at five o'clock in the morning of 24th September.

As their train reached Verviers, the royal travellers received a second telegram, telling them of her death – an event which cast a dark shadow over the longed-for holiday. The duchy was plunged into mourning, and the festivities, which Ernest had planned for their visit, were cancelled. Instead of enjoying fireworks and dances, Albert attended the funeral, which took place in Gotha at seven o'clock in the morning of 27th September as Marie was laid to rest in the Ducal Mausoleum in Glockenburg. The next day Queen Victoria visited the cemetery and thought it was:

> "…such a pretty one, in such a pretty position. Already there are many graves, covered with wreaths and flowers. We went into the beautiful Mausoleum, which has been erected by the whole family, after Albert's and Ernest's designs, carried out by the architect Eberhardt. It is in the Italian style; beautiful inside, with a marble floor and marble altar in the Chapel. There are side-galleries, in which the sarcophagi are placed; dear Papa's [Duke Ernest I of Saxe-Coburg-Gotha] and Albert's own Mother's are already there; but the coffins have not been placed in them. It is beautiful, and so cheerful."[192]

Messages of condolence poured in from across Europe, including one from the Emperor of Austria, delivered by the Queen's cousin, Alexander Mensdorff.

Albert, though, was haunted by the thought that 'poor Mama must have had an infinite deal of suffering'[193] and, barely had the gloom begun to lift, when his own life was seriously endangered. He had set out with only a coachman to carry out some family business in Coburg when the sound of an approaching engine startled the horses, causing them to bolt through a level-crossing, into the path of an on-coming train. Just in time, Albert and the coachman leaped from the speeding carriage, as one horse was struck by the locomotive and the three others raced on towards the

188

town. A railway worker, who had witnessed the event, hurried to offer assistance, taking Albert and the more seriously injured coachman back to his cottage to attend to their wounds. By chance, Albert's equerry happened to travelling along the same road to Coburg when he spotted the bolting horses and realised at once that there must have been an accident. Summoning a doctor, he hastened back along the route, and, on finding the Prince, arranged for him to be moved to the home of Baron Stockmar. By the time that Queen Victoria was told of what had happened, Albert was safely resting in bed having suffered only superficial cuts and bruises, but the shock to his system had been severe and over the next twelve months his health began a more rapid decline.

Six months after Marie's death, Queen Victoria suffered a far more devastating blow, which left her so prostrate with grief that she could no longer continue to carry out her duties. Although, over the past two years, she had noticed that her mother was becoming frailer, the Duchess' cheerfulness and enthusiasm masked the extent of her physical deterioration. She had suffered from a series of painful abscesses on her arm, but, despite causing her to feel weak, they gradually healed until February 1861 when another swelling developed. Neither the Duchess herself nor the members of her household were unduly concerned, as her lady-in-waiting observed that she was less weak than she had been with previous inflammations, and she brightly spoke of her plans to spend that Easter in London. By March, though, the pain was so intense that her doctors decided to drain the abscess, but their efforts had little beneficial affect and, as other sores developed, they concurred that the Duchess was suffering from cancer. Prince Albert was informed of the diagnosis but he kept the information from the Queen, who, nonetheless, noticed her mother's deterioration and urged her eldest daughter to return from Prussia to visit 'dearest grandmama' while there was still time.

Throughout the first fortnight in March, the Duchess's condition was stable, and her lady-in-waiting reported that, despite the difficulties of dressing to many wounds, 'the pain in the back had decreased, and in the breast scarcely at all...She certainly never suffered as people usually suffer in such cases.'[194]

On the afternoon of the 15th, however, she was suddenly struck by a sharp pain in her hand, followed by such excessive shivering that the doctor, fearing that she was dying, sent a message to Prince Albert. By the time he and the Queen arrived at Frogmore, the Duchess had sunk into a coma from which she never recovered.

She died at ten ten o'clock the following morning, prompting Albert, who had loved his aunt deeply, to burst into tears. His expressions of grief were, however, as nothing compared to his wife's inconsolability.

"Oh! the sickness of heart, the agony," she wailed, "the thought of the daily, hourly blank was and is unbearable."[195]

Rather than lessening her sorrow, time only intensified her grief, as every conversation reminded her of her mother's absence, and every family gathering brought home to the Queen how deeply she missed her.

"Her grief is extreme," wrote Albert, "In body she is well, though terribly nervous...she remains almost entirely alone."[196]

At first, he did everything in his power to support and comfort her but, as the weeks passed, and her mourning showed no sign of abating, his patience began to evaporate. Exhausted by the weight of so many responsibilities, and afflicted by numerous painful ailments, he became increasingly short-tempered, as he urged her to resume her duties. Abscesses formed in his gums; his teeth ached; his digestive disorders worsened; rheumatic pains plagued his joints; and he was prone to alternate fits of shivering and fevers.

The business of state, however, continued as usual, and, in mid-November 1861, Albert saw that he had no option but to put aside his own problems to prevent the country from becoming involved in an unnecessary war with the United States.

Throughout Queen Victoria's reign, relations between the two nations had vastly improved since the days of her grandfather, George III, who never recovered from the shock of having 'lost the colonies' in the American War of Independence. By the middle of the nineteenth century, despite a series of relatively minor political disputes, the countries were on a more balanced footing, and, in 1855, the Foreign Secretary, Lord Clarendon, encouraged the Queen to invite President James Buchanan to Windsor. Five years later, Buchanan was happy to return the hospitality when he asked the Prince of Wales, who was about to embark on a tour of Canada, to detour into the United States and visit him at the White House.

The following year, when civil war broke out between the Unionist North and Confederate South, the Queen issued a declaration of neutrality, but, for the next five months, Prince Albert anxiously followed events across the Atlantic, predicting that any minor incident could lead to drag the country into the conflict.

At the beginning of November 1861, two Confederate agents, John Slidell and James Mason, departed Havana for England aboard a British mail ship, the *Trent*. Suspecting that they were planning to garner European support for their cause, the Unionist

191

Captain of the *San Jacinto,* Charles Wilkes, pursued the agents, and prepared to intercept the mail ship as it passed through the Bahamas Channel. As the *Trent* approached, Wilkes ordered a shot to be fired across the bow and, when no response was forthcoming, he ordered a second shot, which brought the ship to a halt. Despite protests from the British captain, officers from the *San Jacinto* boarded and searched the vessel and, finding Slidell and Mason, removed them by force.

In the Unionist north of the United States, Wilkes was feted as a hero, but when the *Trent* returned home to England, news of the 'invasion' led to outrage and calls for war.

> "There never was within memory," wrote an American living in London, "such a burst of feeling as has been created by the news of the boarding of the [*Trent*]. The people are frantic with rage, and were the country polled, I fear that 999 men out of a thousand would declare for immediate war. Lord Palmerston cannot resist the impulse if he would."[197]

Under immense pressure from the press and the public, the British Foreign Secretary, Lord Russell, drafted a forceful letter to President Lincoln, couched in such belligerent terms that it was tantamount to a declaration of war. Fortunately, though, before it could be sent, it required the Queen's approval, and when Prince Albert read it, he was so aghast at its contents that he immediately set to work rewording it in far more conciliatory terms. Wilkes, he said, must have been acting without the authority of Washington, and:

> "...Her Majesty's Government are unwilling to believe that the United States Government intended wantonly to put an insult upon this country, and to add to their many distressing complications by forcing a question of dispute

upon us, and that we are therefore glad to believe that, upon a full consideration of the circumstances of the undoubted breach of International Law committed, they would spontaneously offer such redress as alone could satisfy this country, viz. the restoration of the unfortunate passengers and a suitable apology."[198]

This intervention almost certainly saved Britain from war, and the Prince's efforts were all the more remarkable since, at the time, he felt so ill that he could barely hold a pen. As his physical strength began to fail, so, too, did his spirits, and when, in that dark and damp November of 1861, tragic news arrived from Portugal, he became convinced that his life was nearing its end.

Chapter 18 – 'Too Good For This World'

Maria II de la Gloria – Queen of Portugal
Ferdinand – Prince of Saxe-Coburg-Kohary; titular King of Portugal; husband of Maria II de la Gloria; Queen Victoria's cousin
Pedro – Son of Maria II and Ferdinand
Stephanie of Hohenzollern-Sigmaringen – Wife of Pedro
Luis – Son of Maria II and Ferdinand
Joao – Son of Maria II and Ferdinand

Bertie – Prince Albert Edward; Prince of Wales; eldest son of Victoria and Albert

Ernest – Duke of Saxe-Coburg-Gotha; Prince Albert's brother; Queen Victoria's cousin

George – Duke of Cambridge; Queen Victoria's cousin

King Leopold of the Belgians – Queen Victoria's maternal uncle
King Leopold II of the Belgians – Queen Victoria's cousin
Philippe, Count of Flanders – Brother of King Leopold II; Queen Victoria's cousin
Marie – Wife of Philippe

On 3rd February 1853, Queen Maria II de la Gloria of Portugal, wife of Ferdinand of Saxe-Coburg-Kohary, gave birth to their eleventh child – a boy named Eugenio. Since three of her older children had been stillborn, her doctors had dreaded this confinement, and Maria herself was more anxious than she had been during her previous pregnancies. Initially, however, the birth appeared to have gone well, but, within two hours, both mother and baby died of exhaustion.

The whole of Portugal joined Ferdinand's mourning for the thirty-five-year-old Queen, whose popularity had greatly increased towards the latter part of her reign. So genuine was her subjects' grief that the funeral procession was three miles long, and even the poorest people who lined the route were dressed in black mourning and wept as the cortege passed by.

For the next two years, having lost the title of King, Ferdinand served as regent for his sixteen-year-old son, King Pedro V. A studious boy, known for his love of learning and artistic appreciation, Pedro had already written two scholarly works; and, after coming across the writings of Victor Hugo, he had developed such a passion for literature that he knew most of the works of Dante and Schiller by heart. When, a year after his mother's death, he and his brother travelled to England, Queen Victoria and Prince Albert were so impressed by his intelligence and good manners that they could not help but compare him with their own lackadaisical son, the Prince of Wales.

At his coming of age the following year, Pedro gave every indication that his reign would be characterised by his genuine concern for his people; and, when, at the age of twenty, he married the pretty and pious Princess Stephanie of Hohenzollern-Sigmaringen, the couple's popularity surpassed that of his parents. Although it was an arranged marriage, Pedro and Stephanie soon fell in love and, as one observer noted:

> "In a short time it was clear that the childlike joy of the Queen exercised a most beneficial influence on Dom Pedro's heart. There was a

certain luminous touch of cheerfulness about her appearance…and when he was at her side, everyone could see the quiet happiness of the King's soul."[199]

Fourteen months after the wedding, however, Stephanie bade goodbye to her husband as he set out for a military inspection. On returning to the palace, she complained of a sore throat, which her doctors initially blamed on the smog of Lisbon. Over the next few days, as the condition worsened, she was diagnosed with diphtheria – a highly infectious disease for which there was no effective treatment. Pedro returned home at once to find that she was already dying, but she was able to receive the sacraments and whisper words of comfort to him as he wept by her bedside. When she died, at one o'clock in the morning on 17th July 1859, he was so overcome with grief that he had to be carried, unconscious, from the room.

"She was too good for this world!" sighed a stunned Queen Victoria, who found comfort in the thought that, "God had taken a pure lovely angel to him!"[200]

From then onwards Pedro was prone to bouts of depression, and just three years later, further tragedy struck his loving family. While two of his brothers – 'poor fat' Luis and Joao – were travelling to England, typhoid swept through the Portugal, claiming two of their brothers, Ferdinand and Agosto, as victims. After a few feverish days, the boys began to recover and felt sufficiently well to walk in the gardens but, while fourteen-year-old Agosto went on to make a full recovery, fifteen-year-old Ferdinand suffered a relapse and died on 6th November 1861.

His brother had barely expired when King Pedro complained of a vague rheumatic pain and fever, which Queen Victoria optimistically believed to be, 'nothing but one of those feverish attacks which foreigners so continually have from not attending to their stomach and bowels.'[201] Even when Luis and Joao arrived in England, and told her that he, too, had contracted typhoid, she saw no cause for alarm since he appeared to be stable and she herself had suffered and recovered from the same illness twenty-six years earlier.

Throughout Sunday 10th November, Pedro suffered a series of seizures, compelling the doctors to issue a bulletin warning that he was in grave danger. His brothers rushed to Portsmouth, intending to return home as soon as possible, but on 11th came the news that he had already died.

> "Poor Ferdinand," Queen Victoria wrote to the King of the Belgians, "so proud of his children – of his five sons – now the eldest and most distinguished, the head of the family, gone, and also another of fifteen...Dear Pedro was so good, so clever, so distinguished! He was so attached to my beloved Albert, and their characters and tastes suited so well, and he had such confidence in Albert!...He is happy now, united again to dear Stephanie, whose loss he never recovered...."[202]

Ferdinand's sorrows were not yet over. While he was attending the funeral of the young King in Lisbon, he received word nineteen-year-old Joao – 'the most popular and talented of all the Portuguese Princes'[203] – had also been taken ill at the Palace of Belem.

According to the somewhat unreliable Marquise de Fontenoy, Ferdinand hurried to the palace where:

> "...he found that the young Prince...had been seized that very morning with convulsions, after smoking a few whiffs of a cigar which he had taken from a boxful on the table in his library.

He had quickly thrown it aside, exclaiming in disgust: 'What a vile weed!'"[204]

His Chinese page picked up the cigar but after taking a few puffs of it, he, too was seized with convulsions and both the Prince and the page were dead before nightfall.

Prince Albert, as the Queen told her eldest daughter, was completely crushed by Pedro's death, and developed an almost obsessive fear of 'the fever'. Ironically, though, while dreading the illness, he simultaneously resigned himself to his fate, telling Queen Victoria that:

> "I do not cling to life. You do, but I set no store by it. If I knew that those I love were well cared for, I should be quite ready to die tomorrow...I have no tenacity for life."[205]

He still, however, had duties to perform, one of the most pressing of which concerned some disconcerting rumours about his eldest son, Bertie, the Prince of Wales.

The previous summer, Bertie, had, against the better judgement of his tutors, been allowed to undertake a period of military training in Ireland during a vacation from Cambridge University. When his parents visited Dublin that year, they were delighted to see how well he carried out his duties, and Albert returned home convinced that his son was behaving impeccably. In November, though, a courtier informed him that, while in Ireland, Bertie had embarked on an affair with an actress named Nellie Clifden, and his amorous antics were now the talk of all the clubs in London.

Initially, Albert was reluctant to believe the story, but when his former mentor confirmed that it was true, he was shocked to the core.

"I am fearfully in want of a true friend and counsellor," he wrote to Stockmar, "and that *you* are the true friend and counsellor I want, you will readily understand."[206]

Saddened that Bertie had betrayed his trust, and horrified that the liaison could damage the image of the monarchy which he had tried so hard to maintain, he journeyed to Cambridge to remonstrate with his son. To avoid prying ears, he and Bertie set out for a long walk in the rain to discuss the potential implications of such dalliances. Albert assured Bertie of his forgiveness, and the duly repentant Bertie promised that in future he would behave with greater propriety. The longer they talked, the further they walked until, lost in the Maddingley countryside, both were soaked to the skin, and by the time they made their way back to civilization, Albert was shivering uncontrollably.

Returning to Windsor, he struggled through the next few days, fulfilling his engagements while becoming increasingly disorientated, wandering from room to room, unable to settle or relieve his lumbago, rheumatism and neuralgia. By early December, he had developed a low fever and, unable to rise from a sofa, was haunted by the thought of King Pedro's death. His doctors blithely insisted that there was no cause for alarm and, as late as the 8th December, they issued bulletins stating that, although he had a chill, there were 'no unfavourable symptoms'.

Four days later, there was a marked deterioration, and his daughter, Alice, who barely left his side, urged her mother to summon Bertie from Cambridge. The Queen, unable to accept that 'the beloved Prince' was dying, said there was no need to do so, as it would only cause his father unnecessary alarm. The following day, Alice overruled her mother, and secretly sent an urgent telegram to her brother, who set out at once for Windsor. By the time he arrived in the early hours of the 14th November, Albert appeared much calmer, giving rise to the hope that he had weathered the worst. That afternoon, though, he suffered a relapse and, by evening, even the distraught Queen had to accept that he was dying.

At ten-forty-five, he drew three final gasps, and as Victoria collapsed to her knees 'kissing his heavenly forehead' and sinking 'in mute, distracted despair,' he breathed his last.

The entire country sympathised with the forty-two-year-old widow and her nine children, the youngest of whom was barely out of babyhood. Black-edged newspapers printed eulogies, describing Albert's tireless efforts on behalf of the British people.

"The nation has just sustained the heaviest loss that could possibly have fallen upon it," reported *The Times*. "Prince Albert, who a week ago gave every promise that his valuable life would be lengthened to a period long enough to enable him to enjoy, even in this world, the fruits of a virtuous youth and a well-spent manhood, the affection of a devoted wife, and of a family of which any father might be proud, this man, the very centre of our social system, the pillar of our State, is snatched suddenly away from us, without even warning sufficient to prepare us for a blow so abrupt and so terrible."[207]

News of his death was greeted with equal sadness across most of Europe, as *The Times* correspondent in Paris wrote:

"The news of Prince Albert's death, which circulated here at an early hour on Sunday, was received by all classes of French citizens with expressions of deep and sincere regret and of sympathy for the Queen. These sentiments are faithfully echoed in the press without distinction of party, and I have seen no journal that in its account of the sad event does not dwell on the high qualities of the deceased Prince."[208]

Nowhere, though, was the shock and sadness felt more deeply than among the members of his own extended family.

George, Duke of Cambridge, who had been present throughout Albert's final hours, remained at Windsor to support the Queen, while the late Prince's brother, Ernest, set out at once for England. Messages of condolence poured in from across the globe, including one from Albert's cousin and childhood companion, Arthur Mensdorff, who wrote of his deep sorrow at the passing of 'dear, great Albert.' Responding to a request from Victoria, Arthur promised to write a record of his memories of the youthful prince, and when the Queen sent him some photographs of him, he replied that he treasured them deeply since so many of his own recollections had been 'obliterated' by 'the changes we have had, the wars and revolutions'[209]

As Commander-in-Chief of the army, George of Cambridge issued an order that the drums and regimental standards were to be draped in black, and:

> "When officers appear at Court in their uniforms, they are to wear black crape over the ornamental part of the cap or hat, over the sword-knot, and on the left arm; with black gloves, and a black crape scarf over the sash."[210]

A week later, his sister, Mary, who had been among the first of the Queen's relations to travel to Windsor after Albert's death, found him 'very unwell indeed, his nerves terribly upset,' to the point where his doctors warned him that he was unfit to attend the funeral. George, however, insisted that it was his duty to be there and, in the event, he acted as the supporter of the chief mourner, the Prince of Wales.

It was not until New Year 1862 that George began to recover, by which time the Queen had further cause for alarm as her favourite uncle, King Leopold of the Belgians was also unwell. Although he continued to carry out his duties, he had an 'atrocious pain' in his chest which would continue unalleviated for the next thirteen months.

By June 1864, the pain had become so unbearable that he placed himself in the care of an English doctor named Thompson[w], who told him that, had he been in hospital, he would have recovered in eight to twelve weeks. King Leopold, though, was unconvinced and informed his friends that his sufferings had gone on for so long that there was little hope of a cure.

In March 1865, he travelled to England but the weather was so cold and damp that he barely left his rooms in Windsor Castle and, by the time he returned home, he was suffering from bronchitis. June was particularly wet that year in Belgium, and, not even daring to walk in the gardens for fear of exacerbating his condition, the King told a friend that his health had been 'much shattered by this wretched weather'. In late summer, on the advice of his doctors, he went to Ostend in the hope that the sea air might help to revive him, and, for a while, there seemed to be some improvement. Soon, though, he developed a high fever and thought it prudent to return to Laeken. By September, although he was confined indoors, he appeared to be 'going on

---

[w] His trusted advisor and physician, Baron Stockmar, had died in April 1863

tolerably well,'[211] but as winter approached it was clear to all around him that he was dying.

By 9th December, he was confined to bed, and, the following day, he asked that his sons, Leopold and Philippe, should come to him with their families. On seeing him, Leopold's wife, Marie, felt it her duty to tell him that he was dying and should, therefore, summon a priest and confess his sins.

> "Marie meant well no doubt..." wrote Queen Victoria's eldest daughter, "but to our Protestant ideas it seems cruel to trouble the last moments of the dying."[212]

The King, though, acknowledged her advice and spoke for some time with his chaplain, after which, surrounded by his weeping family, he lay back serenely and died shortly before midnight.

For three days his body lay in state while preparations were underway for a spectacular funeral, attended by numerous royal dignitaries, including George, Duke of Cambridge, and the Prince of Wales, representing Queen Victoria. Noticeable for his absence was the King's nephew, Ernest of Saxe-Coburg-Gotha, who was unwell at the time and unable to attend, but he sent a message of condolence to his successor. The new King Leopold II's first act as sovereign was to erect a statue of his father to 'perpetuate the remembrance of that great reign which had just come to an end.'[213]

Chapter 19 – 'You Know We Are Fallen'

George of Cumberland – King George V of Hanover; Queen Victoria's cousin
Marie of Saxe-Altenburg – Queen Marie of Hanover; wife of George V

> Children of George V and Marie:
> Ernest Augustus
> Frederica
> Marie

Mary of Cambridge – later Princess Mary of Teck; Queen Victoria's cousin
Francis – Prince of Teck; Mary's husband
Augusta of Cambridge – Grand Duchess of Mecklenburg-Strelitz; Queen Victoria's cousin
Frederick – Grand Duke of Mecklenburg-Strelitz; Augusta's husband

William I – King of Prussia
Alexander Mensdorff – Austrian Foreign Minister; Queen Victoria's cousin
Franz Josef – Emperor of Austria

In 1851, Queen Victoria's cousin, George of Cumberland, had succeeded his father as King of Hanover. The early years of his reign were peaceful and quite idyllic as he pursued his passion for music, promoted the arts, and was blessed by the domestic happiness of a loving family.

From the start, his relationship with his wife, Princess Marie of Saxe-Altenburg, had been something like a fairy-tale, since their first meeting took place at his father's romantic summer residence, Schloss Montbrillant, in 1839. A gentle and devout young woman, one year his senior, Marie shared George's interest in the arts and religion, and, following their wedding in February 1843, the couple remained unfailingly devoted to one another. Often, Marie read spiritual tomes to her husband, underlining relevant passages and adding the date and place in which they had discussed them; and, for his part, George never ceased to shower her with tokens of his affection, including the beautiful Marienburg Castle, which he presented to her on her thirty-ninth birthday as a symbol of his undying love.

A year after the wedding, Marie gave birth to a son, Ernest Augustus, who would grow up to be – in the opinion of Britain's Queen Alexandra – 'the ugliest man there ever was made;'[214] and, over the next decade, two daughters were born: Frederica, who resembled George's Hanoverian forebears and, according to one observer, and the shyer Marie, born in 1849.

George and Marie spent much of their time with their children and often they sat in the summer house as the littles played noisy games in the gardens. On one occasion, a guest found the young prince and princesses in filthy clothes as they busily attempted to create a model of Hanover out of mud. On being told that one particularly mound represented the chapel, the visitor suggested that they should also create the chaplain, only to be informed that, "Wir haben nicht Dreek genug!"[x]

Second only to his love for his wife and family, was George's consuming passion for music. He continued to write his own pieces, and encouraged established and rising composers to perform in his Kingdom. A year after his accession, he invited the French composer, Hector Berlioz, to Hanover and was so entranced by his music that he remained for four hours at the final rehearsal before his first concert.

---

[x] 'We don't have enough mud.'

"'I did not believe..." he told Berlioz afterwards, "that anyone could find new beauties in music. You have undeceived me. And how you conduct! I do not see you...but I feel it...I owe much to Providence, which gives me the feeling of music in compensation for that which I have lost.'"[215]

It was largely thanks to George's patronage that the composer gained such popularity in Germany.

The one glitch in George's otherwise idyllic existence was the fact that he was totally ill-equipped for the role of monarch at a time when Germany was facing great upheavals. Even after his marriage, his father had continued to treat him like a child and had consequently failed to introduce him to the workings of government. When, at the age of thirty-two, he ascended the throne, he had little idea how to deal with his ministers; and, irked that, due to his blindness, they had access to all political documents before he did, he dismissed his most able advisors, replacing them with men who were his intellectual inferiors. At the same time, to Queen Victoria's surprise and chagrin, he let it be known that he fully supported his late father's belief in the power of the monarchy, and that he intend to continue his autocratic rule. Moreover, he insisted on maintaining the royal bloodline, to the point where he firmly refused to allow any member of his family to marry beneath their station; and, when his cousin, Princess Mary of Cambridge became engaged to a lowly Prince of Teck, he stated that, as Head of the House of Guelph, he could never openly acknowledge her husband.

In early 1843, Mary's sister, eighteen-year-old Augusta of Cambridge, had married Prince Albert's former university friend, the Hereditary Grand Duke

Frederick William of Mecklenburg-Strelitz. The wedding took place in Buckingham Palace and was chiefly remembered for the rude behaviour of George's father, King Ernest Augustus of Hanover. As the newly-weds signed the register, the King elbowed himself into place beside the Queen to ensure that he would be able to add his name above Prince Albert's. Realising what he was doing, the Queen immediately handed the book to her husband, and to show her displeasure at her uncle's behaviour, she granted King Leopold of the Belgians   precedence over 'Uncle Ernest' at the subsequent celebrations.

The petty dispute on her wedding day was as nothing compared to the trials that Augusta was about to face in Strelitz. Within five years, she had produced two sons, the elder of whom survived for fewer than twenty-four hours; and her grief at his loss was made the more poignant by her reserved husband's disinclination to show her any affection. Her parents-in-law added to her woes, being part of 'the meanest and most immoral [family] in Germany;'[216] and when they visited England in 1846, a lady-in-waiting noted that the Grand Duke 'is so cross there is no living in the house with him.'[217] The Grand Duchess was no more amenable, being in the view of the Crown Princes of Prussia:

> "...the most vulgar, common, disagreeable woman I ever saw and leads poor Augusta a dreadful life as I have plenty of opportunity of seeing."[218]

Augusta, however, was a formidable woman, whose acerbic wit helped her to adapt to life with the difficult family. Moreover, marriage brought with it several benefits, not least of which was her husband's fortune which made him the wealthiest man in Germany after the Kaiser. When, in 1860, he succeeded his father as Grand Duke, Augusta revelled in her new status, being, according the Queen of the Netherlands, 'one of those who keep themselves in hot water about their rank and cannot bear the second place.'[219]

Apart from a shared pride in being a granddaughter of King George III, Mary bore little resemblance to her elder sister. Her cheerful generosity endeared her to the public and made her arguably the most popular member of the British Royal Family. These qualities, though, were of little use in finding her a suitable *parti*, as her want of a fortune and her enormous size deterred several potential suitors.

Throughout the late 1850s, Queen Victoria was becoming increasingly anxious about her unmarried cousin, whose flirtatiousness and lack of inhibitions were becoming distinctly embarrassing. She thought nothing of asking Prince Albert about the most intimate details of his daughter's pregnancy; and her conversation was so shocking to the Queen of Denmark that she ordered her daughters to avoid her. She had, she said:

> "…seen Mary flirt to such an extent that she had said to [her daughter] who was present 'If ever you become such a coquette as Mary you would get a box on the ears.'"[220]

Although Queen Victoria was convinced that marriage was the only solution for her disconcerting behaviour, she was glad to hear that Mary had declined a proposal from the recently-widowed King of Sardinia, on the grounds that she was devoted to her faith and felt that that 'as the Protestant Queen of Sardinia she must be in a false position, and that a wife can never find herself thus placed without injury to her husband.'[221] A few years later, though, when Mary passed her thirtieth birthday all likelihood of her finding a suitable spouse was rapidly fading. Watching her dancing in a 'dirty gown' with neither refinement not decorum, the Queen sighed sadly, 'I fear there is no hope for a husband. All this with her figure is too much.'[222]

Her pessimism was premature, however, for in March 1866, while attending a dinner given by her mother for the Duc D'Aumale, Mary made the acquaintance of a handsome officer in the Austrian army, Prince Francis of Teck. Francis had a fine reputation, having fought beside Queen Victoria's Mensdorff cousins at the Battle of Solferino, after which he had not only been decorated for his courage but had also won the respect and affection of the Austrian Emperor. This, though, could not erase the fact that he was the son of a morganatic marriage – his father, Duke Alexander of Württemberg, having married Countess Claudine Rhédey, who was tragically killed in a cavalry charge after falling from her horse while watching the Austrian military manoeuvres.

The possibility of his securing a 'great match' was remote, but Mary cared nothing for his parentage, seeing only a dashing hero, who shared her interest in religion and music. From their earliest encounters he appeared to be as enamoured with her as she was with him and, within a month, he had proposed. Her mother was overjoyed and, as she extolled his many virtues, she wrote that her daughter was 'a most fortunate creature to have found such a husband.'[223]

Mary's brother, George, Duke of Cambridge, was equally quick to offer his congratulations, and was delighted when he arrived at Kew on the day of their engagement and noticed that:

> "The young couple looked and seemed supremely happy. It is a great event in my family, and I must say I think it is a very happy one. He is a charming person and likely to make dear Mary an excellent husband. It is a real

pleasure to see Mary so thoroughly satisfied at the resolution come to."[224]

In the absence of her father, George gave Mary away at her wedding, which took place just three months after the couple's first meeting. Much to the delight of the people of Kew, Mary had specifically chosen the venue – Kew Parish Church – as, she stated, she wished to be married among her own people. The villagers responded to the gesture by turning out in force to witness the occasion; and the only sour note came from Hanover, from where King George had made a feeble attempt to prevent the ceremony from taking place. On a personal level, he said, he was prepared to welcome Francis, but he could never sanction the marriage of the son of a mere countess, and a granddaughter of King George III. When, some months later, the couple met him in Vienna, he received them warmly but reiterated that he would never accept their union. Ironically, within weeks of their meeting, he would find himself deprived of his status, his crown and his kingdom.

For over half a century, the German-speaking states had been dominated by Austrian policy, but by the mid-19th century a growing sense of nationalism had led to a widespread belief in the need for a more formal union of the independent kingdoms and duchies. While most of the states favoured unification, disagreements arose as to the nature of the new nation. Prussia, supported by fourteen other states, hoped to create a completely independent Prussian-led Empire; but the majority of the southern states envisaged a 'Greater Germany' – a union of all German-speaking peoples under the Austrian Habsburgs.

Ambitious for himself and for his country, Prussia's formidable minister, Otto von Bismarck, refused to compromise and, in his typically Machiavellian manner, sought an opportunity to bring the southern states into line. His chance came in the spring of 1866, when a dispute erupted over the recent Prussian annexation of Schleswig-Holstein, part of which had, until then, been administered by Austria. Negotiations ensued but it was apparent that Bismarck was baying for war, and the Austrian generals warned the Emperor that the country was unprepared for a conflict and he should implement an immediate armament programme. The Foreign Minister, Alexander Mensdorff, disagreed, believing that it would be better for the Emperor to demonstrate the Austrians' good faith and desire for peace by doing nothing. His advice was viewed by many ministers as naïve.

"There is no more sincere, straightforward, chivalrous man in the world than Count Mensdorff;" one commentator noted, "but I think advantage has been taken of this frankness by the enemy."[225]

While Queen Victoria urged King William I of Prussia to do everything in his power to keep the peace, Bismarck was determined to use the dispute to precipitate a war. By May, Alexander, like his Emperor, was 'frantic at being forced into war, but fearing now no more being able to prevent it.'[226]

Ernest of Saxe-Coburg-Gotha, meanwhile, was torn between his own liberal opinions and the benefits of allying his duchy to the more powerful Prussia. Ultimately, he decided in favour of the Prussians, but his initial overtures served only to arouse suspicion in Berlin. Convinced that he was too attached to his cousins, Queen Victoria and Alexander Mensdorff, Bismarck initiated a press campaign against him, portraying him as unreliable and not to be trusted; and, at the same time, he drew King William's attention to a

211

letter which Ernest had written him some years earlier, which had been so offensive that the King refused to meet him. Now, as the country was on the brink of war, the King received further missives from Ernest, which he forwarded to Bismarck.

"The Duke of Coburg," Bismarck replied, "has during the past four years shared in every intrigue against your Majesty's internal and foreign policy. His Highness has largely contributed to the return of democratic representatives in Prussia through his money and influence...I certainly do not go too far when I describe his Highness as one of the most irreconcilable opponents of your Majesty's policy, and state that no devotion to your Majesty's honour and interest is to be expected from him."[227]

Surprisingly, King William was angered by Bismarck's response, and, rather than acting on his advice, rebuked him so firmly for his letter that he was forced to write a more grovelling reply. Claiming that he had been misled by the newspaper articles, Bismarck sought to excuse his mistake as 'human weakness' but he pointedly added that:

"It appeared to me as if your Majesty were yourself indignant at the insincerity of the Duke and of Count Mensdorff; but your Majesty generously pardons the disrespect manifested in such conduct, as also the former hostility of the Duke, who has done more harm to your Majesty and the Prussian State through the favour which he has shown to the democracy, and the disturbance of the relations with England, than he can ever make good through a military convention."[228]

Nonetheless, having won King William's support, Ernest committed his army to the Prussian cause and set out from Coburg to play his role in the conflict.

While the crisis was brewing, Mary of Teck was enjoying her honeymoon in England when Francis received a call to return at once to his native Württemberg.

> "We were," she Mary, "but too soon awakened from our bright dream of life to its terrible reality by having to get ready and start at two days' notice to enable Francis to join the Army."[229]

After visiting Vienna, where he professed his allegiance to Emperor Franz Josef, Francis left his wife in the care of his aunt, the Queen Mother of Württemberg, and re-joined his regiment in preparation for battle.

Mary not only faced the prospect of losing the man whom she had so recently married, but also of finding herself on the opposing side to her sister, Augusta, Grand Duchess of Mecklenburg-Strelitz.

> "Poor Mama," she wrote, "is much shaken by all she has had to undergo and suffer for our sakes! Both her poor daughters in divided camps, though our hearts are naturally all in the one camp of right and justice."[230]

In Hanover, meanwhile, King George failed to grasp the seriousness of the situation, and, trusting to the camaraderie that existed between monarchs, he blithely wrote to the King of Prussia, suggesting further negotiation. He was shocked that his letter remained unanswered but still more horrified when, on the evening of 15th June, he was told that the Prussians had

213

issued an ultimatum guaranteeing the sovereignty of any state which sided with Prussia, but threatening the invasion or annexation of any state that refused to do so.

The day after the declaration of war, Bismarck sent a peace offer to the Austrian Emperor, who replied that he could not accept the Prussian terms without first consulting his Foreign Minister, Alexander Mensdorff. Alexander, though, according to Bismarck, was 'a weak-minded mediocrity, unequal to ideas of that calibre, and he said he must first take counsel with the Ministers,'[231] the majority of whom favoured the continuation of the war.

As the greater part of Franz Josef's army was dispatched to Holstein, Hanover was left totally unprepared and undefended. To the last moment, George naively believed that the Prussians would give the customary six weeks' notice before launching an invasion and, by the time that he and his generals realised that the enemy had crossed their border, it was too late to save the capital city. In a desperate attempt to preserve the army, George followed his troops southwards in the hope that they could join forces with their Bavarian allies, while the citizens of Hanover tore up railways lines in a futile attempt to delay the enemy's entry into the city. At five o'clock in the evening of the 16th June, the Prussians entered the capital and took over the administration of the government.

Morale was sinking rapidly among King George's troops but, on 24th June, his army approached Gotha, which was defended by only six battalions, two squadrons and four guns under the command of Colonel von Fabeck. This was his chance to restore national pride, for, as one contemporary author observed, 'if the King of Hanover had marched rapidly on Gotha that

214

day, Colonel von Fabeck would have been quite unable to hold his position.'[232] George, though, lacked the confidence to march onwards, and instead he sent a note to Duke Ernest of Saxe-Coburg-Gotha, asking him to mediate on his behalf with the Prussians. If, he said, his troops were granted free passage to Bavaria, they would 'pledge themselves to take no share in the war in Germany during six months.'[233]

Ernest asked that the period be extended to a year, and, when George agreed, his proposal was telegraphed to Berlin. An armistice ensued, which was set to expire the following day, but was then extended for a further twenty-four hours, during which time both the Hanoverians and Prussians were able to regroup. King George, in the meantime, received an offer from Prussia: if he disbanded his army and pledged himself to the Prussian cause, he would be free to return to his capital with his sovereignty intact. His generals, however, suggested that instead, the Hanoverians should make use of the superior numbers to fight their way through the enemy ranks to the Bavarian lines. When the armistice expired the following day, the Hanoverians launched their attack and, despite sustaining over a thousand casualties, they achieved a significant victory during the five-hour Battle of Langensalza.

Their triumph was short-lived. By the end of the day, Prussian reinforcements were arriving in such large numbers that George realised that his troops would be massacred if they launched a second attack. Faced with no alternative, he again approached the Prussians for terms, and agreed to disband his army, in the hope that they would deal leniently with his Kingdom. In response, the Prussians permitted his officers to retain their horses and swords and to return safely home with their men, on condition that they

215

refrained from further participation in the war. They were not, however, prepared to allow George to retain his position, and he was told that he and his son could go anywhere they chose providing they left and never returned to the Kingdom.

Ernest of Saxe-Coburg broke the news of George's surrender to Queen Victoria. 'It is too dreadful!' she gasped, 'Where is the poor King and his son?'[234]

George had, in fact, withdrawn to Austria under the illusion that, when the fighting ceased, his Kingdom would be restored to him. Six days after he had been deposed, the Prussians achieved a resounding victory at Königgrätz, and, as it was clear that the war was all but over, he wrote to the King of Prussia, seeking an assurance that he could retain his throne. On Bismarck's advice, the King failed to respond; and, when Queen Victoria interceded of George's behalf, her daughter, the Prussian Crown Princess, responded with uncharacteristic harshness.

> "At this sad time, one must separate one's feelings for one's relations quite from one's judgement of political necessities, or one would be swayed to and fro on all sides…they were told beforehand what they would have to expect…as rivers of blood had flowed and the sword decided this contest, the victor must makes his own terms and they must be hard ones for many…We have made enormous sacrifices and the nation expects them not to be in vain. This is the only answer I can give you at present."[235]

The severity of the terms imposed on Hanover surpassed George's worst expectations. In August, Bismarck introduced a bill to the Prussian House of Deputies, calling for the annexation of the Kingdom

216

along with Hesse-Kassel, Nassau and Frankfurt. The following month, the annexation was effected and, eighteen months later, part of George's private property was seized.

"Poor Hanover!" gasped Augusta of Mecklenburg-Strelitz. "What is to become of our old dynasty?"

Her mother, the Duchess of Cambridge, was even more distressed,

> "Alas!" she sighed, "All the dearest countries that my heart loved best have been stolen (I can't give it another name)...Hanover, which is the cradle of our English family, Hesse is mine, and Nassau was my dearest own Mother's; so you may judge of my feelings at this moment."[236]

Queen Victoria, deeply sympathetic to her cousin's plight, offered him a home in England, which he gratefully declined, informing a member of his household that:

> "We are all so deeply touched at the kindness shown to us by one and all, from the beloved Queen downwards. We are fallen, you know we are fallen, and we can do nothing for those who come to us. It must be genuine loyalty and devotion to our royal family which makes them show such affection and sympathy for us, the blood relations, in our misfortune."[237]

Fortunately, despite the seizure of some of his assets, George had had the foresight to deposit large sums of money in Austrian and British banks before the outbreak of war. He therefore retained a large fortune to fund the small court, which he established in exile, from where he continued to believe that he would eventually be reinstated as King. There were rumours that he also funded several groups of insurgents, whose mission was to drive the Prussians out of Hanover, and he became such a thorn in the side of Bismarck that he was offered a 'magnificent income' to forfeit his claim to the throne. Declining the offer, he insisted on his God-given right to rule – a stance which he maintained for the next twelve years. Even in exile, he clung to his belief in the importance of maintaining the royal bloodline, refusing his daughter, Frederica, permission to marry his former equerry, Baron Alfons von Pawel-Rammingon, with whom she had fallen in love.

The stress of defeat had, however, weighed heavily upon him, and, a year after losing his Kingdom, a more personal tragedy added to his misery. Following the victory at Langensalza, two of his nephews[y], Princes Bernhard and Ferdinand of Solms-Braunfel, had been court martialled for their conduct during the battle, and, although they were acquitted, the stigma of the accusations still hovered over them. After the war, Count Wendel – a Pomeranian who had formerly resided in Hanover – wrote an insulting letter to Prince Bernhard, repeating the charges against him and his brother. The twenty-eight-year-old Prince demanded a retraction and challenged the Count to a duel, which was duly accepted. As a date was arranged for the duel to take place, both men agreed that once the contest was over, the incident would be forgotten, and, since duelling pistols were usually unreliable, neither believed he would seriously injury the other.

They met in Vienna at dawn on 23rd February 1867, and, when they had taken the customary thirty-five paces, the Prince turned to face his opponent, who, after only a moment's hesitation, pulled the pistol's trigger. To his horror, the gun was more accurate than he had anticipated and a fatal bullet entered Prince

---

[y] The Princes were the grandchildren of George's mother, by her second marriage.

Bernhard's chest. As he collapsed to the ground, Wedel ran to him, begging his forgiveness, which the Prince duly granted before being carried home where he died, in intense agony, twenty-four hours later.

George, accompanied by his son and daughter-in-law, attended the funeral a few days later, and other members of the congregation observed that his demeanour demonstrated not only his sorrow at the death of his nephew but also his grief for the loss of Hanover. Over the next decade, he suffered a series of illnesses and, suspecting that he was dying, he urged his son to continue to maintain the claim to the throne of Hanover. He died rather suddenly in Paris, at six o'clock in the morning 12th June 1878, at the age of only fifty-nine.

> "On arrival at the Bristol Hotel, Paris, at seven," wrote his cousin and childhood friend, George of Cambridge, "heard of the serious condition, and immediately afterwards of the death, of the poor King of Hanover. It was, at the last, very sudden, he having been out driving the day before. Saw the Prince of Wales, and drove with him to the King's house, and saw Ernest, the Queen, and Frederica, all in a dreadful state at the sad and most overwhelming loss they had just sustained."[238]

He was greatly mourned in Britain, where, after much negotiation with his son, Queen Victoria arranged his funeral and interment. George, the last King of Hanover, was laid to rest in St George's Chapel, Windsor, on 25th June 1878.

After his death, his widow moved into a villa close to her later husband's castle in Gmunden, where she was attended from time to time by an American dentist.

"The beautiful widowed Queen of Hanover," he wrote, "...came to have an almost pathetic confidence in the value of the treatment I could give her. Her daughters, the Princesses Mary and Frederica, had much of the beauty of the Queen and the dignified stature of the King and were as noble of soul as they were splendid in person."[239]

Following her father's death, Frederica hoped that her elder brother, Ernest Augustus, might now permit her to marry the man whom she loved, but he adopted the same adamant approach as George had done, and threatened to stop her allowance if she flouted his ruling. When Queen Victoria learned of her situation, she encourage Frederica to marry the Baron and offered them both a home in England. The wedding took place in Windsor Castle in April 1880, after which the couple settled in rooms in Hampton Court and were regular guests of the Queen.

Seeing how harshly the victorious Prussians had dealt with Hanover, other defeated German states awaited their fate with trepidation. Queen Victoria's second daughter, Alice, who had married the heir to the Grand Duke of Hesse, cried desperately that the demands for reparations had virtually bankrupted the Grand Duchy. 'We are almost ruined," she wrote to her mother, "and must devote all our energies to the reconstruction of our suffering country;'[240] while the recently-married Mary of Teck was left in limbo as to what would become of her husband.

Francis remained for some weeks in Austria, waiting to discover whether or not the Emperor still required his services.

"After a week of cruel uncertainty for him and terrible anxiety for me," wrote Mary, "during

220

which he vainly sought for an audience, and never even succeeded in seeing any of the military authorities, so great was the general confusion, he gave it up in despair and came back to me."[241]

Like Ernest of Saxe-Coburg-Gotha, Mary's sister, Augusta, was in a far more secure position, as Mecklenburg-Strelitz had been on the winning side; and the Queen's Württemberg cousins fared rather better than they had expected, for, despite being compelled to pay substantial reparations, the Kingdom was permitted to retain its sovereignty.

In the wake of defeat, Alexander Mensdorff was forced to resign as Austrian Foreign Minister, much to the regret of the many foreign diplomats with whom he had had dealings.

"Poor dear Mensdorff! Everybody liked him," wrote one American envoy. "The foreign representatives adored him, one and all. He is one of the most charming types left of the chivalrous, truthful, loyal, high-bred, perfectly naif and perfectly pococurante Austrian."[242]

Soon afterwards, he was appointed Commanding General in Zagreb and Prague.

Chapter 20 – 'They Will Be Killed! They Will Be Killed!'

Leopold I – King of the Belgians; Queen Victoria's maternal uncle

Charlotte (Carlota) – Daughter of King Leopold of the Belgians; Archduchess of Austria; Empress of Mexico; Queen Victoria's cousin

Leopold II – King of the Belgians; brother of Charlotte; Queen Victoria's cousin

Philippe – Count of Flanders; brother of Charlotte; Queen Victoria's cousin

Maximilian – Archduke of Austria; brother of Emperor Franz Josef; Emperor of Mexico; husband of Charlotte

Franz Josef – Emperor of Austria-Hungary

Napoleon III – Emperor of the French

A year after George's expulsion from Hanover, a second of Queen Victoria's cousins was ousted from a throne, but in this case the consequences were far more devastating, leading to insanity and execution.

Following the death of his wife, Queen Louise, in 1850, King Leopold I of the Belgians had grown even closer to his only daughter, Charlotte, with whom he enjoyed discussing politics and international affairs. Charlotte revelled in his attention but, at the same time, dreamed of escaping from her sheltered world into the dazzling glamour of 'society'. Queen Victoria, briefly toyed with the idea that she would make an ideal bride for King Pedro of Portugal, but when, at the age of sixteen, she was permitted to attend a few dances, she welcomed the attentions of several other would-be suitors, including Archduke Maximilian of Austria, a younger brother of Emperor Franz Josef.

Well-read, well-travelled and, like Charlotte, fluent in several languages, the Archduke had enjoyed an impressive naval career and developed a keen interest in botany and natural sciences. He also had a keen political awareness and his views coincided with those of the young Belgian princess. More importantly, in Queen Victoria's eyes:

> "With the exception of his mouth and chin, he is good-looking, and I think one does not the least care for that, as he is so very kind and clever and pleasant."[243]

By February the following year, there was talk of an imminent betrothal and, in response to a request from King Leopold, the Austrian Emperor appointed his brother Viceroy of Lombardy-Venetia.

The wedding took place in Brussels in the summer of 1857, after which the couple set out for Milan to take up their positions as Viceroy and Vicereine. From the start, seventeen-year-old Charlotte made it known that she intended to involve herself fully in all the political and social affairs of the region and, while her beauty and elegance endeared her to the aristocracy, her charitable activities won her the affection of the people. She and Maximilian carried out their duties with tolerance and grace, but their successes were tarnished in the minds of the Emperor's ministers by the lavish balls and expensive entertainments that they hosted. Franz Josef was more alarmed that his brother's popularity exceeded his own, and, after two years, he used the accusations of extravagance to remove Maximilian from his position and recall him to Vienna.

In Milan, Charlotte had grown used to being the centre of attention, but in Vienna her attractions were

223

overshadowed by those of the strikingly beautiful but unhappily married Empress Elizabeth. She began to put on weight, which, according to Queen Victoria, spoiled her appearance, and placed her in an unfavourable light beside the anorexic Empress, whose close relationship with Maximilian, she quickly came to resent. To make matters worse, she soon discovered that her husband enjoyed the services of prostitutes, and gossips claimed that the couple's childlessness was due to the Archduke's having contracted syphilis, which had either left him sterile, or had caused his wife to refuse to sleep with him for fear of the contagion. Whatever the truth of the stories, it did not take long for the ever-observant Queen Victoria to notice that something was amiss in the marriage.

> "She was in Vienna for some time – part of it without Max, who had to go to Venice," the Queen told her eldest daughter, "and now that Max is returned to Vienna she goes to Venice and he remains at Vienna – which I do not approve."[244]

Disillusioned with the capital, the couple retired to their recently-built castle, Miramar, near Trieste, where for a few months Charlotte was able to employ her artistic talents to the full as she and Maximilian devoted themselves to designing and furnishing the interior, and organising the lay-out of the gardens. Whatever the strains in the marriage, the couple appeared perfectly happy in each other's company, but for Maximilian a life of domestic contentment was unfulfilling after his numerous adventures in foreign lands; and Charlotte still dreamed of playing a more glamorous role on the world stage. When, therefore, in 1863, they received the offer of becoming Emperor and Empress of Mexico, it was too attractive an opportunity to dismiss without further consideration.

Since the 15th century, Mexico had been a Spanish colony, but, throughout the early 19th century a struggle for independence had led to the establishment of the First Empire under the Emperor Agustin I. His reign was short-lived as internal disputes wreaked havoc across the country and, after only eight months, the country was declared a republic. For forty years, wrangling continued between the republican Liberals and the monarchist Conservatives, finally erupting into civil war in 1858, leading ultimately to the election of the Liberal president, Benito Juarez.

One of Juarez' first acts as president was to cancel all foreign loans, much to the annoyance of the European countries which were owed large sums of money. A united British, Spanish and French force was dispatched to demand the repayment of the debts, but, when the Spanish and British discovered that Emperor Napoleon III intended to overthrow Juarez and impose a new government on Mexico, they withdrew, leaving the French to continue alone. Juarez was forced into exile, and Napoleon III established a Second Empire, offering the throne to Queen Victoria's cousin, Ferdinand of Saxe-Coburg-Kohary, the former titular King of Portugal.

When Ferdinand quickly declined the offer, Napoleon's agents approached Maximilian, who initially hesitated, insisting he could not accept the crown without the support of the Mexican people and the backing of the Great Powers of Europe. Charlotte, though, was thrilled by the prospect of a new life as an Empress, and, with much encouragement from Napoleon's wife, Empress Eugénie, she urged him to reconsider. Several months of discussions ensued until October 1863, when a delegation of Mexican Conservatives assured the Archduke that he truly was the choice of the people. Six months later, much to Charlotte's delight, he formally accepted the crown.

Few politicians and members of her family shared Charlotte's enthusiasm.

> "The Archduke Maximilian," wrote an American diplomat, "...firmly believes that he is going forth to Mexico to establish an American empire, and that it is his divine mission to destroy the dragon of democracy and re-establish the true Church...Poor young man!"[245]

Queen Victoria considered the decision rash and dangerous; while Charlotte's grandmother cried aloud, 'They will be killed! They will be killed!'

Franz Josef was also opposed to the move on the grounds that, once his brother was crowned Emperor, they would be on an equal footing; and, to prevent him from returning home as a potential rival, he insisted that, before his departure, he must renounce all his Austrian titles and his position in the line of succession. His concerns were not entirely without justification, for, soon afterwards, Maximilian's Private Secretary, M. Eloin, informed him that, while travelling through Austria, he had seen a good deal of evidence of:

> "...the general discontent which is prevailing...The Emperor is disheartened; the people are becoming impatient and publicly demand his abdication. A sympathy for Your Majesty is visibly spreading throughout the territory of the empire. In Venetia there is a party ready to welcome their former governor."

The couple set sail in April 1864, and, after visiting Italy to obtain a papal blessing, they arrived in Vera Cruz on the evening of May 28th. Coming from the majestic splendour of the Viennese court, Charlotte – now styling herself *Carlota* – was disappointed to discover that her new home bore little resemblance to all that she had envisaged. The reception was lukewarm at best and hostile at worst; the accommodation was rundown; and the country was so poor that she and Maximilian would have to use their private savings to fund their everyday requirements. Nonetheless, in an impressive address, the new Emperor laid out his intention of serving the people to the best of his ability, drawing attention to the important role that his wife would play.

> "To the Empress," he said, "is confided the sacred trust of devoting to the country all the noble sentiments of Christian virtue and all the teachings of a tender mother."[246]

Clearly, in his mind, the childless Charlotte was now the mother of the Mexican people, and it was a role she undertook with diligent enthusiasm. The reign began with a tour of the country, which gave her the opportunity to observe the contrast between the life of the wealthy aristocrats and the abject squalor in which the poor eked out an existence. Determined to improve their lot, she rose each morning at six o'clock to visit her husband's most wretched subjects, often tramping over muddy tracks to prisons, hospitals and remote hovels. When she visited the city of Puebla, she was so distressed by the dilapidated state of a homeless shelter that she immediately forwarded to the city's Prefect seven thousand dollars of her own money so that:

> "...the poor of this city may participate in the pleasure which I have experienced among you...[The money] is to be dedicated to the rebuilding of the House of Charity, the ruinous state of which made me feel sad yesterday: so that the unfortunate ones may return to inhabit it who found themselves deprived of shelter."[247]

Unsurprisingly, one witness commented that the Mexican poor never had a truer friend than the Empress Carlota.

Maximilian, meanwhile, attempted to bring his liberal ideas to the country by reducing working hours, abolishing child labour, banning corporal punishment, and introducing various reforms to benefit the poor. His efforts soon backfired as his reforms angered the aristocracy but failed to impress the exiled Juarez' supporters, who resented the paternalistic benevolence of the foreign usurper.

In order to stabilise his position, Maximilian realised that he must secure the succession and decided to adopt two grandsons of the former Emperor Agustin: two-year-old Agustin de Iturbide y Green, and his fourteen-year-old cousin, Salvador de Iturbide y Marzán, both of whom were named as his heirs. Again, his good intentions failed to achieve the desired end, as many Mexicans suspected the adoption was merely a façade, since he had already named his younger brother, Archduke Karl Ludwig, as his heir; and, what was more, the younger boy's mother had not consented to the adoption and loudly proclaimed that the Emperor and Empress had stolen her son.

The accusations were painful for Charlotte, as was the knowledge that, even in Mexico, her husband continued to indulge in his penchant for prostitutes; and, to make matters worse, in December 1865, she heard that her beloved father had died. She had always found great comfort in her religion, but now it seemed that even the Pope had withdrawn his support, as the Papal Envoy was recalled from Mexico due to Maximilian's refusal to restore the Church properties that had been seized by Juarez.

Amid the mistrust and the constant threat from the exiled Juarez' supporters, Maximilian relied heavily on the continued support of Napoleon III. By mid-April 1865, the French troops had driven Juarez back to the Texan border, but, within days, news arrived that the American Civil War was over, and the Monroe Doctrine was again to be enforced. Since the Doctrine contained a clause stating that no foreign troops were permitted to interfere in the government of any country in the Americas, and any breach of this stipulation would lead to war with the United States, Napoleon III lost interest in his Mexican project, and reneged on the agreement that he had made with Maximilian prior to his accepting the crown. Accusing Maximilian and Charlotte of extravagance, he ordered his officers to take charge of the Mexican treasury, and gradually began withdrawing his troops from the country. The Mexican adventure, he said, was over, and he advised Maximilian and Charlotte to return home.

This left Maximilian in a dire position. Not only was he reluctant to abandon the work he had begun, but the prospect of returning to Vienna was all the more depressing since he had already renounced his Austrian titles and would be obliged to seek succour from his brother, Franz Josef. Disillusioned and still grieving for her father, Charlotte was so incensed by Napoleon's duplicity and cowardice that she set out to France to confront him face to face. Arriving in Paris on 9th August, she settled into the Grand Hotel from where she sent several messages to St Cloud, requesting an urgent meeting. For three days she awaited the Emperor's response and, when he finally deigned to receive her, he told her bluntly that he could offer neither money nor military support and reiterated his advice that she and her husband should return home. Refusing to be so easily dismissed, Charlotte requested further meetings but, again, Napoleon kept her waiting for a response. A week passed before he arrived at her hotel where he discovered that her behaviour was becoming increasingly bizarre. Convinced that she was about to be poisoned, she produced a series of outlandish plans for his further intervention in Mexico, leaving him so bemused that he left abruptly without even uttering a word. Some days later, she received formal letter telling her that the Emperor could not help her.

Stressed and exhausted, Charlotte decided to return for a while to her beloved Miramar but, throughout the long journey, her companions were deeply disconcerted by her mental state. Terrified that she was about to be murdered, she hid her face behind a handkerchief, while frantically urging the coachman to drive at full speed. She was persuaded to break the journey at her late father's villa on Lake Como, where doctors prescribed her sedatives, which seemed to restore her equilibrium. After only a few days, she insisted on continuing to Miramar, but had hardly had time to settle there when she received a letter from Maximilian, asking her to travel to Rome to seek the support of the Pope.

Dutifully, she obeyed but, on reaching Bonzano on the Austro-Italian border, she suddenly declared that she could not venture any further as a plot was afoot to poison her when she reached Rome. For a while she insisted that she must return to Miramar but eventually her panic subsided and she was persuaded to complete her mission.

On reaching the Vatican, she initially appeared perfectly balanced, conversing in a variety of languages with the foreign clerics as she described the problems that beset her husband. Then, suddenly, on the fourth day of her visit, her mental state deteriorated as she threw herself at the Pope's feet, hysterically crying that Napoleon's agents were attempting to poison her, and he must have the suspects immediately arrested. She would only eat food that had been specifically prepared for the Pontiff, and pleaded with him to allow her to remain in the Vatican as this was her only safe haven. The astonished Pope agreed to let her to sleep on a sofa, where she spent the night, attended by a lady-in-waiting, a doctor, and the Spanish diplomat, Antonio del Castillo.

Like Napoleon, the Pope finally told her that he could do nothing to support her husband's regime in Mexico, and, the following day when she returned to her hotel, she was even more convinced that she was the intended victim of a would-be assassin. Wearing a black mantilla to conceal her face, she had a carriage drive her through the streets so that she could drink water from fountains and eat the chestnuts that had fallen on the ground. When she was eventually persuaded to take more substantial food, she allowed only one trusted maid to prepare her meals and had live chickens tied to the table legs to provide her with protection.

Word of the Empress' derangement soon spread through the courts of Europe, and, as her Belgian family hurried to Italy, Queen Victoria wrote woefully that her 'state is too sad and dreadful and grieves us deeply. So young, so handsome, and so clever!'[248]

"She who was so quiet and self-possessed," the Crown Princess of Prussia agreed, "so calm and serious and yet of cheerful disposition I cannot understand how such a thing could happen. I love her so much...Dear Charlotte, whom I have never seen agitated, who indeed at times often appeared phlegmatic and inanimate, whose reason and caution was always above her years, what she must have suffered, what she must have gone through to come to that!"[249]

She had been in Rome for just under three weeks when her brother, Philippe, Count of Flanders, arrived to take her back to her beloved Miramar, where he appointed several eminent physicians to attend her, including the Director of the House for the Insane in Ghent, and Dr Riedel, Director of the Lunatic Asylum in Vienna. As she continued under the illusion that her attendants were trying to poison her, the medics were reluctant to prescribe any treatment other than warm baths and plenty of rest. When her condition showed no sign of improvement, her brother, King Leopold II, decided that she should return to Belgium and, accompanied by his wife, Queen Henriette, he travelled to Miramar to collect her. Still terrified that she was about to be murdered, Charlotte kept her face covered throughout the entire journey to her native land, and in an attempt to calm her, Leopold sent orders to clear every station through which the train would pass, to make the route as quiet as possible.

Maximilian was not told the full extent of her condition until the beginning of October, and the news so affected him that for ten days he withdrew from his duties to spend time alone in his apartment. During his seclusion, he received an anonymous letter from a woman who claimed that Charlotte had indeed been poisoned, not by Napoleon's agents but by angry Republican Mexicans.

When he eventually emerged, he faced the more pressing crisis of finding his country on the verge of civil war. As his family and friends urged him to abandon the Mexican adventure, he contemplated abdicating, but the thought that he had already renounced his Austrian titles weighed heavily on him. Moreover, the Mexican monarchists were so reluctant to see him leave that they staged a demonstration to give the impression that the he still had the support of the vast majority of the people. The ruse worked and he agreed to rally his loyal troops to repel the approaching republican militia.

With an army of approximately eight thousand men, Maximilian set out to drive back Juarez' supporters; and, in February 1867, following several skirmishes, he triumphantly entered the city of Queretaro to a rousing reception. Already, though, the republicans were closing in, and, on 14th March, under the leadership of General Mariano Escobedo, a force of almost thirty thousand surrounded the city. Despite being massively outnumbered, Maximilian was determined to hold his position and, throughout the day, he rode back and forth, encouraging his men to stand their ground in the midst of extensive losses. Queretaro, though besieged, remained in his hands and, as he abandoned his former residence to take up a small room in a church, he was confident that, with reinforcements, he could defeat Escobedo. To that end, he ordered General Leandro Marquez to take a thousand men on the four-day journey to Mexico City to gather more divisions and return to him within a fortnight.

Marquez succeeded in collecting reinforcements but, instead of following orders and returning to Queretaro, he staged an unsuccessful attempt to recapture the city of Puebla, and, unable then to reach the Emperor, was forced to go back to the capital. Waiting in vain for his return, Maximilian launched several sorties into the republican lines but, despite a few minor successes, he failed to break the siege. When a fortnight had passed and there was still no sign of Marquez, he ordered his aide-de-camp, Prince Felix Salm Salm, to take the same route and discover what had happened. Barely, though, had the prince set out than he was shot in the foot and was obliged to return to Queretaro.

By the beginning of May, the siege had been in place for almost eight weeks. Supplies were dwindling so rapidly that Maximilian drew up a list of set charges for every edible item to ensure that the poor were not disadvantaged by over-inflated prices, but even then it was not long before the citizens were reduced to eating dead horses. Maximilian shared the same fare, and, like his companions, was plagued by regular bouts of dysentery. Eventually, it was clear that the only alternative to starvation was to make a break through the enemy lines, and secret plans were made to launch the escape on 15th May. Throughout the evening of 14th, a bodyguard was selected for the Emperor, under the command of a Colonel Miguel Lopez, but that night, as a sleepless Maximilian was crushed with abdominal pains and diarrhoea, Lopez made a clandestine visit to the enemy lines. He was taken to General Escobedo and, in return for a substantial payment, he offered to lead a column of republican troops into the city under cover of darkness. Lopez would later falsely claim that he had acted on the orders of the Emperor, and that part of his deal with Escobedo included ensuring Maximilian's safety.

By dawn, unbeknown to Maximilian, Queretaro was swarming with his enemies, and, when Prince Salm Salm discovered their presence, he urged the Emperor to escape while there was still time. Maximilian refused to abandon his loyal supporters and, that morning, he was captured and imprisoned in a convent in the city before being transferred to a Capuchin monastery with Prince Salm Salm and two Generals – Tomas Mejia and Miguel Miramon. On 12th June, Juarez organised a show trial after which Prince Salm Salm was pardoned; while Maximilian and his Generals were sentenced to death by firing squad.

News of the sentence sent shock waves throughout Europe, prompting several monarchs including Queen Victoria to appeal for a reprieve; and, on the day before the execution, Princess Salm Salm approached Juarez directly, begging him to show mercy to the deposed Emperor. Juarez, pale and drawn, replied that he could not alter the court's decision but 'he would not prolong his agony any longer; the Emperor must die to-morrow.'[250]

As Maximilian prepared for his fate, he prepared a letter to be handed to Charlotte after his death:

"My dearly beloved Carlotta,

If one day God permits you to recover and you read these lines, you will learn the cruelty of the ill fortune which has increasingly pursued me since your departure for Europe, You took with you all my soul. So many events and so many sudden blows have broken all my hopes, that death is for me a happy deliverance and not an agony, I fall gloriously as a soldier, as a king; vanquished but not dishonoured. If your sufferings be too great, if God call you speedily to rejoin me, I will bless the Divine hand which has so heavily pressed upon us. Adieu. Adieu. Your poor Max."[251]

His companions, though, led him to believe that his wife was already dead. Initially horrified, he soon came to terms with her loss, saying that her passing made the prospect of his own death easier to bear.

"The hand of God," he said, "...had sent him an emollient in his misfortune – that the death of the Princess Charlotte inspired him with greater fortitude in bidding adieu to the world."[252]

Showing neither bitterness nor fear, he impressed his guards by his serenity and the kindly manner in which he spoke with them, causing one to confess that:

> "…he had been a great enemy of the Emperor; but after having been so long about him, and having witnessed how good and nobly he behaved in his misfortune, and looked in his true, melancholy blue eyes, he felt the greatest sympathy, if not love and admiration, for him."[253]

He was, he said, prepared to forgive Lopez, but Marquez' insubordination was more difficult to accept. The most hurtful experience of all, however, was the fact that his elder brother had compelled him to renounce his Austrian titles. Unbeknown to Maximilian, when Franz Josef heard that one of the reasons for the severity of his sentence was that, with no position in Austria, he would be seen solely as a pretender to the Mexican throne, he offered to restore his titles, but, by then, it was too late.

At five o'clock in the morning of 19th June 1867, Maximilian, Mejia and Miramon were led into a courtyard where the firing squad was stationed. The former Emperor handed out gold coins to the five armed soldiers, asking them to aim for his heart, before bravely standing erect and awaiting his death. His end was horrific as four of the five soldiers missed his heart, causing blood to gush into his throat and windpipe, almost suffocating him. He fell to his knees, pointing desperately at his heart, but the fifth soldier took fright and ran away, leaving him writhing in agony for five minutes before an officer finally fired the fatal shot.

When news of his death was announced there was little rejoicing in Mexico, and, as his body was taken back to the capital, tearful crowds lined the streets, bowing their heads in silent reverence.

It was some weeks before the details of the execution reached Europe, where George of Cambridge noted that it was 'a most terrible event, and produced a profound sensation.'[254]

Queen Victoria cancelled several public engagements, and Britain broke off all diplomatic relations with Mexico.

Charlotte, meanwhile, remained in seclusion unable to believe that her husband was dead. Refusing to get up except at night, she sometimes claimed that Maximilian had faked his own death in order to marry again; and other times, as her brother, King Leopold, told Queen Victoria, she imagined that he was being held prisoner in England. Alternating between abject apathy and frantic activity, in 1869 she was suddenly struck by a desire to claim the throne of Spain, and consequently, according to King Leopold,

'It is necessary at Laeken to shut all the doors and exercise a close watch over her.'[255]

Occasionally, she appeared lucid and calm and, as the Crown Princess of Prussia observed while visiting her, she was able to hold a conversation about insignificant matters, but would never speak of Mexico or of her husband. Later that year, though, when she was taken to Spa in the hope that the waters might revive her, an event occurred which showed that Maximilian was never far from her mind. Suddenly becoming obsessed with the number nineteen – the date on which he had been executed – she insisted on being taken to play roulette, and placed a large sum of money on that number. Much to the astonishment of observers, she won, and, leaving the room, handed all her winnings to a poor man, who happened to be passing, asking him to take it and to pray for her late husband.

Chapter 21 – 'The Exalted Gentleman Had No Courage Whatever'

Ferdinand of Portugal – Prince of Saxe-Coburg-Kohary; Queen Victoria's cousin
Leopold of Hohenzollern-Sigmaringen – Son-in-law of Ferdinand

Alice – Queen Victoria's second daughter
Vicky – Crown Princess of Prussia; Queen Victoria's eldest daughter
Fritz – Crown Prince of Prussia; Vicky's husband

Ernest II – Duke of Saxe-Coburg-Gotha; Prince Albert's brother; Queen Victoria's cousin
Alexandrine – Duchess of Saxe-Coburg-Gotha; wife of Ernest II

Augusta – Grand Duchess of Mecklenburg-Strelitz; Princess of Cambridge; Queen Victoria's cousin
Adolph – Son of Augusta
Mary – Duchess of Teck; sister of Augusta

Alfred – Duke of Edinburgh; heir to the Duchy of Saxe-Coburg-Gotha; Queen Victoria's second son
Marie – Princess of Edinburgh, later Queen of Roumania; daughter of Alfred

In 1870, four years after the resounding Prussian victory in the Austro-Prussian War, Bismarck engineered another conflict to bring his plans for the unification of Germany closer to fruition. Realising that the best means of uniting the different states was to provide them with a common enemy, he created a situation in which the French could be portrayed as aggressors so that all the German kingdoms and duchies would rise up in support of Prussia.

Two years earlier, following a revolution in Spain, Queen Isabella II was ousted, and an invitation was extended to the Royal Houses of Europe to present potential candidates as a replacement monarch. As ever, various names were suggested, including Queen Victoria's cousin, Ferdinand of Saxe-Coburg-Kohary, but when the Prussians proposed Ferdinand's son-in-law, Prince Leopold of Hohenzollern-Sigmaringen, the French, fearing that they would be encircled by the Hohenzollern[z], were outraged. Napoleon III sent an emissary to King William of Prussia, who was staying at the spa town of Ems, to ask him to remove Leopold's name from the candidacy under threat of war.

In fact neither Leopold himself, nor the King of Prussia had ever been in favour of the idea, and when the emissary, Count Benedetti, stated his case, the King graciously acquiesced to his demands. Benedetti, however, went further, demanding guarantees that no other Prussian candidate would ever be submitted, and the King, not a little affronted, gave a non-committal response after which the meeting ended coolly. The episode might have passed unnoticed, had Bismarck not spotted the opportunity for which he was hoping. Having obtained permission to provide a transcript of the meeting to the press, he carefully doctored the King's report before submitting it for publication. In Bismarck's version, the emissary had been extremely discourteous, and the King had responded sternly, in a manner that was insulting to France. To compound the problem, when the report appeared in the French press, some of the terms were mistranslated, making the King's words sound deliberately offensive.

---

[z] Hohenzollern was the family name of the Kings of Prussia

239

Napoleon III, seething at the perceived blow to his country's honour, played directly into Bismarck's hands by impetuously issuing a declaration of war. To the Germans this was an unnecessary act of aggression, which roused such a wave of nationalistic feeling that, as Bismarck had hoped, the majority of the states rallied to the Prussian cause.

"...The provocation of a war such as this," wrote Queen Victoria's daughter, Alice, from Darmstadt, "is a crime that will have to be answered for, and for which there is no justification...there is a feeling of unity and standing by each other, forgetting all party quarrels, which makes one proud of the name of German."[256]

It was a view shared by her sister in Prussia, who likewise wrote to their mother:

"We have been shamefully forced into this war, and the feeling of indignation against an act of such crying injustice has risen in two days here to such a pitch that you would hardly believe it; there is a universal cry 'To arms' to resist an enemy who so wantonly insults us."[257]

When King Leopold II of the Belgians realised that his country was surrounded by opposing armies, he went to great lengths to secure his defences to maintain Belgian neutrality, while other cousins of Queen Victoria were dragged into the conflict.

Augusta, Grand Duchess of Mecklenburg-Strelitz, saw her husband and their son, Adolph, depart at once for the front, while Ernest, Duke of Saxe-Coburg-Gotha, prepared his troops for battle. Unlike the Crown Prince of Prussia, who was sickened by the horrors of war, fifty-two-year-old Ernest appeared to view it as an adventure, despite the fact that, as he told an English observer, he had had to groom his own horse for the first time in three decades. Smoking a large cigar, he was often seen among his men, strolling about in the uniform of the Coburg Cuirassiers – 'a flat white cap with a yellow band, black double-breasted frock with yellow cuffs and collar, and metal buttons, white cords or leathers, and heavy jack-boots.'[258]

Within two months, the Germans had achieved a resounding victory at Sedan; Napoleon III was captured; and Paris was besieged. Ernest based his headquarters in a former casino near Versailles, where, between his military duties, he found plenty of time to pursue his amorous affairs. His behaviour, like that of several other princes, irked many Prussian ministers who complained that he expected to be fed and housed even though he had plenty of money to pay for his own upkeep. When 'reports got abroad' of the decadent lifestyle of his fellow officers and princes, 'some were sent back to the rear or on to the front, the King [of Prussia] wisely thinking them more ornamental than useful in Versailles.'

Augusta's son, Adolph, was also in the vicinity of Versailles, but unlike Ernest, he had little time to squander on entertainment. Shortly before Christmas, his aunt, Mary of Teck, wrote to a friend:

> "...We have thus far had very good accounts of my nephew...who has for the last nine weeks been at Versailles. He is attached to the headquarters of the Crown Prince of Prussia, and was present at the battle of Sedan, and only recently for five or six hours under fire, during one of the sorties from Paris."[259]

A month later, the French surrendered and, as the final preparations were underway for German unification, Ernest again annoyed the ministers by his constant interference in their discussions. Having attended the coronation of the new Emperor William I

241

in the Hall of Mirrors in Versailles, he further irked his detractors by his attendance in the victory parade during which he rode alongside the Crown Prince of Prussia, sporting his recently-awarded Iron Cross. His attempts to portray himself as 'resolute and fearless' were, said one, were risible because 'the exalted gentleman had no courage whatever.'

It was a theme to which his critics would often return. When he later penned his memoirs, describing his youthful courage at the Battle of Eckernforde in the Schleswig-Holstein wars, Bismarck remarked dryly, "He cannot help that, it's his nature – but that he should have had himself painted as a hero – a stage hero!"

His writings not only earned him the mockery of his compatriots, but also alienated him from his extended family. Queen Victoria was furious when he published a series of private letters from Prince Albert, and she was even more incensed by his outspoken criticism of the British, who, he claimed, had supplied arms to the French during the Franco-Prussian War.

"I had a conversation with the Duke of Coburg," said one Englishman, "who shows the liveliest interest in any question which touches England, without ceasing to be a German Prince. Recently several stand of arms have been taken from the French which have had the 'Tower mark' upon them, and the Germans regard this as proof positive that the English Government has been sending rifles to the French."[260]

His suspicions were shared by a good many of his compatriots, and even Queen Victoria's daughter, the Crown Princess of Prussia, warned her mother that:

"The feeling is very general here that England's neutrality afforded France advantages and us disadvantages. France can buy English horses as her ships can reach England, whereas ours cannot on account of the French fleet."[261]

Ernest, however, went further, suggesting that the Crown Princess herself had divided loyalties, and, in 1886, he published an anonymous pamphlet entitled *'Co-Regents and Foreign Influence in Germany'* in which he openly attacked his niece and her husband. Vicky was aghast at his behaviour and saddened by the damage he had done to the Crown Prince's reputation, particularly since, as she told her mother, 'I have always stuck up for Uncle Ernest here, where he has been very unpopular and often unjustly so.'[262] The attacks, however, continued, and when a second pamphlet appeared, criticising both Vicky and her mother, she wrote desperately to Queen Victoria:

> "What is your advice about Uncle Ernest?...This is the second infamous pamphlet written against me, with covert attacks against you, from his pen. This, added to the misrepresentations in his newly issued Memoirs, is doing a great deal of harm and especially creates in the minds of my three elder children a totally false and very mischievous impression. It is too wicked of him."[263]

One staunch supporter of the Crown Prince and Crown Princess, a certain Dr Harmening, flew to their defence by publishing a pamphlet refuting all of 'Uncle Ernest's' claims. Rather than letting the matter drop, however, the Duke sued Harmening for libel, and being 'sly and supported by clever lawyers', he won his case with the result that the doctor was sentenced to six months imprisonment.

> "Uncle Ernest has much to answer for," Vicky wrote to the Queen. "His behaviour to you, to Fritz [the Crown Prince] and to me is simply disgraceful; it is too grievous, as we have all

243

been so kind to him and really fond of him and I never thought he had a bad heart, though I always knew he was most unscrupulous and unprincipled and had an imagination which played him the most extraordinary tricks."[264]

For the sake of her late husband, Queen Victoria refused to sever all correspondence with him but their occasional meetings lacked the affection that had characterised them in the early days of her reign. He was, according to the Marquise de Fontenoy, her 'pet aversion' and, in 1891, when the 'awful looking man' visited her in Grasse, her lady-in-waiting observed that 'the Queen dislikes him intensely.'[265]

Other members of the family found his behaviour and appearance equally repugnant. His nephew and heir, Queen Victoria's second son Alfred – whose own reputation was far from savoury – sought to keep his family away from his court, which he filled with 'adventurers' and 'rather doubtful gentlemen [who] were married to second-rate actresses of compromised reputation and all sorts of semi-cultured, semi-respectable persons of nondescript types.'[266]

On several occasions Alfred and his uncle quarrelled in public; and, when Alfred's wife refused to invite two of his mistresses to a reception, the ensuing argument became so heated that, for over a year, they did not speak to one another.

As he aged, his appearance bore testimony to his years of self-indulgence. He was, wrote Alfred's daughter,

> "...squeezed into a frock coat too tight for his bulk and uncomfortably pinched in at the waist. A sallow face marred by liver spots, a lean, waxed moustache curving down over the corners of his mouth, the ends turning up again. The jaw of a bulldog, the lower teeth protruding

far beyond the upper, and with a pair of bloodshot eyes alive with uncanny, almost brutal intelligence."[267]

In the early 1890s, he suffered from a series of strokes, the most critical occurring in the summer of 1893. Initially, he appeared to be making a good recovery but, by the middle of August, he had sunk into a decline. Alfred hurried to see him at Rheinhardsbrunn in Gotha, from where he sent regular reports of his condition to Queen Victoria, concluding with a message that he had died peacefully, shortly before midnight on 22nd August at the age of seventy-five.

All past grievances forgotten, the Queen wept at his passing, while her eldest daughter, whom he had so maligned, wrote that she 'heartily' forgave him and felt his death 'very deeply.' Few other members of the family shared her grief. Only his wife, the faithful and much-neglected Alexandrine, truly mourned him and was genuinely broken-hearted at his death.

'Indeed, there are few wives of any of the sovereigns now reigning who have been subjected to more constant abuse, neglect, and infidelity than Duchess Alexandrine,'[268] wrote the Marquise de Fontenoy, but no one could deny that she had genuinely loved him. She outlived him by almost a decade, withdrawing into the ancient Schloss Callenberg where she lived simply, attended by only one faithful lady. 'A sad old figure, whose one and only love was the terrible old gentleman who treated her as no one else would dare treat a servant,'[269] recalled Queen Marie of Roumania. She died peacefully in December 1904, at the age of eighty-four.

Chapter 22 – 'He Has Deserved the Queen's Entire Confidence'

George – Duke of Cambridge; Queen Victoria's cousin

Napoleon III – the deposed French Emperor
Prince Imperial – Prince Louis Napoleon; son of Napoleon III

Arthur, Duke of Connaught – Queen Victoria's third son
Beatrice – Queen Victoria's youngest child
Prince Henry Battenberg – Beatrice's husband

The Franco-Prussian War highlighted the deficiencies of the British army, which lacked both the impressive organisation of the German forces, and the most up-to-date weaponry such as the French Chassepot rifle and the German Krupp six-pounder breech-loading cannon. When, therefore, Edward Cardwell was appointed as Secretary of State for War in Gladstone Liberal Government, he announced his intention of introducing a series of military reforms, including the reduction of the number of troops stationed in the colonies; a re-sizing of the peace-time army; the abolition of the archaic practice of purchasing commissions; and a reorganisation of the War Office, making the Commander-in-Chief of the Armed Forces subordinate to the Secretary of State.

While many politicians welcomed Cardwell's plans, the Commander-in-Chief, George of Cambridge, was quick to point out their flaws. As a serving soldier he was, he claimed, more familiar with the needs of the army than was a politician who had no previous experience of the War Office. Moreover, he was convinced that the reforms were merely a money-saving venture on the part of the Liberal Government, and their implementation would compromise the security of the Empire. A reduction in the size of the peace-time army would, he said, place Britain in an inferior position to other European countries, most of which employed compulsory conscription.

> "There cannot be a doubt," he wrote to Cardwell, "in the present state of the world, and more especially of Europe, that, should troubles arise, they are likely to come upon us suddenly and when we may least expect them…It is to meet such sudden contingencies that the great Continental Powers have of late largely increased their already enormous means of military power, and…it would be impossible for us entirely to overlook what our neighbours are doing in this direction without taking warning ourselves in time."[270]

He was equally concerned about the reduction of the numbers of troops in the colonies and drew up detailed lists of the various regiments, warning that they were necessary for the defence of the Empire.

In the House of Lords, he was politely referred to as the 'illustrious gentleman' to whom the troops owed a debt of gratitude, but privately many Members of Parliament mocked his ideas and accused him of being old-fashioned and intransigent.

> "The Duke of Cambridge's manner is uncommonly taking and pleasant and frank," wrote the Undersecretary of State for the Colonies. "But somehow or other he had a jolly big-dog way of blurting out things that made me inclined to laugh, and I felt that if there were not a desk between him and me I should get into a scrape."[271]

When the press, too, began to mock his ideas, Queen Victoria hastened to his defence. She had, she informed Cardwell, complete confidence in his abilities and was aware that, contrary to much of what was reported, he was not opposed to reform. As early as 1860, he had, for example, been instrumental in restricting corporal punishment in the army and had always been keen to be kept abreast of the most up-to-date advances in armaments and other military equipment. It appeared to the Queen, however, that certain Members of Parliament were doing their utmost to undermine him, which made her all the more determined to demonstrate that he had her full support.

"The Duke of Cambridge," she wrote, "has always acted most cordially, as the Queen is sure Mr Cardwell will already have found, with successive Secretaries of State, in promoting and giving effect to all well-considered measures of improvement, and ever since he has been at the head of the Army H.R.H. has deserved the Queen's entire confidence, and is entitled to her best support. Anything that could tend to lower his position in the eyes of the public would, the Queen feels, be a misfortune as regards the public service, and she is confident that Mr. Cardwell will give his sanction to no measure likely to have this effect."[272]

The press, though, continued its relentless criticism, blaming George for the fact that many recently-recruited soldiers were physically unfit for service; implying that his insistence on maintaining the size of the army was due to his desire for a war; and suggesting that no improvements could be made as long as the outmoded Duke remained in office. Stories about his eccentricities abounded, such as when he punished a

248

young lieutenant for his failure to appear properly dressed on parade by ordering him to wear his uniform on every single occasion for the following year; or his habit of carrying an umbrella while reviewing the troops.

In the midst of the verbal attacks, George was confronted with a more direct assailant when, in January 1874, a stranger approached him as he stood looking in a shop window opposite Marlborough House. Accusing him of having done great wrong, the stranger suddenly struck him on the chest and, before George had time to respond, he launched a second more violent attack, which would have continued had a passing constable not seized him and taken him into custody. It was soon revealed that the assailant was a retired officer, Captain Charles Studdert Maunsell, who had been denied a promotion for which he had been hoping. He was, thought George, 'evidently mad' – a view shared by Queen Victoria, who wrote to him at once expressing her horror at the outrage. Three days later, George attended Maunsell's trial and was satisfied by the sentence of one month's imprisonment, but even then he was reproached by the press for failing to defend himself or apprehend his attacker. Throughout the 1870s, the criticism became more intense, culminating in 1879 in a vitriolic attack, blaming him for the death of the young Prince Imperial.

Prince Louis Napoleon, the only son of Emperor Napoleon III, had been familiar with war from an early age. When he was fourteen years old, he had witnessed the Battle of Sedan – his father having him removed from the scene shortly before the French defeat and his own capture and subsequent ousting from the throne. He was taken first to Belgium then to England where he lived with his parents in Camden Place, Chislehurst, receiving regular visits from Queen Victoria. When his father died three years later, the young prince became the focus of attention of French royalists, who hoped to see a return of the monarchy in France. By then, though, Louis Napoleon had embarked on a military career in England, having begun his cadetship in the Royal Artillery at Woolwich.

The Prince Imperial was a diligent and gifted student, outshining boys who were several years his senior, and winning various riding and fencing competitions. On the completion of his training, he hoped to enter active service, but, in view of his status, Queen Victoria asked the Duke of Cambridge to find him a safer position on his own staff. Over the next two years, George developed a paternal affection for the young man, whose enthusiasm and commitment impressed all his senior officers. It was clear, though, that he was frustrated by his sedentary role and, in January 1879, he requested permission to participate in the South African campaigns.

The previous year, Sir Bartle Frere had been appointed as the Governor of Cape Colony with orders to form a confederation of the British colonies in the region. Within twelve months, he came to the conclusion that he could not carry out his mission until the powerful neighbouring Zulu Kingdom had been suppressed. Consequently, he asked for more troops to be sent to the region but, as the British Government was desperate to avoid further conflicts, the Colonial Secretary, Sir Michael Hicks Beach responded to his request:

> "We cannot now have a Zulu war, in addition to other greater and too possible troubles,"

Frere, though, was determined to crush the Zulus and, in December 1878, he issued an ultimatum to King Cetawayo, demanding the he should disband his army under threat of war.

After much deliberation, George agreed to allow the Prince Imperial to participate in the campaign but purely in the role of a volunteer attached to the staff of Lord Chelmsford, the commander of the British troops in South Africa. George's only concern was that the young man was 'too go-ahead and plucky', but, as he told Chelmsford, he was:

> "...a fine young fellow, full of spirit and pluck, and having many old fellow-cadet friends in the Artillery, he will doubtless find no difficulty in getting on. If you can help him in any other way, pray do so."[273]

Under orders to protect the Prince, Chelmsford permitted him to become involved in intelligence gathering in the area around Rorke's Drift but it was not long before his recklessness in charging alone after enemies caused such concern that he was reassigned to a safer role behind the lines.

Initially, the British suffered a series of dramatic defeats but, towards the end of May 1879, reinforcements arrived and Chelmsford planned an invasion of Zululand. On June 1st, as the army prepared the advance, the impetuous Prince seized the chance to resume active service. Without having obtained official permission from his superior officers, he set out on a scouting expedition with six other men under the command of Lieutenant Carey. In the mid-afternoon, having scoured the region and found no evidence of a Zulu presence, the patrol stopped in a disused camp to review the situation. While relaxing over coffee, they were suddenly confronted by a group of about forty warriors, who killed two members of the party in an instant. In a panic, the others fled the scene but, as Louis Napoleon attempted to mount his horse, it bolted in fear and he was left alone, surrounded by enemies.

The following morning, when British officers, alerted by Carey as to what had happened, arrived on the scene, they found the naked body of the Prince Imperial, riddled with eighteen spear wounds, all of which were to the front, demonstrating that he had been killed as he vainly attempted to fight off his assailants. Alongside him lay the corpse of his faithful fox terrier, who had also been speared to death.

Almost two weeks passed before George heard what had happened.

> "This news is overpowering in its terribleness," he wrote. "...No words can describe the dismay it has caused. How it could have happened that the Prince should have been allowed to get into so exposed a position is quite inexplicable...I feel quite broken-hearted."[274]

The fact that Prince Louis had been abandoned by his companions made the event even more shameful, and, like everyone else in the country, Queen Victoria wanted to know why the 'good, exemplary, brave but alas! far too daring young man' had been placed in such a dangerous situation.

The press immediately seized upon George as a scapegoat, one journalist stating:

> "The Duke of Cambridge will be false to the responsibilities of the great position which he holds if he does not, with more vigour than he has lately shown, order the strictest inquiry into the affair."

An inquiry had, in fact, been established and, in the interim, Carey faced a Court Martial for cowardice. After studying all the details of the case, however, George ensured that he was found innocent and he was equally quick to vindicate Chelmsford and all of the officers involved. The outcome led to further censure from the press, which accused George of covering up the crime and allowing those responsible to walk free.

Apart from the damage to his own reputation, George was deeply saddened by the death of his protégé, and, when his body was eventually returned to England for interment beside his father in Chislehurst, he acted as one of the pall bearers at the funeral.

Throughout the next decade, criticism of George's methods continued with, perhaps, greater justification. In 1882, during the Anglo-Egyptian War, he dismissed the suggestion that officers should discard their scarlet jackets, which made them more visible to the enemy, stating that they should be proud to be seen by those against whom they were fighting on behalf of the Empire. Even following the success of the campaign, journalists mocked him relentlessly, one paper reporting that while the army was fighting the Battle of Tel el-Kebir, the Duke:

> "...aware somehow of fighting, rose two hours earlier than usual, shouldered his umbrella, charged an imaginary enemy at the head of imaginary troops and fell with an imaginary bullet in his shoulder."

As he grew older, George became even more set in his ways, and, like his siblings, took great pride in being part of what was known as 'the Old Royal Family.' Ironically, considering that he had married a commoner[aa], he was particularly affronted by the fact that Queen Victoria had permitted her youngest child, Princess Beatrice[bb], to marry Prince Henry of Battenberg – the son of a morganatic marriage. When he discovered that he was to be placed beside Prince Henry during a formal dinner, he adamantly refused to

[aa] See Chapter 24
[bb] Prior to his death, there were rumours that Beatrice was about to be betrothed to the Prince Imperial.

253

sit down, bellowing, "I'm damned if I'm going to sit there!"

By the mid-1890s his position as Commander-in-Chief was becoming so untenable that even the Queen's son, Arthur, Duke of Connaught, was anxious to see him replaced. Queen Victoria conceded that a younger man would be better suited to the role, and, in November 1895, she persuaded her cousin to resign. As the day of his departure from office approached, she wrote to him sympathetically:

> "It is with much pain that I see you leave the high, important, and responsible office which you have held so worthily for nearly forty years. Accept also my sincerest thanks for the great services you have rendered to the Country, to the Army, and myself, which be most gratefully remembered. Believe me that I feel deeply for you – this severance of a tie which existed so largely between you and the Army...I need not...say that I shall be glad to have your opinion on affairs of importance connected with the Army."[275]

Her sympathy did not lessen the disappointment that he felt, not least because he had been pressurised into resigning rather than doing so of his own volition.

> "I never resigned nor even contemplated resignation," he wrote to a friend, "but when told that these proposed changes were to be carried out, I had no choice left but that of not offering any resistance in my person and thus it has, alas! come about. It simply amounts to my being most summarily turned out, and at the shortest notice without my retirement being awarded to me!! Strong order this I think!!! after 39 years in my present high position."[276]

To soften the blow, Queen Victoria appointed him her personal aide-de-camp, to attend her during all public displays and military engagements but he felt his enforced resignation keenly and, for some time, was so low-spirited that, when he visited Queen Victoria's daughter at Homburg, he 'was rather depressed, he talked about having arranged his grave at Kensal Green Cemetery in London, and of having built himself a little mausoleum.'[277]

His preparations were premature, as he survived for almost another decade, outliving Queen Victoria by three years.

Part IV – Partners, Parents & Potentates

Chapter 23 – 'The Same Self-Centred Taciturn Man'

Leopold II – King of the Belgians; Queen Victoria's cousin

Marie-Henriette – Queen of the Belgians; Leopold II's wife

Children of Leopold II & Marie-Henriette:
Louise
Leopold
Stephanie
Clementine

Philippe – Count of Flanders; Leopold II's brother; Queen Victoria's cousin

Marie – Countess of Flanders; Philippe's wife

Children of Philippe & Marie
Baudouin
Henriette
Josephine
Albert

Augustus of Saxe-Coburg-Kohary – Queen Victoria's cousin

Clementine of Orléans – Wife of Augustus

Philip of Saxe-Coburg – Son of Augustus and Clementine; husband of Louise of Belgium

Franz Josef – Emperor of Austria-Hungary

Rudolf – Son of Franz Josef; Crown Prince of Austria-Hungary; husband of Stephanie of Belgium

As the eldest surviving son of her favourite uncle, Leopold II of the Belgians, had always had a special place in Queen Victoria's heart. During her uncle's lifetime, she had taken a great deal of interest in his upbringing and, when he was eighteen years old, she was happy to hear that his father had arranged for him to marry the beautiful and vivacious Marie Henriette of Austria, a daughter of Archduke Joseph, Palatine of Hungary.

Although it was reported that Leopold and Marie Henriette were truly in love, their characters and interests could not have been more disparate. Where he was withdrawn, diffident, self-indulgent and studious, she was outgoing, sporty and deeply religious. Although both enjoyed studying botany, Leopold was far more interested in architecture, while nothing brought Marie Henriette more pleasure than her overriding passion for horses. She not only enjoyed galloping apace but also possessed a remarkable gift for communicating with the animals, teaching them tricks, calming them when they were skittish and even training them to come indoors and climb the stairs to her rooms.

> "She knew how to control the wild Hungarian horses which were only safe with her," her daughter later recalled. "…They flew like the wind; one might have said that she guided them by a thread, but in reality she made them obedient to the sound of her voice…What amused her most was to drive two or four different animals at once who had never been harnessed, and who were so high-spirited that no one dared to drive them. By dint of patience and the magnetic charm of her voice the most restive animal eventually became docile."[278]

She was also an avid photographer and later became a skilled conjurer, having studied the art in private under the guidance of a renowned magician, Professor Herrmann. So different was the high-spirited bride from her introverted groom that a joke spread through Brussels that this was to be a marriage of a stable boy and a nun – Marie being the stable boy, and Leopold the nun.

The wedding took place in August 1853, and after touring Belgium, the couple accompanied King Leopold I to England. While visiting the Royal Stables at Windsor, Marie impressed Queen Victoria by her knowledge of their inhabitants, but, at the same time, the Queen suspected that something was amiss in her relationship with her husband. When it gradually became apparent that Leopold had failed to consummate the marriage, the Queen asked Prince Albert to undertake the delicate task of advising their cousin on the practicalities of producing an heir.

Whether or not the advice was heeded, it was five years before Marie Henriette gave birth to their first child – a daughter, Louise, whose arrival prompted the Prussian Crown Princess to echo the sighs of the parents:

'What a disappointment that it is a little girl!'[279]

Leopold's lack of interest in his daughter was matched only by his indifference to his wife. Already Queen Victoria had observed that his want of affection had dampened Marie-Henriette's natural exuberance, and Louise would later report that she could not remember 'a single act of kindness or tenderness on his part towards my mother,' but rather he remained 'the same self-centred and taciturn man in his relations with her.'[280]

There was still, however, the necessity of producing an heir and, when, fourteen months after Louise's birth, a boy – also named Leopold – was born, his parents were overjoyed. Little Leopold became the sole object of his father's attention as he showered on him the affection which was singularly lacking in his relationship with his wife and daughter. When a second little girl, Stephanie, was born in 1864, Leopold showed no interest in her, and 'fatherly caresses were rare and brief'[281] as he was frequently absent attending to his duties or spending time with his mistresses.

Little Leopold's special status did not damage relations between him and his sisters. All three children played happily together with their dolls, and, as he had inherited his mother's kind nature, he endeared himself to his relations, all of whom agreed that the 'sweet little boy' would one day make an excellent King of the Belgians.

Tragically, it was not to be. While playing in the gardens of Laeken Palace during the winter of 1868, he slipped into a pond and caught a chill which soon developed into pneumonia. For several weeks he lay in a critical condition, and, while his family prayed for a full recovery, the nine-year-old boy felt certain that he was about to die. On 14th January 1869, he asked his doctor how much longer he had to live, and when he was told that he was improving, he replied gravely, 'No, I am sure that my life's end draws near.'

Five days later, he became delirious and, as his distraught father came and went, his mother dared not leave his side. For three days she sat at his bed, neither resting nor changing her clothes until, shortly before noon on 22nd January he calmly passed away. King Leopold threw himself onto a couch, crying so hysterically that he had to be taken from the room, as his daughters were hastily dispatched to Brussels to come to terms with their loss. For Louise, however, the sorrow was so great that even fifty years later she still wept for her brother whose death had, she wrote:

"...lacerated my whole being...I remember then that I dared curse God and disown Him...Leopold, handsome, sweet, sincere, tender and intelligent, embodied for me, after our mother, all that was most precious in the world – I could no more conceive existence without him than the day without light. But he could not stay…"[282]

Rather than bringing his parents closer together, the loss of a son served only to drive them further apart. Marie Henriette withdrew from the public gaze to mourn in seclusion, while Leopold used his mistresses as a distraction from his grief. Colder and even more hard-hearted than he had been previously, his son's death had, according to one commentator, 'soured a nature that was at no time genial.'[283]

In spite of the intensity of his sorrow, the King carried out his duties, aware that chief among them was to produce a male heir. In the summer of 1871, therefore, he effected a brief reconciliation with Marie Henriette, and by Christmas she was pregnant for a fourth time. The following July when a third daughter, Clementine, was born, Leopold abandoned all hope of fathering a future monarch and centred his attention on his young nephew, Baudouin, the eldest son of his brother, Philippe of Flanders.

'Good' Philippe, Count of Flanders, had little in common with his elder brother beyond a dedication to study and a great love of their homeland. Scholarly, cultured and loyal, he had declined the thrones of Greece and Roumania, preferring to serve in the Belgian army, and assist first his father then his brother in carrying out their kingly duties. He was, however, well-travelled and, during his many visits to England, he endeared himself to the Queen and her people, being 'so kind and amiable and clever.'

While staying in London in 1856, he first met his future wife, Marie of Hohenzollern-Sigmaringen, a younger sister of the late Queen Stephanie of Portugal. Since, at the time, Marie had not yet reached her twelfth birthday, neither she nor nineteen-year-old Philippe had any inkling that one day they would marry, and it was not long before the pretty princess was being pursued by several European princes.

Queen Victoria, who considered 'good excellent Marie' far more beautiful than Queen Stephanie, was so delighted by her 'lovely little mouth and nose…sweet eyes and eyebrows, and the forehead and shape of the face'[284] that she was convinced she would have made a perfect Princess of Wales, were it not for her Roman Catholicism.

"Oh," she sighed, "why can't Marie H. become Protestant?"[285]

Resigned to the impossibility of her ever becoming Princess of Wales, the Queen came to the conclusion that she would be perfectly placed in predominantly Catholic Belgium. With her usual penchant for matchmaking, she began working towards bringing Philippe and Marie together, and her efforts soon proved successful.

The wedding took place in Berlin on 25th April 1867 – a splendid occasion on which, according to the Crown Princess of Prussia, the bride looked 'very pretty' despite her unbecoming and tasteless dress.

Unlike Leopold and Marie Henriette, Philippe and Marie had many common interests, particular their love of art and their devotion to their religion. Two years after the wedding, little Leopold's death raised Philippe to the position of heir and when, six months later, Marie gave birth to a son, Baudouin, it appeared that the dynasty would be secured through the Flanders line.

By then, Queen Victoria had altered her once high opinion of Marie. Now she found her overbearing; 'rather abrupt and decided in her tone,' and, most annoyingly of all, she entirely dominated Philippe[286], while her devotion to her native Prussia was certain to trouble her sister-in-law, the Austrian Marie Henriette.

To Marie Henriette's daughters, however, 'Aunt Marie' was the epitome of kindness, as she cared for them like a surrogate mother when their parents' duties kept them away from home. Marie would become the chief confidante of both Louise and Stephanie; and, to her own children, too, she was a kindly and affectionate mother.

A year after Baudouin's birth, twin daughters, Henriette and Josephine, were born, the latter of whom survived for only six weeks. When a third daughter was born in 1872, she was also named Josephine; and three years later, the family was completed with the birth of a son named Albert after Philippe's cousin, the late Prince Consort.

Philippe and Marie took a personal interest in every detail of their children's lives, spending at least two hours a day in their company, and overseeing their studies and recreations. In the summer, they withdrew to their country estate, Chateau Amerois, near the town of Bouillon, but, each Sunday when they were living in Brussels, the family walked through the avenues and parks, mixing with the ordinary people before taking lunch with King Leopold and Queen Marie Henriette.

During these family gatherings, the King developed a paternal bond with his nephew, whom he viewed as his successor; and, from the time that Baudouin was five years old, he began to acquaint him with the art of kingship. The young prince was an attentive student who eagerly absorbed his lessons and, before his twentieth birthday, he solemnly declared that his rule would be governed solely by tradition. In the meantime, he progressed through military college and was commissioned in the Grenadier Guards, rising to the rank of Captain Commandant and earning the respect of his colleagues and of the country.

Although he had been deprived of his son, through Baudouin, King Leopold saw the possibility of his playing a part in the succession, by arranging for his nephew to marry his own youngest daughter, Clementine. Their betrothal was about to be announced in the winter of 1890 when Baudouin's brother, Albert, contracted an influenza-like illness which quickly spread through the family. Baudouin's favourite sister, Henriette, was the worst affected, her condition becoming so critical that bulletins warned that she was close to death. Baudouin remained night and day by her bedside, praying for her recovery and, by mid-January, his prayers had been answered as her doctors announced that she was out of danger.

The following day, 17th January 1891, Baudouin began showing signs of the same illness but his symptoms were so mild that he was able to continue his duties. Three days later, though, on returning from a carriage ride, he felt so ill that he took to his bed and was unable to rise the next morning. Pneumonia developed bringing with it complications that affected his kidneys, and he began to deteriorate so rapidly that his chaplain was called to administer the Last Rites. King Leopold and Queen Marie Henriette hurried to join his parents at his bedside, and were present when died shortly before two o'clock in the morning of January 23rd.

While Belgium was plunged into mourning, the popular press around the world invented all kinds of bizarre explanations for his early demise. Some reports claimed that he had been suffering from smallpox, while others suggested that he had been poisoned. To his family, though, his death was simply an utter

266

tragedy, as Queen Victoria commented sadly, he was such a 'promising boy', who was:

> "The hope of the country, the pride of his poor parents and the comfort of poor Leopold who treated him like a son!"[287]

The loss of his nephew did nothing to improve the King's relationship with his daughters. Renowned for his parsimoniousness, he was particularly miserly when it came to providing them with a reasonable allowance and made no effort to prepare them for their future roles. Their mother often took them to the Sacred Heart School in Jetti, founded in 1836 by the future saint, Madeleine Sophie Barat, where they followed some of the classes and regularly participated in religious services, but little was done to familiarise them with wider society. Queen Victoria was shocked to discover that, at the age of sixteen, Stephanie never attended plays or dances, but was 'completely shut up never seeing anyone.'[288]

Their father viewed them solely as useful tools in creating dynastic alliances, and, while they were still young, he began to consider potentially profitable marriages. When Louise was barely fifteen years old, the King was reviewing prospective bridegrooms when he was approached by Philip of Saxe-Coburg Kohary, the eldest son of Queen Victoria's cousin, Augustus, and his wife, Clementine of Orléans. Despite an age difference of fourteen years, Philip asked King Leopold's permission to marry his daughter but, hopeful that a more prestigious suitor might yet be found, the King advised him to travel the world and return to Brussels after Louise's sixteenth birthday. Soon afterwards, though, a second proposal came from Prince Frederick Hohenzollern, and the King was so anxious to prevent a Prussian match that he advised Louise to accept Philip's offer.

267

Eager to escape from the confines of her home, Louise naively anticipated a glamorous life in Vienna and looked forward to her wedding with undisguised excitement. She was soon to be dramatically disillusioned when, having been told nothing of what to expect, her wedding night was a horrific experience, which left her so 'bruised and mangled in her soul'[289] that she fled in her nightdress through the gardens to 'hide her shame' in the greenhouses that her father had built at Laeken. When her mother eventually found her, she upbraided her for her over-sensitivity, and reminding her of her duty, explained that now her future was laid out and she must act accordingly.

This was but the beginning of the disaster of Louise's marriage. Two days later, she and Philip set out for Austria, breaking their journey with a visit to the home of Ernest, Duke of Saxe-Coburg-Gotha and his wife, Duchess Alexandrine. Their kindness temporarily soothed Louise's sadness, but, on reaching the Coburg Palace in Vienna, her spirit sank to their nadir. Nothing about the place appealed to her tastes, and, what was worse, her worldly husband, she claimed, constantly plied her with alcohol, instructed her to read sordid books and took great pleasure in recounting salacious stories to her.

> "Mon Dieu!" she gasped half a century later, "when I think of all this – the stuffed birds, the unhealthy books, the dirty jokes, and the daily miseries of my life – I am at a loss to know how I endured it."[290]

But she did not endure it for long. Although she bore her husband three children, she frequently separated herself from him and gained a reputation for her extravagance and the lavish lifestyle that she adopted.

In her loneliness, it occurred to her that the presence of a sister in Vienna might help assuage her nostalgia; and, as Crown Prince Rudolf, the heir the Austro-Hungarian Empire, was an eminently eligible suitor, she set about trying to bring him together with her younger sister, Stephanie.

Rudolf had already enjoyed numerous affairs and, in view of his taste for glamorous older women, the shy and plain Stephanie was not an attractive prospect. Under pressure, though, from his father, Emperor Franz Josef, he visited Brussels, secretly bringing his latest mistress with him. Half-heartedly, he spoke of the purpose of his visit and as 'his proposal for her hand was jumped at by grasping old King Leopold...the Crown Prince accepted his fate most philosophically.'[291]

> "Dear little Stephanie's marriage is very sudden," wrote the Prussian Crown Princess when the engagement was announced in the spring of 1880. "And taking such a great leap all of a sudden is of course very trying to a young girl's mental and moral development. It will be a great trial to the poor dear child to be grown up on such short notice and engaged to a young man she does not know, and had never seen."[292]

The wedding took place the following year in Vienna where society ladies openly made disparaging comments about the appearance of the bride, who:

> "...looked her worst in her bridal attire; her arms were red, and her dull yellow hair was most unbecomingly dressed. Stephanie was very tall, and her figure in those days was most deplorable...She had no eyebrows or eyelashes, and her one beauty was her exquisite biscuit-china complexion."[293]

269

Nonetheless, for a while it appeared that she and Rudolf were happy together, but their happiness was short-lived. Within two years, when Stephanie gave birth to a daughter, it was clear that the couple no longer enjoyed one another's company. Ill after her confinement, Stephanie disregarded Rudolf's wishes, and left Vienna for Jersey, remaining there far longer than her husband believed was necessary. Worse was to follow when he was told that she would not be able to have any more children, depriving him of the possibility of fathering an heir. He began drinking to excess and spending more and more time with his mistresses, which Stephanie might have endured in silence were it not for the interference of her sister, Louise, who 'fostered her jealousy and told her all kinds of things about the Crown Prince, who gradually found her unbearable to live with.'[294]

Rudolf planned to petition the Pope for an annulment of the marriage but, as his father refused to countenance the idea, he sank deeper and deeper into despair. In January 1889, he travelled with his young mistress, Maria Vetsera, to his hunting lodge at Mayerling where, on the morning of the 30th both were found shot dead. Later that day, Stephanie was handed a letter, which had been found in Rudolf's desk, informing her that he intended to take his own life.

Stephanie refused to wear mourning for her husband, and in 1900, much to her father's chagrin, she renounced her Austrian titles in order to marry a Hungarian Count, Elemer Lonyay de Nagy, with whom, it was rumoured, she had long been having an affair.

Louise, meanwhile, continued to despise her husband, 'fat Philip', and in 1895 embarked on a liaison with Lieutenant Mattachich, an officer in the Austrian army. Two years later, she fled with Mattachich to France, hoping that this would prompt Philip to divorce her. Realising, though, that he stood to lose her substantial Belgian inheritance, Philip refused to do so, and instead challenged Mattachich to a duel in the Riding School in Vienna. Mattachich accepted the challenge but, when handed a pistol, he deliberately missed his opponent, who duly returned the favour. The two men were then given swords and Mattachich made a slight cut on Philip's hand, after which the contest was over.

Just three weeks later, Mattachich was arrested on trumped-up charges of forgery and, as he was sentenced to four years in prison, Louise was declared insane and taken to the Doebling Lunatic Asylum in the outskirts of Vienna. There she remained confined for six years until Mattachich, released from prison, assisted her to escape and flee with him to Paris.

Having seen the heartache caused by his two elder daughters' disastrous marriages, King Leopold might have taken greater care of his youngest child, but when Clementine begged him to allow her to marry the love of her life, Prince Napoleon, he adamantly refused and warned that if she persisted in her request she would be disinherited[cc].

Unsurprisingly, Leopold's daughters viewed him as a domestic tyrant, and most of his contemporaries shared their opinion. In Belgium, he was:

> "...liked well enough as a King, but greatly disliked as a man. The last fact cannot really be wondered at, for a more cold and repellent manner than his it would be impossible to meet with. His face looks as if it were cut out of wood while he talks to you, and then there is a low

---

[cc] Clementine did, in fact, marry Prince Napoleon after her father's death, and enjoyed a very happy marriage.

cunning expression always lurking in his eye which is in the highest degree offensive."[295]

His demeanour and his behaviour towards his daughters was, though, as nothing compared to the reputation he would acquire as 'the Butcher of the Congo,' responsible for one of the most horrific genocides of the 19th and 20th centuries.

Chapter 24 – 'A Veritable Hell on Earth'

Leopold II – King of the Belgians; Queen Victoria's cousin

At the time of his accession, Queen Victoria had high hopes for the reign of King Leopold II, whom she considered 'amiable, sensible and tactful' and willing 'to give himself so much trouble to do his duty in his position in every way he can.'[296]

From the outset, Leopold stated his intention of ensuring peace and prosperity for Belgium, and raising the country to the status of the other Great Powers of Europe. His vision exceeded that of the majority of his ministers, most of whom were happy with the status quo, their neutrality guaranteed by international agreement. Like his father, however, Leopold believed that the agreement could easily be broken by any of the guarantors if it should prove to be in their interest to do so, and therefore it was necessary to build defences and ensure that his kingdom was viewed as a powerful independent nation by improving the structure of the cities and acquiring overseas possessions.

Five years prior to his accession, he had addressed the Senate on the need for improvements to Ghent, Namur, Mons, Liege, Charleroi, and Verviers; and, inspired by his love of architecture, he had proposed a prize of ten thousand francs for the best design for the appearance of Brussels. He planned to create imposing cities to rival Paris, London and Berlin, and, in a speech of which his cousin, Prince Albert, would certainly have approved, he told the Senate that:

> "...The embellishment of towns advances step by step with the increase of public welfare...The working populations have a right

to our full solicitude. We must exert ourselves to improve their dwellings and give them light and air."[297]

After his accession, he was even more determined to place his kingdom on an equal footing with her neighbours by continuing his building programme and acquiring colonies, which would increase trading outlets and turn his relatively small country into a mighty empire. He looked first to the Americas but, seeing that there was little possibility of territorial gains, he unsuccessfully tried to obtain the Philippines from Queen Isabella of Spain. Undeterred, by the early 1870s, his thoughts had turned to Africa – the 'dark continent' into which British and French pioneers were gradually delving.

Fascinated by the accounts of such explorers as Henry Morton Stanley, Leopold realised that the vast expanses of Central Africa were largely undiscovered and filled with potentially lucrative natural resources. In 1876, therefore, he organised and presided over an International Geographical Conference in Brussels, the ostensible aim of which was to end the slave trade that was still operant in the area. Addressing delegates from Britain, France, Germany, Austria, Italy and Russia, he gave an impassioned speech, calling for a united force to combat the 'plague' that was a blight on civilization.

"The horrors of that traffic," he said, "the thousands of victims massacred each year through the slave trade, the still greater number of perfectly innocent beings who, brutally reduced to captivity, are condemned en masse to forced labour in perpetuity, have deeply moved all those who have even partially studied this deplorable situation; and they have conceived the idea of uniting together and concerting, in a word, for the founding of an International

Association to put an end to an odious traffic which makes our epoch blush, and to tear aside the veil of darkness which still enshrouds Central Africa."[298]

Appearing as a great philanthropist, he claimed that the purpose of the International Organisation was to build hospitals and schools and to bring to the 'savages' the blessing of Christianity. To his surprise, few of the delegates shared his enthusiasm for his plans but he obtained the assurance that no one would object to his forays into the region, on condition that other countries were free to do likewise.

This was the perfect outcome for which he had been hoping, and, when his own ministers refused to support his dream of colonial expansion, he decided to embark on the project as a private enterprise, funded partly by a government loan, and partly from his own private funds, including those of his sister, Charlotte, whose financial affairs he had managed since she had been declared insane. Before the conference was over, he contacted the explorer, Stanley, who had already made several journeys through the Congo, and agreed to return and claim the land on Leopold's behalf.

To Leopold's delight, Stanley was hugely successful in making 'trade agreements' with the local chiefs by duping them into signing contracts – which they could neither read nor understand – agreeing to hand over their land to him in exchange for something as small as a piece of linen or a similar item. In this way, he amassed sufficient territory to form a successful colony, which in 1884, Leopold named the Congo Free State and declared himself its sovereign.

In order to do so, he needed the backing of the Great Powers, and, by chance, that year Bismarck had organised an International Conference in Berlin. The aim of the conference was to prevent the tensions that arose from the European 'scramble for Africa' from escalating into war, by dividing the continent into zones, which would be shared out among the conference participants. Leopold's emissaries reassured the other delegates that his primary aim in the Congo remained to improve living conditions and suppress slavery, and, with the promise of maintaining free trade in the region, he won international support for the official establishment of the Congo Free State.

In reality, Leopold, who in the opinion of the Spanish Infanta, 'was less like a king in his palace than like a banker in his counting-house', intended to make a fortune from the sale of ivory. Thousands of elephants were slaughtered, but the return on the King's investment was paltry, and the entire Congo project was on the verge of becoming a financial disaster, when fate turned dramatically in Leopold's favour. Although pneumatic tyres had first been invented by Charles Goodyear and Robert William Thompson in the 1840s, it was not until 1888 that they began to be widely used, thanks to the work of a Scottish vet, John Dunlop, who created inflatable rubber tyres for bicycles. The sudden popularity of both bicycles and motor cars, led to an urgent demand for rubber – a product that was plentiful in the Congo.

Leopold was quick to see the potential and ordered Stanley to employ local people to undertake the laborious work of collecting it. At first his efforts were unsuccessful as the majority of Congolese were too busy on their own small farms and had little desire to work for European masters. When Stanley reported that they were 'idle' and money was no incentive to them, Leopold established a mercenary army, known as the Force Publique, to compel them collect the rubber for him. The methods of the Force Publique became increasingly horrific, as women and children were taken

276

hostage to force their menfolk to work, and, if they failed to meet their daily targets, they faced flogging, torture, beatings and even castration or the amputation of their hands. When some attempted to return home to tend their own plantations, their crops were set alight and they were driven into the forests at gunpoint and left to starve to death.

Leopold, reaping the profits, continued to present himself to the world as a great philanthropist, telling a credulous Queen Victoria of his difficulties in forming an army of natives to bring stability and order in the region.

> "To civilise the negroes," he claimed, "it is necessary to educate them, and their education can only be effected by leading them into the paths of profitable labour. It was to this end – to civilise, not to oppress them – that the laws entailing the necessity of labour upon the native races were introduced into the Congo State at the same time as slavery was forbidden by law in that State."[299]

The Queen was not alone in believing that his enterprise was altruistic and designed solely for the benefit of a people of whom the rest of the world was barely aware. Politicians and monarchs across Europe praised his endeavours and the vast amounts of his own money that he had invested in the region, unaware of the profits he was making or the depths of depravity to which his agents had sunk.

Not everyone was so convinced of his motives, as many had observed his behaviour during Queen Victoria's Golden Jubilee celebrations when he refused to sit beside the Queen of Hawaii simply because she was black. Others were aware of the unwelcome advances he had made to the Prince of Wales' one-time mistress, Lillie Langtry, and, as one of Queen

Victoria's equerries observed, even his body language suggested that he bore little resemblance to the powerful image that he desperately tried to portray.

> "He seemed very nervous & frightened of [Victoria] and sat twisting his hands like a schoolboy. It was curious that she should like him because his morals were notorious, but the Queen seemed to overlook this."[300]

As he had stated that he intended to evangelise the region, Leopold could not ban missionaries from entering the Congo, but he attempted to gain the Vatican's support in granting permission only to Belgian Catholics, in the certainty that he could prevent them from reporting anything untoward that they witnessed.

> "Our missionaries are expected to keep silence," one Belgian Member of Parliament observed, "…There is therefore, a gag. The gag is only placed in the mouths of Belgian missionaries, and it was to ensure this result that the Congo State urged the Vatican to agree that Catholic evangelisation on the Congo should be confined exclusively to Belgium."[301]

In spite of his efforts, it was impossible for the atrocities to remain undetected indefinitely as journalists and missionaries began to move freely in the region. Word leaked out that women were regularly raped by the colonists, who thought nothing of shooting the natives if they were deemed too idle to work. The Congolese who joined Leopold's militia were issued with a set number of bullets each day, and, to make sure that they had not wasted any, they were ordered to bring back a severed hand for every shot that they fired to prove that they had killed their intended targets. Sadistic governors collected whole baskets of hands as trophies, symbolising their power over the natives; and it was not unknown for those who had wasted their bullets, to sever the hands of living women or children, merely to make up the count at the end of the day.

Those who escaped corporal or capital punishment were liable, for the slightest hint of insubordination, to be confined in the unhygienic hovels that were called state prisons, where disease and malnutrition were rife and death was commonplace. One missionary, seeking to discover the truth of what was happening in the Congo, interviewed many guards and officials before reaching the conclusion that 'during the last seven years, this 'domaine privé' of King Leopold has been a veritable hell on earth.'[302]

By 1895, even Queen Victoria was beginning to suspect that the actuality of Leopold's private enterprise was very different from a benevolent venture aimed to improve the lives of the Congolese. Two years later, she was faced with evidence presented to the House of Commons by a Member of Parliament who demanded an immediate inquiry into the subject. As an increasing number of shocking reports were presented to the public, Leopold tried to distance himself from the crimes, and when, that year, he visited Queen Victoria, her lady-in-waiting noted that:

> "He is an unctuous old monster, very wicked I believe, we imagine he thinks a visit to the Queen gives him a fresh coat of whitewash, otherwise why does he travel five hundred miles in order to partake of lunch?"[303]

Even his appearance had become more like an archetypal villain, with his large hooked nose, and such long nails that he could only 'shake hands with two fingers as...he dare not run the risk of injuring them.'[304]

By the turn of the century, damning reports were being widely distributed throughout Europe and the United States, containing interviews with officials who admitted that the less they cost him, the happier the King was, and therefore it was imperative to ensure that the natives were paid such a pittance that they were basically working for nothing. Documents, which Leopold tried to suppress, also came to light, including a circular sent by a district commissioner in January 1897, stating that:

"Where the natives refuse obstinately to work, you will compel them to obey by taking hostages."[305]

This was the slave labour that Leopold claimed he had set out to eliminate and yet he had turned the Congo into his own plantation, and the Congolese into his slaves.

"And as slaves I have observed," wrote one eye-witness, "they must sometimes make bricks without straw, as when one must furnish fish nearly the year round, and he can catch fish only at certain seasons. Then one is forced to buy in other parts, paying in this way ten to forty times what will be received in return from the State Post. To meet these obligations one of the remaining members of a once large family had to pawn, or sell into slavery, a younger member of his family."[306]

In response to such reports, the British Government prohibited the King's agents from recruiting workers in British-controlled areas of Africa, and sent several messages to Leopold, urging him to establish reforms to prevent further outrages. It was not, however, until after Queen Victoria's death that the full extent of the horrors came to light, thanks partly to Joseph Conrad's novel *Heart of Darkness*, and the writings of a British journalist named Edmund Dene Morel.

While working in a shipping office in Liverpool, Morel had been perplexed by the amount of ammunition that was sent to the Force Publique, and eventually he began to suspect that the ivory and rubber that was being brought from the Congo had been obtained through slave labour. He set out to discover the truth for himself by travelling to Africa to see the situation first-hand. On his return home, he documented his findings in two damning books, which laid charges at the feet of Leopold that could not be ignored.

When the British Consul in the area, Roger Casement, also produced a report that presented Leopold in a most unfavourable light, demands were made that he should relinquish the Congo to the control of either his own or a foreign government. He was not, though, prepared to yield easily. Instead, he presented his own defence, shamelessly claiming that he had been given international support for his ventures, and adding that atrocities had been committed by other nations, drawing particular attention to the British treatment of the Boers. Initially, the Belgian press supported the King but, in 1904, under pressure from Britain and Germany, his own government insisted on establishing an enquiry into the affairs of the region. The results revealed that Leopold could no longer plead ignorance of the crimes that were committed in his name, since many missionaries and journalists had written to him describing in vivid detail the barbarism of his agents but he had done nothing to restrain them.

Leopold attempted to assuage what little conscience he had by stating that the conditions had been harsh in the Congo long before his agents arrived; and, what was more, he had used a great part of his profits for the public good – funding extensive building projects in Belgian cities and improving the health of his people by providing hygienic housing and better medical care. On the twenty-fifth anniversary of his accession, he had declined the offer of expensive celebrations, using the money to establish instead a fund for injured workmen, as his thoughts had always been how best to improve the lot of his countrymen. His excuses earned him little sympathy, as one politician called out in the parliamentary Chamber in Brussels:

> "I tell him that this money, these profits, these presents are shameful things because they are the result of the exploitation of a whole people."[307]

The international outcry ultimately forced the King to hand over to his government his personal rule of the region. Conditions immediately began to improve but there was no escaping from the fact that during the twenty-seven years he had ruled the country, an estimated ten million people had died.

By the time that Leopold lost the Congo, he had already outlived his only son and his estranged wife, Queen Marie Henriette. In 1895, the Queen had purchased a former hotel in Spa where she pursued her interests in riding and music, patronising artists and composers and continuing her extensive charity work. By the turn of the century, her health was visibly failing, and, on the evening of Friday 19th September 1902, she rose from her chair after supper to retire to her room. As soon as she stood up, she collapsed in pain and moments later she died.

It was several days before Leopold deigned to travel to Spa to pay his respects but, on being told that his daughter, Stephanie, had also arrived to bid farewell to her mother, he refused to enter the room until she had left. Worse was to follow for Stephanie and her sisters as, under the terms of their mother's will, they stood to inherit not only a large share of her private property but also, eventually, that of their father. Immediately, he instigated a law suit against the will, and ultimately he disinherited his daughters.

"King Leopold," reported one Austrian newspaper, "has not even a heart of a stone; he has a heart of gold, which is harder than stone."[308]

Alongside the fortune that he had spent on beautifying the cities of Belgium, Leopold also used the profits from the Congo to fund a lavish lifestyle for his mistress, Caroline Lacroix – a former barmaid and prostitute, whom he met when she was sixteen years old and he was already in his mid-sixties. Granting her the title Baroness Vaughan, he showered her with expensive gifts, rented for her two majestic estates, and, after Marie Henriette's death, he married her in a private ceremony, which was recognised as lawful by the Roman Catholic Church, but viewed as morganatic by the Belgian authorities. In 1906, she bore him a child – who reputedly bore a resemblance to his legitimate son, the late Leopold – on whom he later conferred the title Count de Revenstein. A second was born soon afterwards, and, while the press speculated as to whether Leopold was actually his father, foreign journalists pointed out the irony of the fact that the boy was born with one hand missing – a misfortune that appeared strangely karmic for the son of a king whose agents had amputated the hands of so many Congolese people.

Leopold did not have long to enjoy the pleasures of his second marriage, for, despite having been assured by his doctors that he was in good health, he contracted a liver complaint and died quite suddenly, shortly before Christmas in 1909. He had already made plans for his own funeral, which, he stated, must be a simple affair, but he could not have predicted that he would have become so unpopular that his cortege was jeered as it was taken for interment at the Church of Our Lady of Laeken in Brussels. His will created a further furore when it was discovered that he had left a relatively small sum to be shared among his daughters, but to Caroline he had left a substantial fortune.

As Caroline's sons were barred from the succession, the throne passed to his nephew, Albert, whose father, Philippe of Flanders, had died four years earlier.

Chapter 25 – 'She Has Thought of Nothing Else'

George, Duke of Cambridge – Queen Victoria's cousin
Augusta of Cambridge/ Grand Duchess of Mecklenburg-Strelitz – Queen Victoria's cousin
Mary Adelaide of Cambridge – Duchess of Teck
Francis – Duke of Teck; Mary Adelaide's husband
>   Children of Mary Adelaide & Francis
>   Adolphus (Dolly)
>   Francis (Frank)
>   May
>   Alexander

Duchess of Cambridge – Mother of George, Augusta and Mary Adelaide

Eddy – Prince Albert Victor; eldest son of the Prince of Wales
George – Second son of the Prince of Wales

Empress Frederick – Queen Victoria's eldest daughter, Vicky

In the autumn of 1873, Queen Victoria's aunt by marriage, the Duchess of Cambridge, suffered a stroke while staying with her daughter, Augusta, in Strelitz. As soon as Queen Victoria heard that she was partially paralysed and confined to a chair, she bombarded the Duchess' son, George, with letters, asking him 'what sort of Physician have they at Strelitz' and telling him that he could go there at a moment's notice 'without asking my permission, beyond just telegraphing to let me know you are going.'[309]

A month later, when no such telegram had been sent, the Queen wrote more directly to him:

> "I think you ought to go for a week to see your dear Mother...I fear she is not getting on as well or as quickly as we could wish...If you left at the end of this week, you could spend New Year at Strelitz, which would be as good almost as Christmas."[310]

George decided to postpone his visit until the following Easter, but, shortly before his planned departure, he received a letter from Augusta, telling him that their mother was in such a 'nervous state' that she could not receive him. Her children feared the worst, but the Duchess was of hardier stock than they had realised and, within a month, she was sufficiently recovered to be brought back to England, where George thought that she appeared frail but far better than he had anticipated.

A few months later, she suffered a heart attack, which again left her in a critical condition and brought another barrage of letters from Queen Victoria. This time, knowing of the Duchess' aversion to doctors, the Queen suggested sending her own physician, William Gull, under the pretext that he was bringing a message from the sovereign. Once more, though, the Duchess regained sufficient strength to continue her charitable works and pay attention to the affairs of her family.

One of her greatest causes of concern was the financial situation of her youngest daughter, Mary Adelaide, Duchess of Teck. The £5000 per year, which her brother had secured for her, was insufficient to fund Mary's lifestyle and the charitable donations which she gave so freely. Occasionally, she scrimped and saved, using half-sheets of paper for her letters, and reusing envelopes, but, as a friend observed, she had 'chronic habit of giving away just twice as much again as she could well afford.'[311]

Her situation was not helped by her penniless husband, Francis, who was equally economically inept, and, despite the romance of the early months of their marriage, was not above seeking distraction elsewhere. According to the Marquise of Fontenoy, on one occasion he ran off with his children's governess and had to be brought back from Vienna by Mary Adelaide's brother, George.

> "Nor," claimed the Marquise, "was this the only incident of the kind, and 'keeping brother-in-law Frank straight' has taken up almost as much of the Duke of Cambridge's time as his duties of Commander-in-Chief of the British Army."[312]

In spite of her impecuniousness and her husband's roving eye, Mary Adelaide never lost sight of her status as a granddaughter of King George III. She insisted on dressing her footmen in royal livery and having her carriages painted with the royal emblem. This extravagance, and her love of hosting expensive parties, led to the acquisition of debts, which, by the early 1880s, were estimated to have reached £70,000.

Mary Adelaide appealed to her cousin for assistance, but the Queen, who had already provided her with rooms in Kensington Palace, and a country house, White Lodge in Richmond Park, refused to give her more money, suggesting instead that she and Francis should live within their means.

As creditors came knocking on the door, the Tecks organised an auction of family heirlooms and historic artefacts in Kensington Palace in what was seen as a shocking and demeaning display. So annoyed was the Queen that her birthplace had been transformed into a public market, that she withdrew the Tecks' right to remain in the palace, and, supported by the Duchess of

Cambridge, *advised* Mary Adelaide and Francis to live abroad to put their finances in order.

For two years, the family stayed in Florence and Germany, returning to England in 1885. Four years later, Mary Adelaide's siblings joined her to celebrate George's seventieth birthday but hardly had Augusta returned to Strelitz when news reached her that the ninety-one-year-old Duchess was dying. As George was away in Ireland, and Mary was also some distance from London, Augusta made hurried arrangements to race back to England. Just as had been the case with her father, she arrived too late to say a final goodbye.

> "The end was so sudden," wrote Mary Adelaide's daughter, "that we arrived one and a half hours after all was over and dearest Grandmama had passed calmly and peacefully into Her everlasting rest. For Her it is indeed a mercy that all suffering is now over, but the blank in our lives will, as you know, be very great, and we shall miss the kind words and smile."[313]

The Queen invited the family to have their mother interred at St. George's in Windsor, but the Duchess had left specific instructions that she was to be buried beside her husband in the grounds of St Anne's church in Kew. Her wishes were honoured but, in 1930, both she and Adolphus were exhumed and reinterred in the royal vault at Windsor.

Meanwhile, Mary Adelaide's sons, Adolphus ('Dolly'), Francis ('Frank') and Alexander, were enrolled in boarding schools, where Frank, having already gained a reputation for misbehaviour, was finally expelled for allegedly throwing his headmaster over a hedge. After school, the boys went on to pursue military careers via Sandhurst, but for her only daughter, May, Mary Adelaide had far more ambitious plans.

May was the very antithesis of her mother. Slim and studious, she was often embarrassed by the Duchess' obesity and lack of financial acumen; and, where the Duchess was warm and outgoing, May was shy and aloof.

"She has something very cold & stiff & distant in her manner," wrote Queen Victoria's daughter, " – each time one sees her again one has to break the ice afresh;…she is a little heavy & silent…but I should say she…would certainly never do – or say a foolish thing."[314]

It was an opinion shared by a lady-in-waiting, Marie Mallet, who thought her, 'very stiff. I am sure she means to be kind but in her case it is often necessary to take the will for the deed.'[315]

To Queen Victoria, though, May was 'unfrivolous,' and well-brought-up, in spite of her mother's often feckless behaviour; and, since she was eminently sensible, she might make an ideal bride for the Queen's somewhat wayward grandson, Prince Albert Victor.

As the eldest son of the Prince of Wales, Prince Albert Victor ('Eddy') was second-in-line to the throne, so the choice of a bride, who would eventually become Queen Consort, was a matter of great importance to Queen Victoria. May was not her first choice of candidate – she had already tried to arrange a match with one of her granddaughters, Alix of Hesse; and the German Empress Frederick had proposed her own youngest daughter. When neither plan came to fruition, the Queen decided to look further afield.

Mary Adelaide, eager to see her child in the 'highest position there is', was quick to draw attention to May, and in the spring of 1891, Queen Victoria invited her to Balmoral for a thorough inspection. Throughout the ten day visit, May could not have pleased her more, and, as the Prince of Wales was equally impressed, he agreed to recommend her to his son. Arrangements were made for the couple to spend time together at Luton Hoo, the home of the Danish ambassador, in early December, and, although Eddy was simultaneously in love with a French princess, Héléne d'Orléans, and the daughter of the Earl of Rosslyn, he proposed to May far sooner than anyone had expected.

Mary Adelaide was overjoyed, since, as the Empress Frederick observed, 'for years and years it has been her ardent wish, and she has thought of nothing else. What a marriage, and what a position for her daughter!'[316] Her excitement though was soon to be dashed when, during a family gathering at Sandringham, several guests and members of the family were struck with influenza. While the other patients began to recover, Eddy's condition worsened and by the 11th January 1892, his doctors feared he had developed pneumonia.

> "I cannot conceal from you," Mary Adelaide wrote to a friend, "that we are very anxious and must continue so, until the crisis is over and the inflammation has begun to subside...May is wonderfully good and calm, but it is terribly trying for her."[317]

Like Queen Victoria, Mary Adelaide took comfort from the fact that Eddy was younger than many who had survived the same illness, but her brother, George of Cambridge, was less optimistic, recording in his diary:

> "Heard to-night...that dear Eddy had been attacked at Sandringham by Influenza in a very serious form, which distresses me much."[318]

His anxieties were well-founded. Throughout 13th January 1892, Eddy became delirious, crying out 'Hélène! Hélène!' before expiring at nine-thirty the following morning.

"Was there ever a more terrible catastrophe?" Queen Victoria wrote to the poet, Lord Tennyson. "A wedding with bright hopes turned into a funeral."[319]

Shocked and saddened, Mary Adelaide withdrew with her daughter to White Lodge to live quietly, out of the public gaze. It was not long, though, before journalists observed that they received frequent visits from Eddy's younger brother, George, who now stood second-in-line to the throne. As George and May comforted one another, a friendship developed between them, and the press did not fail to observe that the Russian Tsarina – a sister of the Princess of Wales – had once found herself in a similar situation to that of Mary Adelaide's daughter. Like May, the Tsarina had been betrothed to the heir to a throne but, when her fiancé died before the wedding, she transferred her affection to his younger brother and subsequently married him.

Although her mother was delighted by the prospect of her daughter gaining a throne after all, May found the speculation oppressive and intrusive.

'It is too cruel too cruel!' she sobbed, 'Why may I not have the privilege of privacy at such a time as this, which every other girl in private life may have?'[320]

The Empress Frederick empathised:

"[May's] position is most difficult and embarrassing. She is still in mourning for our poor darling Eddy, and the newspapers are constantly writing about her becoming engaged to Georgie, and the whole of the public seem to wish it ardently."[321]

Mary Adelaide wish for it ardently, too, and gave the couple every encouragement. George, though, was reticent about expressing his feelings and it was not until his sister, Louise, engineered a meeting of the couple at her home in Richmond that he summoned the courage to propose. Again, May accepted him without hesitation, much to the delight of her mother, and the satisfaction of the Queen.

In the weeks leading up to the wedding, Mary Adelaide interested herself in every detail of her daughter's trousseau, insisting that it should be completely manufactured in Britain.

> "I am determined," she said, "that all the silk shall come from England, all the flannel from Wales, all the tweeds from Scotland, and every yard of lace and poplin from Ireland."[322]

By the time that the wedding took place on 6th July 1893, Mary Adelaide was already entertaining the idea that another of her children might marry into the family of the Prince of Wales. His youngest daughter, Maud, had developed a 'malheureuse passion' for her second son, Frank; and Mary Adelaide contemplated their potential union with growing excitement. Unfortunately, unlike his elder brother, Dolly – 'a charming sensible boy, so amiable and with such nice manners'[323] – Frank's misbehaviour during his schooldays had progressed into a disreputable lifestyle. A renowned philanderer and gambler, Frank did not reciprocate Maud's feelings and, when it was discovered that he was conducting an affair with an older married woman, any hope of his marrying the princess came to an end.

Disappointed in her son, Mary Adelaide continued to dedicate much of her time to charity work, visiting hospitals and hospices, and involving herself in several children's foundations, as well as the Royal Cambridge Asylum, founded in honour of her father. She was instrumental, too, in promoting the London Needlework Guild – a cause which would be eagerly adopted by her daughter after her death.

Her exhausting programme of official visits was taking a toll on her health, and, in the autumn of 1896, she was advised to take a cure at the spa at Nauheim. On returning home to White Lodge in October, she was obliged to decline several invitations to charity events, explaining that:

"I have for these last four or five years so overworked myself that I quite broke down at the end of the season, and though St. Moritz and Nauheim have to a great extent restored me, I still feel the need of rest and care."[324]

Her condition was exacerbated by anxiety about her husband, who was rapidly drifting into dementia, and her son, Frank, who had been sent to India in the hope that he would extricate himself from his unsuitable romantic liaison. Towards the end of April 1897, she suffered from such acute pains that her doctors deemed surgery necessary, despite the risk that her heart might not be able to withstand an anaesthetic. To her family's relief, she recovered more quickly than anyone had anticipated and, when her brother, George, visited her later in the day, he found her 'comfortable in bed, with a strong voice and no fever, which all looks hopeful,' although her husband was 'very agitated.'[325]

Within a few weeks, she resumed some of her charity work and was able to participate in Queen Victoria's Diamond Jubilee celebrations. As the Queen no longer felt capable of walking the length of Westminster Abbey, the Thanksgiving Service was held on the steps of St Paul's Cathedral, so that she could remain in her carriage, prompting Mary Adelaide's sister to ask wryly,

"Why is she thanking God in the street?"

Four months later, while travelling home from a Sunday service to White Lodge, Mary Adelaide began to feel unwell and thought she was developing a cold. By Tuesday, her health had deteriorated so rapidly that a doctor was summoned and, having examined her, announced that a second emergency operation was necessary. That night, she appeared to be recovering when suddenly she suffered a relapse and died shortly before three o'clock in the morning on 27th October, at the age of sixty-three.

Mary Adelaide's death came as a great shock to her siblings, both of whom had believed that her first operation had been such a success that she was fully recovered. For Augusta, the news was all the more difficult to bear as it came at the time when a shocking family scandal had become the talk of Berlin.

Chapter 26 – 'Immoral, Deplorable and Universally Mismanaged'

Augusta of Cambridge – Grand Duchess of
Mecklenburg-Strelitz; Queen Victoria's cousin
Frederick William – Grand Duke of Mecklenburg-
Strelitz; Augusta's husband
Adolf Frederick – Son of Augusta and Frederick
William
Elizabeth (Elly) of Anhalt – Adolf Frederick's wife
   Children of Adolf Frederick & Elly:
   Adolf Frederick
   Marie
   Jutta
   Karl Borwin

George – Duke of Cambridge; Queen Victoria's cousin

  Proud as she was of her role as Grand Duchess of Mecklenburg-Strelitz, Augusta never lost her nostalgia for her native land. Signing her name always as a Princess of Great Britain and Ireland, she read the English daily papers and followed all the vagaries of British politics. Her heart was forever in England, wrote her companion, Lady Eva Dugdale:

> "It was pathetic to watch her feeding on every memory, every relic, every association with England…None cared as she cared about what was happening in England; as a mother knows every mood and motive in the working of her child's heart, so she knew England."[326]

She had involved herself in finding a suitable bride of the Prince of Wales, allowing his sister and his future fiancée to meet at her home in Strelitz; and, decades later, she was overjoyed to hear of the betrothal of her favourite niece to the Prince's son. Augusta had always enjoyed a special relationship with May of Teck, with whom she shared an interest in art and literature and, above all, a great respect for the British monarchy. After the death of May's mother, Mary Adelaide, the two women had become even closer, and in many ways May became for Augusta the daughter that she never had.

The bond she shared with May was all the more important to Augusta, since her relations with her son, Adolf Frederick, had become increasingly strained since his marriage in 1877. She disapproved of his militaristic plans for the Grand Duchy; and rivalry rather than affection characterised her relationship with his wife, Elizabeth Elizabeth (Elly) of Anhalt. Elly had come from one of the most traditional courts in Germany, where, according to Queen Victoria's granddaughter, Marie Louise, who married into the Anhalt family, all kinds of strict protocols had to be observed at the expense of common sense. When, for example, Marie Louise wished to take a carriage ride with her sister-in-law, she could not simply approach her directly but must first summon her lady-in-waiting, who would pass on her message via a footman to the lady-in-waiting of her sister-in-law, who in turn would eventually bring the message to its intended recipient. Elly brought the same strict adherence to convention to Mecklenburg-Strelitz, including the idea that royal parents need not spend much time with their children. She and Adolf Frederick rarely saw their two sons – Adolf Frederick and Karl Borwin – as, following an early education under private tutors, they were enrolled in a gymnasium in Dresden; and still less consideration was given to their two daughters – Marie and Jutta – who were placed under the care of governesses in remote nurseries.

Relations with her husband, Grand Duke Frederick William, were also increasingly difficult for Augusta. He had, she claimed, never understood her, and before his seventieth birthday he had not only lost his sight but was also losing his mind. Although Augusta nursed him faithfully, he was 'not an easy patient', for, as his thoughts became more erratic, he became so dependent on her that, if she took a little time for herself, he became very angry and accused her of neglecting him. To avoid such confrontations, she fussed over him, and let witnesses observe her tender ministrations. When, for example, they attended Queen Victoria's Golden Jubilee Thanksgiving Service in 1887, a fellow guest noticed how she led him down the aisle, then:

> "...she seated him on a bench...then she proceeded to adjust his necktie, she pulled down his coat and smoothed it out, and arranged other parts of his uniform to suit her own taste. Finally when his appearance seemed to her satisfactory she left him."[327]

Appearances were of vital importance to the Mecklenburg-Strelitz family, which made the scandal which broke in 1897 all the more excruciating.

It was the custom in German palaces for a footman to extinguish the lamps in the bedrooms each evening, and for many years an elderly servant had carried out that service for Augusta's granddaughters. On his retirement, the old retainer was replaced by a younger married man named Hecht, who, having been attached to the household for seven years, was deemed equally trustworthy. In autumn 1897, however, it was brought to Elly's attention that her elder daughter, nineteen-year-old Marie, was in what Queen Victoria euphemistically referred to as 'an unfortunate condition.'

The girl had lived such a sheltered existence that when she was told that her cousin, May, was expecting a baby, she had reputedly asked in amazement how such a thing was possible since there were no storks in England. Unsurprisingly then, her pregnancy came as much as a shock to her as it was to her parents, who, after much questioning, were able to discern that Hecht was the father.

The footman was summarily dismissed but when he applied for a post in another house and references were required, Marie's parents claimed that he had lost his position because he had been caught stealing. Incensed by the false accusation, Hecht approached a socialist lawyer who happily leaked the story to the press and, in early October, the German Empress Frederick informed Queen Victoria that news was about to break which would bring great shame on the Anhalt and Mecklenburg-Strelitz families.

Intrigued, Queen Victoria was desperate to know the details of the scandal, and scolded her daughter, the Empress, for providing her with insufficient information.

> "I shall now try," she wrote, "...to find out from other sources, as it is too unpleasant to have such mysterious hints thrown about."[328]

It did not take her long to get to the root of the matter and she could only conclude that the unfortunate girl must have been drugged or hypnotised. By November, the affair had become the talk of all the clubs and courts in Europe, and even American newspapers carried the story. Some claimed that Marie intended to marry the footman in order to legitimise the child, one journalist writing that Hecht was now to 'crown his ignominy by winning the girl'; while others alluded to similar events in recent history, including the case of the daughter of a Prince of Hohenlohe-

Schillingsfürst, who had become pregnant by a gamekeeper.

In reality, much to Queen Victoria's horror, Marie's parents sent her away to France and gave orders that her name must never be mentioned within their household. Considering the affair 'deplorable,' 'most immoral' and 'universally mismanaged', the Queen asked Marie's cousin, May, to visit her and to make a point of being seen with her in public.

Augusta refused to abandon her granddaughter, and, when the baby was born in March 1898, she arranged for him to be adopted. A few months later, she took Marie to Nice, where Queen Victoria happened to be staying and invited them both to visit her in her hotel.

Although she had been permitted to return to her family, the strained relations between Marie and her parents convinced Augusta that she should marry as soon as possible. In view of the scandal, a royal match was out of the question but, during a visit to Paris, Marie met George Jametel, the thirty-nine-year-old son of a banker, whose services to the Pope had earned him the papal title of Count.

Jametel was only too willing to marry Marie in return for a substantial settlement from her father, and it was agreed that the wedding would take place in England in June 1889. The days leading up to the ceremony foreshadowed the troubled years that lay ahead, for, once it was agreed that there should be both a Roman Catholic and a Protestant rite, an argument erupted which threatened to disrupt the whole event. The Catholic service, presided over by a priest named Father Bagshawe and a French monsignor, was set to take place in a small church not far from White Lodge in Richmond, but when the Roman Catholic Cardinal Vaughan discovered that it would be followed by the

Protestant ceremony in Kew, he sent a message to Jametel, forbidding him from setting foot in the Anglican Parish Church. The Roman Catholic Duke of Norfolk was asked to intervene on behalf of the Mecklenburg family, but his efforts were of little avail and the wedding was postponed for several hours. Eventually, the Catholic ceremony took place but the couple had barely left the church when Father Bagshawe received a letter from Cardinal Vaughan, ordering him to prevent Jametel from going on to Kew. The family gathered in the presbytery where a loud argument ensued, during which the bride's great-uncle, the Duke of Cambridge was heard to use extremely offensive language. Jametel, whom the Duke described as 'cheerful and pleasing', finally yielded to his threats and set out with the rest of the party for Kew. The situation was made all the more difficult by the fact that Jametel did not speak English and therefore remained silent throughout the entire Protestant ceremony.

The Duke's account of the day made no mention of the furore.

> "At 11, drove to the Roman Catholic church in Richmond," he wrote in his diary, "to attend the marriage of dear Marie with Count Jametel, a short ceremony performed by a French Monsignor. All the Strelitz family were present, besides a few others...The whole thing passed off quite satisfactorily, and without a hitch of any kind, though the previous arrangements had been troublesome, but dear Augusta was very calm and judicious and got over every difficulty with great prudence — so all's well that ends well!"[329]

All, though, did not end well.

The couple moved into an expensive property in the Faubourg St. Germain in Paris, where, in 1904 and

1905, Marie gave birth to two children – a son and a daughter. Jametel, however, blatantly enjoyed numerous affairs, including a very public liaison with Infanta Eulalia of Spain. Aware that he had married her solely for her money, Marie sought a divorce, and when her younger brother, Karl Borwin, who was serving in Alsace-Lorraine, realised how deeply she had been humiliated, he challenged Jametel to a duel.

On 24th August 1908, Jametel answered the challenge, leaving Karl Borwin fatally wounded. When he died a few days later, his family claimed that his death was caused by heart failure, but the fact that only his father and brother attended his funeral, fuelled suspicion about the family's version of events, and left gossips to suggest that he had killed himself, due to the shame of what had happened to his sister.

Marie's divorce was finalised four months later but by then Jametel had spent her fortune and not until August 1914, as Europe was exploding into war, did she finally happiness with a new husband, Prince Julius Ernst of Lippe.

It was unsurprising that George, Duke of Cambridge, sympathised with Marie's plight and raised no objections to her marriage to a man of inferior rank, for, despite his renowned devotion to the monarchy and his shabby treatment of Prince Henry of Battenberg, in his private life, he willingly flouted tradition. Arranged marriages, he said, were 'doomed to failure,' and therefore he had always insisted that he would only marry for love. At the age of twenty he developed an infatuation with Princess Louise of Hesse-Kassel, who had been 'a very great friend' and of whom he was 'exceedingly fond...so that I naturally take a double interest in everything that concerns her, dear little soul.'[330] Their relationship, however, remained platonic and, in

1842, Louise married her second cousin, Prince Christian of Schleswig-Holstein-Sonderburg-Glucksburg, eventually becoming the Queen of Denmark and mother of Britain's Queen Alexandra and Russia Empress Marie Feodorovna.

George's infatuation with Louise did not prevented him from enjoying several affairs, for, despite his unprepossessing appearance, his status and kindly manner gave him a certain attraction particularly to women 'of the lower orders'. As a regular theatre-goer he had made the acquaintance of many performers and, in 1840, at the age of twenty-one, he met an Irish actress named Sarah Louisa Fairbrother. Four years older than he was, Louisa was the ninth child of a servant and had begun her theatrical career as a ballet dancer when she was twelve years old. She soon progressed to appearing as the principal boy in pantomimes, and often performed in theatres in Covent Garden, the Lyceum and Drury Lane. According to Lady Dorothy Nevill, she:

> "...was not perhaps one of those brilliant constellations of the theatrical firmament the announcement of whose appearance ensures crowded houses, but possessed a graceful and winning personality, which lingers pleasantly in the recollection."[331]

She certainly lingered pleasantly in George's recollection and, within a short time, the couple began an affair. In view of her humble origins, George had little hope of ever obtaining royal approval to marry her, and, to make matters worse, she already had two illegitimate children by different fathers – the 1st Viscount of Canterbury, who was thirty-five years her senior; and an Irish officer and landowner named Thomas Bernard. Unperturbed by her past, George fell deeply in love and the passionate liaison continued for

302

seven years, during which time Louisa bore him two sons, George and Adolphus. When, in 1847, she was pregnant by him for a third time, she finally persuaded him to marry her.

The quiet wedding took place in Clerkenwell in January 1847, after which Louisa was installed in a house in Mayfair where she styled herself Mrs FitzGeorge. For a while, her husband spent every possible spare moment in her company but, with time, his passion waned and her former attractions were insufficient to maintain his fidelity.

Within two years of the wedding, he had begun another long-term affair with yet another Louisa – Mrs Louisa Beauclerk, whom he called 'the idol of my life and existence.'

By 1867, Mrs FitzGeorge's health was failing, leaving her a semi-permanent invalid, and although George continued to provide for her and their children, his affection for Louisa Beauclerk far exceeded that which he felt for her. When Louisa Beauclerk died suddenly of a blood clot three days after Christmas 1882, he was utterly broken-hearted and, following her interment in Kensal Green cemetery, insisted that he wished to be buried beside her. A year later, he wrote to his friend, Lady Dorothy Nevill:

> "To me the time is a most painful one, for my thoughts are entirely absorbed by the events of this time last year, which you can well imagine cause very sad reflections and give me so much sorrow and grief. Friday next, 28th, was the sad day which ended my happiness in this world."[332]

Mrs FitzGeorge survived her by eight years, dying in January 1890. Although the marriage had lasted for over four decades, she had never been accepted into the Royal Family, and, even in death she was not free of her rival for George's affection, being interred close to Louisa Beauclerk in Kensal Green cemetery.

Chapter 27 – The Dressmaker's Daughter

George, Duke of Cambridge – Queen Victoria's cousin

Ernest of Württemberg – Queen Victoria's cousin
Alexander of Württemberg – Brother of Ernest; Queen Victoria's cousin

Leopold of Saxe-Coburg-Kohary – Queen Victoria's cousin
Ferdinand of Portugal – Prince of Saxe-Coburg-Kohary; brother of Leopold; Queen Victoria's cousin
Gusti (Augustus) of Saxe-Coburg-Kohary; brother of Leopold and Ferdinand
Clementine of Orléans – Daughter of King Louis-Philippe; wife of Gusti

Alexander Mensdorff-Pouilly – Queen Victoria's cousin
Alfonse Mensdorff-Pouilly – elder brother of Alexander; Queen Victoria's cousin
Arthur Mensdorff-Pouilly – youngest brother of Alexander and Alfonse; Queen Victoria's cousin

Queen Victoria, repeatedly stressing that, since marriage is a sacrament, no distinction could be made between one union and another, dismissed the notion of morganatic marriages, whereby a wife and children could be barred from inheriting the husband's title or position. Disdainful of what she viewed as German snobbery, she raised no objections when her daughter, Louise, married the 'mere' Marquis of Lorne; and when her youngest daughter, Beatrice, married the son of a morganatic marriage, she vehemently defended him from his Prussian detractors. Less judgemental than the majority of her fellow monarchs, she pitied Prince Albert's mother, whose liaison had led to her banishment; she supported a granddaughter who had deserted her homosexual husband; and she sympathised with the plight of the pregnant Marie of Mecklenburg-Strelitz.

It was necessary, though, to maintain the balance between tolerance and upholding the image of a morally exemplary monarchy. She refused, therefore, to receive divorcees at court, and, because George of Cambridge's wife had a 'reputation', she could never acknowledge her or granted her a title.

George's marriage to Louise Fairbrother, was strikingly similar to that of another of the Queen's cousins, Ernest of Württemberg. Like George, Ernest was once in love with a princess – Marie of Baden, the youngest child of a Grand Duke, and a cousin of Napoleon III – but nothing came of the romance and, in 1842, Marie married the future Duke of Hamilton.

Ernest remained single for the next eighteen years, focussing his attention on his duties in the Russian army, until a visit to the Coburg Theatre in Gotha led to an encounter which would alter his life. The theatre was of particular significance to him, since it had been opened in honour of the forty-first birthday of his sister, Marie – the wife Ernest I of Saxe-Coburg Gotha. Following her husband's death four years later, Marie and her stepson and cousin, Duke Ernest II, continued to support the theatre, inviting several notable composers, including Franz Liszt, Hector Berlioz and Richard Wagner, to have their works performed there. Such was the theatre's reputation that Wagner had pleaded with Liszt to introduce him to Duke Ernest II, who was, in Wagner's opinion, a man of 'superior intelligence [with] a personal love of music.' Nothing, said Wagner, could be better for him than for the Duke to join his other two patrons – the Princess of Prussia and the Grand Duke of Weimar.

"I would willingly surrender my whole artistic activity to these three protectors as a kind of equivalent," he wrote to Liszt, "and they would have the satisfaction of having kept me free and ready for my art. I cannot ask for myself nor find the proper form for the necessary agreement, but you can, and you and your intercession will succeed."[333]

Initially, Hector Berlioz was far less enthusiastic about accepting an invitation to Gotha, since the Duke, whom he described as 'a knowledgeable judge of music,' had recently poured scorn on his opera *Benvenuto Cellini*. Ernest II, however, had not invited him to perform his own compositions but rather to conduct the orchestra in a performance of the opera, *Santa Chiara,* which the Duke himself had written.

Singers were as keen to perform in the theatre as composers were to have their music performed, and many a musical career was made by an appearance in front of an illustrious and wealthy audience. Wilhelmine Seebach and Marie Rémond became renowned soloists after performing for the Duke, and, in 1858, a twenty-two-year old soprano, Natalie Eschborn, arrived in Gotha, after making a name for herself in various major European venues.

As the daughter of a musical director and a singer, Natalie was surrounded by music from her earliest childhood, and, a year before her arrival in Coburg, she had gained fame for translating into German Verdi's *La Traviata,* in which she played the lead role of Violette at the premier in Hamburg.

Soon afterwards, while visiting his ailing sister in Gotha, forty-three year old Ernest of Württemberg heard Natalie sing and was so enchanted by her performance that the seemingly staid bachelor fell in love. When the couple married in 1860, Natalie was granted the title Baroness Grünhof, and the following year, their only child – a daughter, Alexandra – was born. The marriage was happy but tragically brief, for, just eight years later, Ernest died and was interred near his late sister in Glockenburg Cemetery in Coburg.

Natalie devoted herself to raising their daughter, who eventually became a professional pianist, and, while performing in Rome, she came to the attention of the German ambassador to Italy, Baron Robert Keudell. The Baron's love of music had created a rapport between him and Queen Margarita, with whom he often played duets on the piano. When, though, the Queen heard that he had married Alexandra, she was horrified by his *mésalliance,* and the breakdown of their relationship led to his being recalled to Germany. Natalie remained living with her son-in-law and daughter, moving between their homes in Wiesbaden, Frankfurt and Berlin until her death in April 1905.

Since their earliest meetings before her accession, Queen Victoria had seen so little of her Württemberg cousins that Ernest's death passed her by almost unnoticed; and, when his brother, Alexander, passed on thirteen years later, she recorded the event merely as an afterthought. She had, though, kept in closer contact with her Saxe-Coburg-Kohary relations, one of whom, Leopold – a one-time candidate as consort of the Queen of Spain – also caused a scandal by marrying a former child-actress named Constance Geiger.

Miss Geiger, however, did not fit the popular image of a disreputable actress, for, as a highly gifted musician, she had been viewed as a child prodigy and had progressed from acting to performing as both a soprano and concert pianist. To supplement her income she also gave music lessons in Vienna but, when her father died, her mother opened a dressmaker's shop in which Constance was forced to work as a saleswoman.

By chance, one of her regular clients was the wife of the proprietor of a local hotel where Prince Leopold regularly dined. One day, the two men fell into a conversation about music, during which the proprietor mentioned his wife's connection to the former child prodigy, Constance Geiger. Intrigued, Leopold visited the shop and, after speaking with Constance, was so enamoured that he made many more visits until a liaison developed, resulting the birth of a son in April 1860.

Constance's many accomplishments could not compensate for her lack of royal blood, and the Austrian court was aghast when Leopold chivalrously announced his intention of marrying her. When his request for a title for her was denied, he demonstrated his respect and love for his bride, by arranging a lavish public wedding, presided over by Joseph Rauscher, the Cardinal Archbishop of Vienna. On the way to the church, Leopold rode proudly beside Constance's carriage, which was emblazoned with his coat of arms and surrounded by footmen and outriders; and, once inside, he further asserted her right to be viewed as his equal by offering her his right hand, rather than the left, which was the usual custom in the case of a morganatic marriage. When questioned about this, he boldly replied that, since his own mother was not of royal blood, he and Constance were equal in the sight of God, and, by rights, in the eyes of society.

Fifteen months later, Constance was granted the title Baroness Ruttenstein, but, while Queen Victoria and Leopold's brother, the former King Ferdinand of Portugal, welcomed her into the family, his other brother, Gusti, was pressed by his wife, Clementine of Orléans, to refuse to acknowledge her. Viennese society was equally disdainful of the dressmaker's daughter so the couple lived mainly in Paris, where Leopold purchased a villa near the Bois de Boulogne. There, they formed a cultured and lively circle of friends, including such luminaries as the actress, Sarah Bernhardt, and the Swedish soprano, Christine Nilsson. Leopold, according to Count Paul Vasili,

> "…aimait la France, la belle France, comme il l'appelait: ses deux plus grands plaisirs, disait-il, étaient une promenade, le soir, au bois de Boulogne, et une chasse au coq de bruyère, le matin, en Styrie."[dd][334]

Few guests appreciated their visits to Paris more than Leopold's brother, Ferdinand of Portugal, for whom the couple's marriage was to prove an inspiration. At the very time that Leopold was falling in love with Constance, the widowed Ferdinand had himself become entranced by an opera singer and actress named Elisa Hensler.

While still a child, Elisa and her parents had emigrated from her native Switzerland to the United States where her many talents soon became apparent. A gifted linguist who could speak seven languages fluently, she also demonstrated a remarkable flair for the arts – most notably sculpting and music. Returning to Europe, she performed at La Scala in Milan, and, when, in April 1860, she played the role of Oscar in Verdi's *Un Ballo in Maschera* in Lisbon, Ferdinand happened to be in the audience. Enraptured by her voice, he became her most ardent supporter, and despite a twenty-year age gap and their very different

---

[dd] '…he loved France, beautiful France, as he called it; his two greatest pleasures, he said, were a walk in the evening in the Bois de Boulogne, and hunting grouse in the morning in Styria.'

backgrounds, the couple soon discovered they had much in common. They began a liaison, which continued for almost a decade until 1869 when they were married in a private ceremony, much to the annoyance of Gusti, who again refused to acknowledge his sister-in-law. Ferdinand's cousin, Duke Ernest II of Saxe-Coburg-Gotha, bestowed on Elisa the title Countess Edla, and such was her husband's devotion to her that, when he was offered the throne of Spain, he declined it because the Spanish refused to accept Elisa as his official consort.

Both of the Kohary marriages were remarkably happy, and just as Leopold created the beautiful Villa Constance for his wife, Ferdinand created a Chalet in Sintra where he and Elise indulged their passion for art and sculpture, and where they planted a garden filled with exotic and rare species of plants from all over the world.

Sadly for Constance, the romantic idyll came to a sudden end when, in the spring of 1884, Leopold died quite suddenly of an inflammation of the brain in the same hotel in Vienna where the couple had first met. Having lived for so long in France, he had become a stranger to Viennese society but, as one contemporary reported:

> "...ceux qui avaient connu jadis le bel officier d'infanterie, à la haute taille, à la longue moustache blonde, se rappelaient toujours son cœur sincère, son âme aimante, son esprit bienveillant. Sa mort a été un grand chagrin pour ses amis."[ee335]

[ee] '...those who had known of old the handsome infantry officer with his tall figure and long blonde moustache, remembered always his sincere heart, he loving soul, and his welcoming spirit. His death was a great sorrow for his friends.'

Trusting that his family would respect his unwritten wish to bequeath all his property to his wife and their son, Franz, he had not seen fit to make a will. No sooner did the news of his death reach his sister-in-law, Clementine[ff], than she and her sons had his estates seized, claiming the marriage had been illegal and consequently his widow and child were entitled to nothing.

A lengthy court battle ensued, but, as Constance had been deprived of her assets, she was unable to afford skilful lawyers to promote her claims. Clementine, on the other hand, not only had sufficient wealth to hire legal experts but also had the full backing of the Austrian court. With this assistance of her son, Philip – the estranged husband of Louise of Belgium – she succeeded in compelling Constance to settle for a relatively small allowance of ten thousand dollars a year for her son, on condition that she never used the name Princess of Coburg and would not ever return to Vienna.

Throughout her marriage, Constance had adopted numerous charities, and, despite her reduced circumstances, she was reluctant to neglect them. Her benevolence reduced her to selling all her jewellery and ultimately the homes which she and Leopold had so lovingly created. Ferdinand's wife, Countess Edla, sympathising with her position, offered what help she could but Constance's heart was broken by Leopold's loss, and she survived him only by five years, dying in Paris at the age of fifty-five. In death, however, she had the final say, as her tombstone is engraved with the name 'Constance de Saxe-Coburg Gotha.'

Nineteen months after Leopold's demise, sixty-nine-year-old Ferdinand followed him to the grave,

---

[ff] Her husband, Leopold's brother, Gusti, had died in 1881.

having outlived eight of his eleven children. He had bequeathed his estates in Pena, including the Chalet and Gardens, to Elise, but his son, King Luis I, contested the will and a five-year court battle ensued. Eventually an agreement was reached whereby the property passed to the state but Elise would be allowed to remain there for her lifetime with a grant of sufficient funds to maintain the estates. In 1904, at the age of sixty-five, she left Pena to live with her son and daughter-in-law in Lisbon, where she died of kidney failure on 21st May 1929, the day before her ninety-third birthday.

If the Viennese were shocked by Leopold's marriage, nothing could have prepared them for them for Arthur Mensdorff-Pouilly's choice of a bride. Like so many of the Coburg cousins, he had once seemed destined for greatness, but, of his own volition, he thwarted such promise to the great disappointment of his family.

In 1843, his elder brother, Alfonse, married Teresia ('Resi') Dietrichstein, the daughter of a wealthy nobleman whose family had done much to promote the arts throughout Bohemia. The marriage was financially advantageous to Alfonse but this was a genuine love match which, despite a thirteen year age difference, had developed over twenty-four months since the couple first met at a ball in Vienna in 1841.

Alfonse had little interest in a political or a military career and, following his wedding, he focussed most of his attention on improving farming on his estates and renovating his property, Castle Nectiny in Pizen, erecting monumental battlements and neo-gothic towers. He was equally involved in raising his growing family, as, between 1843 and 1848, Resi gave birth to four daughters[gg], and four years later, to a longed-for

313

son, Arthur. The joy of Arthur's birth was overshadowed by the rapidly declining health of Alfonse's father, who died peacefully in Vienna a few weeks later, and whose death marked the beginning of a series of tragedies for his family.

In 1853, Alfonse's six-year-old daughter died and, in the winter of 1856, Resi contracted scarlet fever which led to a fatal paralysis of the heart. Alfonse inherited the Dietrichstein Boskovice Castle, built on the site of an ancient Dominican convent, in the vicinity of which he established a cloister for the Sisters of Mercy in memory of his wife. Misfortune, though, continued to plague him, as, six years after Resi's death, ten-year-old Arthur died; and just two months later, his twelve-year-old daughter, Antonia, also passed away.

In his grief, Alfonse he found comfort in the arms of a new bride – Maria von Lamberg, the daughter of an Austrian soldier and statesman, who had been savagely murdered during the Hungarian uprising of 1848. It was a happy marriage which produced three sons and a daughter, but it was not long before further tragedy beset Alfonse's second family. His little girl died at the age of three, and his youngest son, one day before his third birthday. In 1876, forty-two-year-old Maria contracted a fatal typhoid, leaving Alfonse widowed for a second time.

In spite of so many sorrows, his religious faith remained unshaken as he continued to support local churches and funded the building of a chapel, remaining devoted to his extended family until his

---

gg Most family trees show only three daughters born during this period, but an entry in Queen Victoria's journals refers to the death of a third daughter who died at the age of six, and whose dates do not coincide with those given on the usual genealogical tables.

death from an inflammation of the lungs in 1894 at the age of eighty-five.

At the time of Alfonse's first marriage, his elder brother Hugo had yet to find a bride, despite pressure from his family to marry and father an heir. As the eldest son he was expected to continue the family line but, while he enjoyed many liaisons, he was particularly reluctant to commit himself to a wife. Various suitable women were paraded before him, including Alfonse's sister-in-law, Maria Dietrichstein, but he tactfully refused them all and, despite frequent prompting from his father and brothers, remained single throughout his relatively short life.

The third brother, Alexander, was far more willing to marry but his military duties had left him little time for romance until 1852 when, in his thirtieth year, he met another member of the Dietrichtstein family – Alexandra ('Aline') – at a dinner in Prague. The only child of the wealthy Prince Joseph von Dietrichstein, Aline had many attractions but Alexander's peripatetic lifestyle prevented him from pursuing her with any ardour and it would take five years and a great deal of effort on the part of her sister, Clotilde, to finally spur him to propose.

The couple married in 1857, and, three years later, Aline came into her inheritance, including the medieval castle of Nikolsburg, which was requisitioned as the headquarters of the King of Prussia during the Franco-Prussian War. Due to the cost of its renovation and maintenance, the Moravian edifice came as a mixed blessing to the couple, and, since Alexander was frequently away from home, it fell to Aline to supervise its upkeep – a task which she performed with skill and diligence. In spite of the financial difficulties and Alexander's frequent absences, the marriage was happy and produced four children – Marie; Hugo; Albert; and Clotilde.

In 1868, having been created Prince of Dietrichstein zu Nikolsburg, Alexander resigned his diplomatic position although he continued to take his seat in the Upper House in Vienna and was persuaded to accept the post of Stadtholder of Bohemia. The stresses of the Austro-Prussian War and his subsequent appointments had, though, weakened his constitution, and in February 1871, at the age of fifty-seven, he contracted bronchitis and died 'to the profound regret of all who knew him [as] one of the most sympathetic and attractive of men.'

After his death, Aline and her family regularly visited England, where the Queen sympathised with the young widow; and her son, Albert, became 'a great favourite, especially in the time of Queen Victoria.'[336] Back in Vienna, she resumed her social activities and, according to one of her guests:

> "The princess is today one of the best, the most affable and the most welcoming great ladies of Vienna, and in her salon...one can find the most charming of pleasures."[337]

Meanwhile, Arthur, the youngest of the Mensdorff brothers, had watched Alexander's rapid rise through the Austrian ranks with a modicum of envy. Overshadowed by his brother, he failed to gain the promotions that he felt he deserved and was equally disillusioned by a series of unfulfilling romantic affairs. In 1852, at the age of thirty-five, his spirits were plunged to the depths by the death of his beloved father, and, in a moment of apparent madness, he fell madly in love with a seventeen-year-old circus artiste named Magdalena ('Ellen') Kremzow.

At a time when actresses were viewed as women of dubious reputation, the performers in

Alessandro Guerra's circus acts were seen as positively immoral. The Italian entrepreneur, who had worked his way up from humble origins, had created some of the most fabulous and exotic equestrian displays in which nubile young women danced semi-naked on horseback in a glamorous array of colours, feathers and ribbons. Among the riders was the Hungarian Magdalena, whom Guerra claimed to have bought as a child and to have trained to become one of his star attractions. She travelled with his company throughout Europe and, during a performance in Italy, Arthur first set eyes upon her.

Few of his friends or kinsmen would have cared in the least had he taken Magdalena as his mistress but, in 1853, to the amazement of his fellow officers and the horror of his brothers, he announced that he had married her in a secret ceremony in Venice. His brother, Alfonse, was so disgusted that he made an excuse for not inviting the couple to his wedding in 1862; and many of his former friends deserted him as he resigned from the Austrian army. The more tolerant Queen Victoria maintained her correspondence with him, and after Prince Albert's death asked him to write his recollections of their childhood, but his sense of having failed his family was so intense that he largely withdrew from all social occasions for several years.

His situation might have been more bearable had he and Magdalena enjoyed one another's company, but his was a case of 'marry in haste, repent at leisure', and, as the couple had little in common, they were soon living separate lives, ultimately resulting in a divorce in 1882. For the next twenty years, Arthur remained single until 1902 when, at the age of eighty-five, he married a sixty-five-year old widow, Baroness Bianca von Wickenburg, who remained with him until his death, two years later.

Part V – After Victoria

Chapter 28 – 'A Fearful Blow and A Great Catastrophe'

George, Duke of Cambridge – Queen Victoria's cousin
Augusta of Mecklenburg-Strelitz – George's sister;
Grand Duchess of Mecklenburg-Strelitz
Frederick William – Grand Duke of Mecklenburg-
Strelitz; Augusta's husband
Adolf Frederick V – Augusta's son
Adolf Frederick VI – Augusta's grandson

Bertie – Prince of Wales; King Edward VII
May of Teck – Wife of King George V of Great
Britain; daughter of Queen Victoria's cousin, Mary
Adelaide

Alexander Mensdorff – Queen Victoria's cousin
Arthur Mensdorff – Brother of Alexander; Queen
Victoria's cousin

Leopold II – King of the Belgians; Queen Victoria's
cousin
Philippe – Count of Flanders; Leopold II's brother;
Queen Victoria's cousin
Charlotte – Empress of Mexico; Leopold II's sister;
Queen Victoria's cousin

In December 1900, Queen Victoria left Windsor for the Isle of Wight to spend Christmas in the seclusion of Osborne House. In recent months, her physicians and attendants had observed a steady deterioration in her health, which so concerned her doctor, Sir James Reid, that a fortnight before her departure for Osborne, he had written to the Prince of Wales, warning him that, although there was no evidence of organic disease, his mother had 'gone downhill' in the past year and:

> "In the course of nature this must be progressive, though with constant care and attention, I trust it may be slow. Of course, there is in addition, always present the risk of some sudden illness which would be very serious at the Queen's age and in her enfeebled state."[338]

At Osborne, the Queen complained of feeling particularly weary and tired, and the joy of the season was overshadowed by the sudden death of her friend and Lady of the Bedchamber, Jane Churchill, who was found dead in her bed on Christmas morning.

By mid-January, the Queen had lost her appetite and was becoming increasingly confused, and, on 18th of the month, she took to her bed. As word of her condition spread, members of her large family flocked to the island, gathering at Osborne until, as her equerry recorded, 'the whole house was crammed, and even all the houses in the vicinity were full.'[339]

For the next three days, she lingered until on the evening of 22nd January 1901, she died in the arms of her grandson, Kaiser Wilhelm II.

> "The Duke of Argyll told me," wrote Frederick Ponsonby, "that the last moments were like a great three-decker ship sinking. She kept on rallying, then sinking....The [German] Emperor never moved for two and a half hours and remained quite still."[340]

She had outlived her husband, three of her children and no fewer than nineteen of her cousins of whom only six were still living: George and Augusta of Cambridge; Leopold, Philippe and Charlotte of Belgium; and Arthur Mensdorff.

Eighty-one-year-old George of Cambridge was in Paris when he heard he received a telegram informing him of the 'dear Queen's' death.

"It is a fearful blow and a great catastrophe," he wrote, "not only for England, but for the world at large."[341]

He set out at once for England, and, when the Queen's body was returned to the mainland for her funeral on February 2nd, he rode with other dignitaries to await the arrival of the coffin at Victoria Station. From there, the cortege was taken by train to Paddington and on to Windsor, where he insisted on walking in the procession through the town but was obliged to lean for support on the arm of his nephew Dolly of Teck. By the time the ceremonies were over, he was, he said 'dead beat' and could only crawl into bed to try to sleep.

Tributes to the late Queen were published all over the world – a Zulu chief observing that there would be one more star in the sky; and the members of the American Columbia Historical Society noting that:

"As a friend of international peace, and especially as an advocate of perpetual friendly relations between Great Britain and the United States of America, she has won the respectful admiration of the American people...Her name and fame will be among the treasures preserved in the hearts of all who speak the language of our race."[342]

Her British subjects were still more effusive, bombarding the press with mournful or eulogistic poems.

"An Empire joins in mourning for its Queen,
The noblest of all Royal womankind,
Who, summoned by One greater, has resigned

324

The sceptre she upheld with gracious mien..."[343]
wrote one. While another claimed that:
"In times to come, when nations yet unborn,
Shall speak with glowing pride of freedom's
morn;
The place of honour, then, as now, we ween,
Shall still be given to our beloved Queen."[344]

As grief gave way to optimistic expectations of the new reign, George of Cambridge found himself in more or less continuous mourning. Shortly before the Queen's death, he had visited her eldest daughter, Empress Frederick, who was suffering from cancer, and found her 'most changed in appearance, and was very much shrunk up, and she is evidently in very delicate health, and can hardly walk.'[345] Six months after attending Queen Victoria's funeral, he travelled to Kronberg for that of the Empress.

A glimmer of hope of brighter days came in the summer of 1902 with the conclusion of the Boer War, to be followed by the coronation of King Edward VII. Queen Victoria had reigned for so long that no one could remember the details of the ceremony, prompting ministers to turn to George and his sister, Augusta, for advice. Both had attended not only their cousin's coronation but also that of King William IV in 1831, and Augusta's memory was so sharp that she was able to furnish them with a full description of both events. In June 1902, she travelled to England to watch the new King being crowned, when suddenly word reached the gathering guests that the event must be postponed as the King had been taken ill and required an emergency appendectomy.

"A lovely morning and dry," George wrote wryly on 26th June. "It would have been perfect for the Coronation, but alas! it was not to be!"[346]

Instead, he and Augusta went to St. Paul's Cathedral to join in a service of prayers for the King's recovery, and, within a few weeks, their intercessions had had been answered, as Bertie – now Edward VII – was sufficiently recovered to attend the re-scheduled ceremony.

Fewer guests were present than had originally been intended, and the day was dull and cloudy. Nonetheless, the crowds cheered wildly as the procession set out from Buckingham Palace to the Abbey – George riding in the first carriage with the late King of Hanover's daughter, Frederica, and the King's sister-in-law and niece, the Duchess and Princess Alice of Albany.

Augusta, accompanied by her son, also returned for the occasion, as did Alexander Mendorff's son, Albert, who was soon to be appointed as the Austro-Hungarian Ambassador to London. The late Queen's Belgian cousins were represented by Philippe's son, Albert, who, seven years later would succeed his uncle, Leopold II, as King.

The day was a highlight in an otherwise increasingly sad era for George of Cambridge. As his contemporaries aged, he found himself attending so many funerals that, at the end of the year, he sighed sadly:

> "It is terrible to think how many of one's friends are taken daily during this sad season. The last day of a very eventful and very sad year. May the coming one turn out more satisfactorily to myself and all concerned, though I am afraid I can hardly hope for or expect that as regards myself."[347]

He continued, though, to play an active role during the new reign, reviewing the troops and making regular visits to the London Hospital of which he had been a patron and president for several decades. In February 1904, he suffered the first of a series of severe stomach haemorrhages which continued intermittently until 17th March when he lapsed into unconsciousness. Later that morning, surrounded by his sons, he died peacefully in his London home.

A month later, Arthur Mensdorff-Pouilly died at his home in Wöllan in Slovenia at the age of eighty-six; and the following year, Philippe, Count of Flanders, passed away in Laeken Palace.

The death of his brother made King Leopold II more anxious about his own mortality, and, during one of his regular visits to his physician in Paris, he asked whether he would live long enough to complete all his plans for the country. After examining him, the doctor assured him that he had many more years left but the King replied that even a decade would not be sufficient to bring all his dreams to fruition. He did not, though, survive for a decade and his final years were marred by continuing disputes with his daughters and his growing unpopularity among many of his own people. He died quite suddenly on December 17th 1909 and was interred with his father, son and nephew, Baudouin in the Church of Our Lady of Laeken in Brussels.

Two months after the death of George of Cambridge, his brother-in-law, Frederick William of Mecklenburg-Strelitz, died at the age of eighty-four, forcing his reluctant widow, Augusta, to hand over her authority to the new Grand Duchess, her daughter-in-law, Elly. Relieved of her responsibilities, she was free to continue her travels to and from her beloved England, but, by the time that her niece, May of Teck, was crowned as Queen Consort in 1911, she felt too old and frail to make the crossing.

Further heartache awaited her, for just three years later, her only son, Adolf Frederick died, and within two months, the outbreak of the First World War made her an enemy of the country to which she was so devoted. The British Government pronounced her an alien and deprived her of the annuity, which she had been receiving since her wedding seventy-one years earlier.

In spite of this slight, she lost none of her devotion to her native country and, fiercely loyal to tradition, she refused to abide by the Kaiser's decision to put the clocks forward an hour in the summertime – and consequently all her engagements were an hour behind everyone else's.

In spite of her advanced age, she worked tirelessly on behalf of British prisoners-of-war, forwarding lists of names to the Princess of Pless, in the hope that she might locate them so that their families could be told where they were being held. Having succeeded in locating all the names on the list, the Princess wrote to Augusta's grandson, the new Grand Duke of Mecklenburg-Strelitz, who replied:

> "I would be so much obliged if you would kindly help me again to find out where a few other English officers are. I enclose my Grandmother's letter, in which she mentions the names. [It would be so kind of you to] let the Crown Princess of Sweden know where the officers are. From here it is rather impossible to write to her. About Lord Gerald and Hugh [Grosvener]hh, my Grandmother must have made a mistake, but meanwhile I have written to her."348

It was a measure of his fondness for Augusta that he also asked the Princess to return to him all his grandmother's letters, as he liked to collect them.

---

hh The sons of the Duke of Westminster

The Princess was equally enchanted by the aged Grand Duchess, as, 'one feels so young next to her, and to see her dear little proud face would make one do anything.'

> "If I had one-tenth of the intellect that she has, I should be thankful," she wrote. "The power of remembrance with her is absolutely uncanny. Most people when they are old wander in their mind, but she can talk of the present and the past; how diplomatically Peace could have been arranged before this, and could be arranged even now..."[349]

So keen was Augusta to see peace restored that the Princess insisted,

> "She has got to live...to see realized the future plans for a peaceful Europe, which will be formed after this war. She must live for this, and I am going to pray for it..."[350]

It was not to be. In November 1916, she became ill and, for almost four weeks ate next to nothing. Towards the end of the month, having told her family that she knew she was dying, she lost her power of speech and was in such obvious pain that she was prescribed narcotic injections. Her grandson, the Grand Duke, spent every possible moment with her until her death on the morning of 5th December.

> "As long as the coffin was open," he wrote later, "I could go and look into her dear face and kiss her most darling hand. I had long talks with her...I sat there for a long time and had the true feeling that her spirit was with me and peace came over me. And now I know, that she will be with me all my life. The darling was and will be for all my life my best and most dear friend."[351]

His own life was tragically brief. On 23 February 1918, he set out for a walk and never returned.

His body was found in a lake with a bullet through his head. Rumours surfaced that he had killed himself either because he was about to be discredited by a series of lovers, or because he had been spying for England and was about to be captured. His friend, the Princess of Pless, however, was convinced that he had never recovered from the loss of his grandmother, and his depression was exacerbated by the horrors of a war that made her beloved England his enemy.

By the time that the Armistice was signed in November 1918, only one of Queen Victoria's cousins was still living. Charlotte of Belgium, the former Empress of Mexico, had spent the past four decades in Bouchout Castle near Meise. When the Germans invaded Belgium, they agreed to protect the castle and leave its inmates undisturbed, due partly to Charlotte's mental condition and partly due to the fact that she was the sister-in-law of their ally, Emperor Franz Josef.

Barely aware of the tragedy being enacted around her, Charlotte continued her quiet existence, outliving all of her paternal cousins. It was not until 1927, that she finally succumbed to pneumonia, dying on 19th January at the age of eighty-six.

By the same author:

Biography

Queen Victoria's Granddaughters 1960-1918
Queen Victoria's Grandsons 1859-1918
Alice, the Enigma – A Biography of Queen Victoria's Daughter
Dear Papa, Beloved Mama – An intimate portrait of Queen Victoria & Prince Albert as parents
The Innocence of Kaiser Wilhelm II

Historical Fiction

Most Beautiful Princess – A Novel Based on the Life of Grand Duchess Elizabeth of Russia
Shattered Crowns: The Scapegoats
Shattered Crowns: The Sacrifice
Shattered Crowns: The Betrayal
The Fields Laid Waste

Novels

The Counting House
By Any Other Name

Children's Books

Wonderful Walter

Poetry

Child of the Moon
The Ragamuffin Sun

References

[1] Malmesbury, James Harris 1st Earl of, *Diaries & Correspondence of the 1st Earl of Malmesbury Vol III* (Richard Bentley 1844)

[2] Malmesbury, James Harris 1st Earl of, *Diaries & Correspondence of the 1st Earl of Malmesbury Vol III* (Richard Bentley 1844)

[3] Malmesbury, James Harris 1st Earl of, *Diaries & Correspondence of the 1st Earl of Malmesbury Vol III* (Richard Bentley 1844)

[4] Langdale, Charles *Memoirs of Mrs Fitzherbert* (Richard Bentley 1856)

[5] Clerici, Graziano Paolo (translated by Frederic Chapman) *A Queen of Indiscretions; The Tragedy of Caroline of Brunswick, Queen of England* (Bodley Head 1897)

[6] Pearce, Charles E. *The Beloved Princess, Princess Charlotte of Wales* (Stanley Paul & Co. 1911)

[7] Stockmar, Baron von E. *Memoirs of Baron Stockmar Vol I* (Longmans, Green & Co. 1873)

[8] Campbell Bury, Lady Charlotte *The Diary of a Lady-in-Waiting* (John Lane 1908)

[9] Campbell Bury, Lady Charlotte *The Diary of a Lady-in-Waiting* (John Lane 1908)

[10] Corti, Egon Caesar *Leopold I of Belgium, Secret Pages of European History* (T. Fisher Unwin Ltd. 1923)

[11] Hamilton, Lady Anne *Secret History of the Court of England From the Accession of George the Third to the Death of George the Fourth* (L.C. Page & Company 1901)

[12] Brougham, Henry Lord *The Life & Times of Henry, Lord Brougham Vol II* (Harper & Brothers 1871)

[13] Pearce, Charles E. *The Beloved Princess, Princess Charlotte of Wales* (Stanley Paul & Co. 1911)

[14] Pearce, Charles E. *The Beloved Princess, Princess Charlotte of Wales* (Stanley Paul & Co. 1911)

[15] Knight, Cornelia *Autobiography of Miss Cornelia Knight, Lady Companion to the Princess Charlotte of Wales Vol II* (W.H. Allen 1861)

[16] Brougham, Henry Lord *The Life & Times of Henry, Lord Brougham Vol II* (Harper & Brothers 1871)

[17] Brougham, Henry Lord *The Life & Times of Henry, Lord Brougham Vol II* (Harper & Brothers 1871)

[18] Clerici, Graziano Paolo (translated by Frederic Chapman) *A Queen of Indiscretions; The Tragedy of Caroline of Brunswick, Queen of England* (Bodley Head 1897)

[19] Panam, Pauline *Memoirs of a Young Greek Lady* (Fairburn 1823)

[20] Pearce, Charles E. *The Beloved Princess, Princess Charlotte of Wales* (Stanley Paul & Co. 1911)

[21] Bauer, Karoline (translated by Charles Nesbit) *Caroline Bauer & the Coburgs Vol I* (1887)

[22] Stockmar, Baron von E. *Memoirs of Baron Stockmar Vol I* (Longmans, Green & Co. 1873)

[23] Stockmar, Baron von E. *Memoirs of Baron Stockmar Vol I* (Longmans, Green & Co. 1873)

[24] Corti, Egon Caesar *Leopold I of Belgium, Secret Pages of European History* (T. Fisher Unwin Ltd. 1923)

[25] Pearce, Charles E. *The Beloved Princess, Princess Charlotte of Wales* (Stanley Paul & Co. 1911)

[26] Rees Price *A Critical Inquiry Into the Nature and Treatment of the Case of Her Royal Highness the Princess Charlotte of Wales and her Infant Son* (1817)

[27] Stockmar, Baron von E. *Memoirs of Baron Stockmar Vol I* (Longmans, Green & Co. 1873)

[28] Stockmar, Baron von E. *Memoirs of Baron Stockmar Vol I* (Longmans, Green & Co. 1873)

[29] Hamilton, Edwin B. *A Record of the Life & Death of Her Royal Highness, Princess Charlotte* (J. Bumpus 1817)

[30] Brougham, Henry Lord *The Life & Times of Henry, Lord Brougham Vol II* (Harper & Brothers 1871)

[31] Doran, John *Memoir of Queen Adelaide, Consort of William IV* (Richard Bentley 1861)

[32] Bauer, Karoline (translated by Charles Nesbit) *Caroline Bauer & the Coburgs Vol 1* (1887)

[33] Gurney, Mrs Gerald *The Childhood of Queen Victoria* (James Nisbet & Co 1901)

[34] Greenwood, Grace *Queen Victoria, Her Girlhood and Womanhood* (1883)

[35] Gurney, Mrs Gerald *The Childhood of Queen Victoria* (James Nisbet & Co 1901)

[36] Wilkinson, Rev. Alex *Reminiscences of the Court & Times of King Ernest of Hanover Vol 1* (Hurst & Blackett 1886)

[37] Heneage Jesse *Memoirs of King George III Vol 5* (1902)

[38] Wilkinson, Rev. Alex *Reminiscences of the Court & Times of King Ernest of Hanover Vol 1* (Hurst & Blackett 1886)

[39] Bauer, Karoline (translated by Charles Nesbit) *Caroline Bauer & the Coburgs Vol 1* (1887)

[40] Brougham, Henry Lord *The Life & Times of Henry, Lord Brougham Vol II* (Harper & Brothers 1871)

[41] Greville, Charles C.F. *The Greville Memoirs Vol 1.* (Longmans, Green & Co. 1874)

[42] Greville, Charles C.F. *The Greville Memoirs Vol 1.* (Longmans, Green & Co. 1874)

[43] Wilkinson, Rev. Alex *Reminiscences of the Court & Times of King Ernest of Hanover Vol 1* (Hurst & Blackett 1886)

[44] Benson, Arthur & Esher, Viscount *The Letters of Queen Victoria Vol 2* (John Murray 1907)

[45] Benson, Arthur & Esher, Viscount *The Letters of Queen Victoria Vol 2* (John Murray 1907)

[46] HRH The Crown Prince of Hanover *Ideas & Reflections on the Properties of Music* (Henry Colburn 1841)

[47] Hansard *HC Deb 26 May 1825 vol 13 cc836-7*

[48] Hansard *HC Deb 06 June 1825 vol 13 cc1047-58*

[49] Lyttelton, Lady Sarah *Correspondence of Sarah Spencer, Lady Lyttelton* (John Murray 1912)

[50] Tooley, Sarah A. *The Personal Life of Queen Victoria* (Hodder & Stoughton 1897)

[51] Sheppard, Edgar (editor) *George, Duke of Cambridge – A Memoir of his Private Life Based on the Journals and Letters of His Royal Highness* (Longmans, Green & Co. 1906)

[52] Kinlock Cooke, C. *A Memoir of Her Royal Highness Princess Mary Adelaide, Duchess of Teck* (John Murray 1900)

[53] Kinlock Cooke, C. *A Memoir of Her Royal Highness Princess Mary Adelaide, Duchess of Teck* (John Murray 1900)

[54] Lyttelton, Lady Sarah *Correspondence of Sarah Spencer, Lady Lyttelton* (John Murray 1912)

[55] Lyttelton, Lady Sarah *Correspondence of Sarah Spencer, Lady Lyttelton* (John Murray 1912)

[56] Sheppard, Edgar (editor) *George, Duke of Cambridge – A Memoir of his Private Life Based on the Journals and Letters of His Royal Highness* (Longmans, Green & Co. 1906)

[57] Lyttelton, Lady Sarah *Correspondence of Sarah Spencer, Lady Lyttelton* (John Murray 1912)

[58] Kinlock Cooke, C. *A Memoir of Her Royal Highness Princess Mary Adelaide, Duchess of Teck* (John Murray 1900)

[59] Kinlock Cooke, C. *A Memoir of Her Royal Highness Princess Mary Adelaide, Duchess of Teck* (John Murray 1900)

[60] Kinlock Cooke, C. *A Memoir of Her Royal Highness Princess Mary Adelaide, Duchess of Teck* (John Murray 1900)

[61] Sheppard, Edgar (editor) *George, Duke of Cambridge – A Memoir of his Private Life Based on the Journals and Letters of His Royal Highness* (Longmans, Green & Co. 1906)

[62] Sheppard, Edgar (editor) *George, Duke of Cambridge – A Memoir of his Private Life Based on the Journals and Letters of His Royal Highness* (Longmans, Green & Co. 1906)

[63] Grey, C. The Early Life of His Royal Highness, the Prince Consort (Smith, Elder & Co. 1867)

[64] Benson, Arthur & Esher, Viscount *The Letters of Queen Victoria Vol 1* (John Murray 1907)

[65] Benson, Arthur C. *The Letters of Queen Victoria, Volume 1, 1837-1843) A Selection from Her Majesty's Correspondence Between the Years 1837 and 1861* (Longmans, Green & Co. 1907)

[66] Rappoport, Angelo S. *The Curse of the Romanovs* (Chatto & Windus 1908)

[67] Waliszewski, K. *Paul the First* (William Heinemann 1913)

[68] Grey, C. *The Early Life of His Royal Highness, the Prince Consort* (Smith, Elder & Co. 1867)

[69] Grey, C. *The Early Life of His Royal Highness, the Prince Consort* (Smith, Elder & Co. 1867)

[70] Rappoport, Angelo S. *The Curse of the Romanovs* (Chatto & Windus 1908)

[71] Rappoport, Angelo S. *The Curse of the Romanovs* (Chatto & Windus 1908)

[72] Grey, C. *The Early Life of His Royal Highness, the Prince Consort* (Smith, Elder & Co. 1867)

[73] Rapp, Comte Jean *Memoirs of General Count Rapp; First Aide-de-Camp to Napoleon* (Henry Colburn & Co. 1823)

[74] Esher, Viscount (editor) *The Girlhood of Queen Victoria* (John Murray 1912)

[75] Bauer, Karoline (translated by Charles Nesbit) *Caroline Bauer & the Coburgs Vol 1* (1887)

[76] Walford, Edward *The Life of the Prince Consort* (Routledge, Warne & Routledge 1862)

[77] Bauer, Karoline (translated by Charles Nesbit) *Caroline Bauer & the Coburgs Vol 1* (1887)

[78] Nichols, William *The Beloved Prince a Memoir of the Prince Consort* (1880)

[79] Bauer, Karoline (translated by Charles Nesbit) *Caroline Bauer & the Coburgs*

335

Vol 1 (1887)

[80] Grey, C. *The Early Life of His Royal Highness, the Prince Consort* (Smith, Elder & Co. 1867)

[81] Ernest II, Duke of Saxe-Coburg & Gotha *Memoirs of Ernest II, Duke of Saxe-Coburg & Gotha Vol 1* (Remington & Co. 1888)

[82] Grey, C. *The Early Life of His Royal Highness, the Prince Consort* (Smith, Elder & Co. 1867)

[83] Bauer, Karoline (translated by Charles Nesbit) *Caroline Bauer & the Coburgs Vol 1* (1887)

[84] Grey, C. *The Early Life of His Royal Highness, the Prince Consort* (Smith, Elder & Co. 1867)

[85] Ernest II, Duke of Saxe-Coburg & Gotha *Memoirs of Ernest II, Duke of Saxe-Coburg & Gotha Vol 1* (Remington & Co. 1888)

[86] Grey, C. *The Early Life of His Royal Highness, the Prince Consort* (Smith, Elder & Co. 1867)

[87] Grey, C. *The Early Life of His Royal Highness, the Prince Consort* (Smith, Elder & Co. 1867)

[88] Hohenlohe-Schillingsfürst, Chlodwig, Prince of *Memoirs of Prince Chlodwig of Hohenlohe-Schillingsfürst* (William Heinemann 1906)

[89] Bauer, Karoline (translated by Charles Nesbit) *Caroline Bauer & the Coburgs Vol 1* (1887)

[90] Ernest II, Duke of Saxe-Coburg & Gotha *Memoirs of Ernest II, Duke of Saxe-Coburg & Gotha Vol 1* (Remington & Co. 1888)

[91] Esher, Viscount (editor) *The Girlhood of Queen Victoria* (John Murray 1912)

[92] Esher, Viscount (editor) *The Girlhood of Queen Victoria* (John Murray 1912)

[93] Benson, Arthur C. *The Letters of Queen Victoria, Volume II A Selection from Her Majesty's Correspondence Between the Years 1837 and 1861* (Longmans, Green & Co. 1907)

[94] Ernest II, Duke of Saxe-Coburg & Gotha *Memoirs of Ernest II, Duke of Saxe-Coburg & Gotha Vol 1* (Remington & Co. 1888)

[95] Lyttelton, Lady Sarah *Correspondence of Sarah Spencer, Lady Lyttelton* (John Murray 1912)

[96] Lyttelton, Lady Sarah *Correspondence of Sarah Spencer, Lady Lyttelton* (John Murray 1912)

[97] Corti, Egon Caesar *Leopold I of Belgium, Secret Pages of European History* (T. Fisher Unwin Ltd. 1923)

[98] Fuehr, Alexander *The Neutrality of Belgium* (Funk & Wagnalls Company 1915)

[99] Juste, Theodore (translated by Robert Black) *Memoirs of Leopold I, King of the Belgians Vol 1* (Samson, Lowe and Marston 1868)

[100] Fuehr, Alexander *The Neutrality of Belgium* (Funk & Wagnalls Company 1915)

[101] Juste, Theodore (translated by Robert Black) *Memoirs of Leopold I, King of the Belgians Vol 1* (Samson, Lowe and Marston 1868)

[102] Merode, Comte Felix de *Memoirs* (publisher unknown)

[103] Rappoport, Angelo S. *Leopold II, King of the Belgians* (Hutchinson 1910)

[104] Rappoport, Angelo S. *Leopold II, King of the Belgians* (Hutchinson 1910)

[105] Martin, Percy F. *Maximilian in Mexico; The Story of the French Intervention* (Constable & Company 1914)

[106] Wilkinson, Rev. Alex *Reminiscences of the Court & Times of King Ernest of Hanover Vol 1* (Hurst & Blackett 1886)

[107] Wilkinson, Rev. Alex *Reminiscences of the Court & Times of King Ernest of Hanover Vol 1* (Hurst & Blackett 1886)

[108] Sheppard, Edgar (editor) *George, Duke of Cambridge – A Memoir of his Private Life Based on the Journals and Letters of His Royal Highness* (Longmans, Green &

Co. 1906)

[109] Sheppard, Edgar (editor) *George, Duke of Cambridge – A Memoir of his Private Life Based on the Journals and Letters of His Royal Highness* (Longmans, Green & Co. 1906)

[110] Kinlock Cooke, C. *A Memoir of Her Royal Highness Princess Mary Adelaide, Duchess of Teck* (John Murray 1900)

[111] Kinlock Cooke, C. *A Memoir of Her Royal Highness Princess Mary Adelaide, Duchess of Teck* (John Murray 1900)

[112] Esher, Viscount (editor) *The Girlhood of Queen Victoria* (John Murray 1912)

[113] D'Auvergne Edmund B. *The Coburgs; The Rise of a Great Royal House* (Stanley Paul & Co. 1911)

[114] Esher, Viscount (editor) *The Girlhood of Queen Victoria* (John Murray 1912)

[115] Benson, Arthur & Esher, Viscount *The Letters of Queen Victoria Vol 1* (John Murray 1907)

[116] Benson, Arthur & Esher, Viscount *The Letters of Queen Victoria Vol 1* (John Murray 1907)

[117] Ernest II, Duke of Saxe-Coburg & Gotha *Memoirs of Ernest II, Duke of Saxe-Coburg & Gotha Vol 1* (Remington & Co. 1888)

[118] Ernest II, Duke of Saxe-Coburg & Gotha *Memoirs of Ernest II, Duke of Saxe-Coburg & Gotha Vol 1* (Remington & Co. 1888)

[119] Ernest II, Duke of Saxe-Coburg & Gotha *Memoirs of Ernest II, Duke of Saxe-Coburg & Gotha Vol 1* (Remington & Co. 1888)

[120] Ernest II, Duke of Saxe-Coburg & Gotha *Memoirs of Ernest II, Duke of Saxe-Coburg & Gotha Vol 1* (Remington & Co. 1888)

[121] Dyson C.C. *The Life of Marie Amelie, the Last Queen of the French* (D. Appelton & Co. 1910)

[122] Bush, Mrs Forbes *The Queens of France* (Hart 1852)

[123] Bazin, René *Le Duc de Nemours* (Emil Paul 1907)

[124] Stockmar, Ernst *Memoirs of Baron Stockmar Vol. 1*, (Longmans, 1872)

[125] Stockmar, Ernst *Memoirs of Baron Stockmar Vol. 1*, (Longmans, 1872)

[126] Greenwood, Grace *Queen Victoria, Her Girlhood and Womanhood* (1883)

[127] Stockmar, Ernst *Memoirs of Baron Stockmar Vol. 1*, (Longmans, 1872)

[128] Grey, C. *The Early Life of His Royal Highness, the Prince Consort* (Smith, Elder & Co. 1867)

[129] Grey, C. *The Early Life of His Royal Highness, the Prince Consort* (Smith, Elder & Co. 1867)

[130] Stockmar, Ernst *Memoirs of Baron Stockmar Vol. II*, (Longmans, 1872)

[131] Stockmar, Ernst *Memoirs of Baron Stockmar Vol. II*, (Longmans, 1873)

[132] Argyll, John Sutherland, Duke of *The Life of Queen Victoria* (George Bell & Son 1909)

[133] Tappan, Eva March *In the Days of Queen Victoria* (Hutchinson 1905)

[134] Hope, Eva *Our Queen: A Sketch of the Life and Times of Victoria, Queen of Great Britain and Ireland* (1884)

[135] Hope, Eva *Our Queen: A Sketch of the Life and Times of Victoria, Queen of Great Britain and Ireland* (1884)

[136] Stockmar, Ernst *Memoirs of Baron Stockmar Vol. II*, (Longmans, 1873)

[137] Argyll, John Sutherland, Duke of *The Life of Queen Victoria* (George Bell & Son 1909)

[138] Ernest II, Duke of Saxe-Coburg & Gotha *Memoirs of Ernest II, Duke of Saxe-Coburg & Gotha Vol II* (Remington & Co. 1888)

[139] Ernest II, Duke of Saxe-Coburg & Gotha *Memoirs of Ernest II, Duke of Saxe-Coburg & Gotha Vol II* (Remington & Co. 1888)

[140] Nichols, William *The Beloved Prince a Memoir of the Prince Consort* (1880)

[141] Benson, Arthur C. *The Letters of Queen Victoria, Volume 1, 1837-1843 A Selection from Her Majesty's Correspondence Between the Years 1837 and 1861*
[142] Ernest II, Duke of Saxe-Coburg & Gotha *Memoirs of Ernest II, Duke of Saxe-Coburg & Gotha Vol II* (Remington & Co. 1888)
[143] Martin, Theodore *The Life of His Royal Highness the Prince Consort Vol 1* (Smith, Elder & Co. 1875)
[144] Fulford, Roger (Editor) *Dearest Child; Letters Between Queen Victoria and the Princess Royal 1858-1861* (Evans 1964)
[145] Ernest II, Duke of Saxe-Coburg & Gotha *Memoirs of Ernest II, Duke of Saxe-Coburg & Gotha Vol II* (Remington & Co. 1888)
[146] Stanley, The Hon. Eleanor (Edited by Mrs Stuart Erskine) *Twenty Years at Court* (Nisbet & Co. 1918)
[147] Raikes, Thomas *The Private Correspondence of Thomas Raikes with the Duke of Wellington and other Distinguished Contemporaries* (Richard Bentley 1861)
[148] Hohenlohe-Schillingsfürst, Chlodwig, Prince of *Memoirs of Prince Chlodwig of Hohenlohe-Schillingsfürst* (William Heinemann 1906)
[149] Ernest II, Duke of Saxe-Coburg & Gotha *Memoirs of Ernest II, Duke of Saxe-Coburg & Gotha Vol II* (Remington & Co. 1888)
[150] Ernest II, Duke of Saxe-Coburg & Gotha *Memoirs of Ernest II, Duke of Saxe-Coburg & Gotha Vol II* (Remington & Co. 1888)
[151] Raikes, Thomas *The Private Correspondence of Thomas Raikes with the Duke of Wellington and other Distinguished Contemporaries* (Richard Bentley 1861)
[152] Fulford, Roger (Editor) *Your Dear Letter; Private Correspondence of Queen Victoria and the Crown Princess of Prussia, 1865-71* (Evans 1971)
[153] Dyson C.C. *The Life of Marie Amelie, the Last Queen of the French* (D. Appelton & Co. 1910)
[154] Bazin, René *Le Duc de Nemours* (Alfred Mame et Fils 1900)
[155] Dyson C.C. *The Life of Marie Amelie, the Last Queen of the French* (D. Appelton & Co. 1910)
[156] Raikes, Thomas *The Private Correspondence of Thomas Raikes with the Duke of Wellington and other Distinguished Contemporaries* (Richard Bentley 1861)
[157] Raikes, Thomas *The Private Correspondence of Thomas Raikes with the Duke of Wellington and other Distinguished Contemporaries* (Richard Bentley 1861)
[158] Raikes, Thomas *The Private Correspondence of Thomas Raikes with the Duke of Wellington and other Distinguished Contemporaries* (Richard Bentley 1861)
[159] Motley, John Lothrop *The Correspondence of John Lothrop Motley Vol. 2* (John Murray 1889)
[160] Lyttelton, Lady Sarah *Correspondence of Sarah Spencer, Lady Lyttelton* (John Murray 1912)
[161] Lyttelton, Lady Sarah *Correspondence of Sarah Spencer, Lady Lyttelton* (John Murray 1912)
[162] Stanley, The Hon. Eleanor (Edited by Mrs Stuart Erskine) *Twenty Years at Court* (Nisbet & Co. 1918)
[163] Hohenlohe-Schillingsfürst, Chlodwig, Prince of *Memoirs of Prince Chlodwig of Hohenlohe-Schillingsfürst* (William Heinemann 1906)
[164] Louise, Princess of Belgium *My Own Affairs* (George H. Doran Co. 1921)
[165] Louise, Princess of Belgium *My Own Affairs* (George H. Doran Co. 1921)
[166] Benson, Arthur & Esher, Viscount *The Letters of Queen Victoria Vol 3* (John Murray 1908)
[167] Benson, Arthur & Esher, Viscount *The Letters of Queen Victoria Vol 3* (John Murray 1908)
[168] Stockmar, Baron von E. *Memoirs of Baron Stockmar Vol 2* (Longmans, Green & Co. 1873)

[169] Sheppard, Edgar (editor) *George, Duke of Cambridge – A Memoir of his Private Life Based on the Journals and Letters of His Royal Highness* (Longmans, Green & Co. 1906)

[170] Sheppard, Edgar (editor) *George, Duke of Cambridge – A Memoir of his Private Life Based on the Journals and Letters of His Royal Highness* (Longmans, Green & Co. 1906)

[171] O'Rourke, Rev. John *The History of the Great Irish Famine* (James Duffy & Co. 1902)

[172] Sheppard, Edgar (editor) *George, Duke of Cambridge – A Memoir of his Private Life Based on the Journals and Letters of His Royal Highness* (Longmans, Green & Co. 1906)

[173] Hansard *HC Deb 22 July 1848 vol 100 cc696-743*

[174] Sheppard, Edgar (editor) *George, Duke of Cambridge – A Memoir of his Private Life Based on the Journals and Letters of His Royal Highness* (Longmans, Green & Co. 1906)

[175] Martin, Theodore *The Life of His Royal Highness, the Prince Consort Vol 2* (Smith, Elder & Co. 1876)

[176] Ernest II, Duke of Saxe-Coburg & Gotha *Memoirs of Ernest II, Duke of Saxe-Coburg & Gotha Vol 1* (Remington & Co. 1888)

[177] Wilkinson, Rev. Alex *Reminiscences of the Court & Times of King Ernest of Hanover Vol 2* (Hurst & Blackett 1886)

[178] Wilkinson, Rev. Alex *Reminiscences of the Court & Times of King Ernest of Hanover Vol 2* (Hurst & Blackett 1886)

[179] Wilkinson, Rev. Alex *Reminiscences of the Court & Times of King Ernest of Hanover Vol 1* (Hurst & Blackett 1886)

[180] Wilkinson, Rev. Alex *Reminiscences of the Court & Times of King Ernest of Hanover Vol 2* (Hurst & Blackett 1886)

[181] Stanley, The Hon. Eleanor (Edited by Mrs Stuart Erskine) *Twenty Years at Court* (Nisbet & Co. 1918)

[182] 'An Officer' *The Battle of Alma* (T. Hatchard 1854)

[183] Verner, William Willoughby Cole & Parker, Erasmus Darwin *The Military Life of H.R.H. George, Duke of Cambridge* (1906 John Murray)

[184] Skene, John Henry *With Lord Stratford in the Crimean War* (R. Bentley 1883)

[185] Verner, William Willoughby Cole & Parker, Erasmus Darwin *The Military Life of H.R.H. George, Duke of Cambridge* (1906 John Murray)

[186] Stanley, The Hon. Eleanor (Edited by Mrs Stuart Erskine) *Twenty Years at Court* (Nisbet & Co. 1918)

[187] Dunant, Henri (translated by Mrs David H. Wright) *Un Souvenir de Solferino* (1911)

[188] Martin, Theodore *The Life of His Royal Highness the Prince Consort Vol 1* (Smith, Elder & Co. 1875)

[189] Martin, Theodore *The Life of His Royal Highness the Prince Consort Vol 1* (Smith, Elder & Co. 1875)

[190] Martin, Theodore *The Life of His Royal Highness the Prince Consort Vol 1* (Smith, Elder & Co. 1875)

[191] Anonymous *Empress Frederick, A Memoir* (Dodd, Mead and Co. 1914)

[192] Martin, Theodore *The Life of His Royal Highness the Prince Consort Vol 5* (Smith, Elder & Co. 1875)

[193] Martin, Theodore *The Life of His Royal Highness the Prince Consort Vol 5* (Smith, Elder & Co. 1875)

[194] Stanley, Lady Augusta *The Letters of Lady Augusta Stanley* – edited by the Dean of Windsor and Hector Bolitho (Gerald Howe Ltd. 1927)

[195] Martin, Theodore *The Life of His Royal Highness the Prince Consort Vol 5*

(Smith, Elder & Co. 1875)

[196] Martin, Theodore *The Life of His Royal Highness the Prince Consort Vol 5* (Smith, Elder & Co. 1875)

[197] Adams, Charles Francis *The Trent Affair* (The American Historical Review Vol. 17 April 1912)

[198] Martin, Theodore *The Life of His Royal Highness the Prince Consort Vol 5* (Smith, Elder & Co. 1875)

[199] Schelhorn, Emil von *Dom Pedro V* (1866)

[200] Fulford, Roger (Editor) *Dearest Child; Letters Between Queen Victoria and the Princess Royal 1858-1861* (Evans 1964)

[201] Fulford, Roger (Editor) *Dearest Child; Letters Between Queen Victoria and the Princess Royal 1858-1861* (Evans 1964)

[202] Benson, Arthur & Esher, Viscount *The Letters of Queen Victoria Vol 3* (John Murray 1908)

[203] Fontenoy, Marquise de *The Marquise de Fontenoy's Revelation of High Life Within Royal Palaces; the Private Life of Emperors, Kings, Queens, Princes, and Princesses* (1892)

[204] Fontenoy, Marquise de *The Marquise de Fontenoy's Revelation of High Life Within Royal Palaces; the Private Life of Emperors, Kings, Queens, Princes, and Princesses* (1892)

[205] Martin, Theodore *The Life of the Prince Consort Vol 5* (Smith, Elder & Co. 1875)

[206] Martin, Theodore *The Life of the Prince Consort Vol 5* (Smith, Elder & Co. 1875)

[207] Rimmer, Alfred *The Early Homes of Prince Albert* (William Blackwood & Sons 1883)

[208] Walford, Edward *Life of the Prince Consort* (Routledge, Warne & Routledge 1862)

[209] Martin, Theodore *The Life of His Royal Highness the Prince Consort Vol 5* (Smith, Elder & Co. 1875)

[210] Walford, Edward *Life of the Prince Consort* (Routledge, Warne & Routledge 1862)

[211] Juste, Theodore *Memoirs of King Leopold I of the Belgians Vol. 2* (Samson, Lowe & Marston 1868)

[212] Fulford, Roger (Editor) *Your Dear Letter; Private Correspondence of Queen Victoria and the Crown Princess of Prussia, 1865-71* (Evans 1971)

[213] Juste, Theodore *Memoirs of King Leopold I of the Belgians Vol. 2* (Samson, Lowe & Marston 1868)

[214] Pope-Hennessey, James *Queen Mary* (George Allen & Unwin 1959)

[215] Bennett, Joseph *Hector Berlioz* (Novello, Ewer & Co. 1884)

[216] Mallet Marie (edited by Victor Mallet) *Life With Queen Victoria; Marie Mallet's Letters from Court 1887-1901* (John Murray 1968)

[217] Stanley, The Hon. Eleanor (Edited by Mrs Stuart Erskine) *Twenty Years at Court* (Nisbet & Co. 1918)

[218] Fulford, Roger (Editor) *Dearest Child; Letters Between Queen Victoria and the Princess Royal 1858-1861* (Evans 1964)

[219] Pope-Hennessey, James *Queen Mary* (George Allen & Unwin 1959)

[220] Fulford, Roger (Editor) *Dearest Child; Letters Between Queen Victoria and the Princess Royal 1858-1861* (Evans 1964)

[221] Benson, Arthur & Esher, Viscount *The Letters of Queen Victoria Vol 2* (John Murray 1907)

[222] Fulford, Roger (Editor) *Dearest Child; Letters Between Queen Victoria and the Princess Royal 1858-1861* (Evans 1964)

340

[223] Kinlock Cooke, C. *A Memoir of Her Royal Highness Princess Mary Adelaide, Duchess of Teck* (John Murray 1900)

[224] Sheppard, Edgar (editor) *George, Duke of Cambridge – A Memoir of his Private Life Based on the Journals and Letters of His Royal Highness* (Longmans, Green & Co. 1906)

[225] Motley, John Lothrop *The Correspondence of John Lothrop Motley Vol. 2* (John Murray 1889)

[226] Alice, Grand Duchess of Hesse (Editor by Princess Helena of Schleswig-Holstein) *Alice, Grand Duchess of Hesse & Princess of Great Britain & Ireland; Letters to Her Majesty the Queen* (John Murray 1885)

[227] Busch, Moritz *Bismarck; Some Secret Pages of his History Vol. 2* (Macmillan 1898)

[228] Busch, Moritz *Bismarck; Some Secret Pages of his History Vol. 2* (Macmillan 1898)

[229] Kinlock Cooke, C. *A Memoir of Her Royal Highness Princess Mary Adelaide, Duchess of Teck* (John Murray 1900)

[230] Kinlock Cooke, C. *A Memoir of Her Royal Highness Princess Mary Adelaide, Duchess of Teck* (John Murray 1900)

[231] Busch, Moritz *Bismarck; Some Secret Pages of his History Vol. 2* (Macmillan 1898)

[232] Hozier, Henry Montague *The Seven Weeks War & Its Antecedents* (1871)

[233] Hozier, Henry Montague *The Seven Weeks War & Its Antecedents* (1871)

[234] Lee, Sir Sidney *Queen Victoria* (Smith, Elder 1902)

[235] Fulford, Roger (Editor) *Your Dear Letter; Private Correspondence of Queen Victoria and the Crown Princess of Prussia, 1865-71* (Evans 1971)

[236] Kinlock Cooke, C. *A Memoir of Her Royal Highness Princess Mary Adelaide, Duchess of Teck* (John Murray 1900)

[237] Wilkinson, Rev. Alex *Reminiscences of the Court & Times of King Ernest of Hanover Vol 2* (Hurst & Blackett 1886)

[238] Legge, Edward *King George & the Royal Family Vol 1* (G. Richards 1918)

[239] Jenkins, Newell Sill *Reminiscences of Newell Sill Jenkins* (1924)

[240] Alice, Grand Duchess of Hesse (Editor by Princess Helena of Schleswig-Holstein) *Alice, Grand Duchess of Hesse & Princess of Great Britain & Ireland; Letters to Her Majesty the Queen* (John Murray 1885)

[241] Kinlock Cooke, C. *A Memoir of Her Royal Highness Princess Mary Adelaide, Duchess of Teck* (John Murray 1900)

[242] Motley, John Lothrop *The Correspondence of John Lothrop Motley Vol. 2* (John Murray 1889)

[243] Martin, Percy F. *Maximilian in Mexico; The Story of the French Intervention* (Constable & Company 1914)

[244] Fulford, Roger (Editor) *Dearest Child; Letters Between Queen Victoria and the Princess Royal 1858-1861* (Evans 1964)

[245] Motley, John Lothrop *The Correspondence of John Lothrop Motley Vol. 2* (John Murray 1889)

[246] Taylor, John M. *Maximilian & Carlota; A Story of Imperialism* (G.P. Putnam's & Sons 1894)

[247] Hall, Frederic *Life of Maximilian I, Late Emperor of Mexico: With a Sketch of the Empress Carlota* (James Miller 1868)

[248] Fulford, Roger (Editor) *Your Dear Letter; Private Correspondence of Queen Victoria and the Crown Princess of Prussia, 1865-71* (Evans 1971)

[249] Fulford, Roger (Editor) *Your Dear Letter; Private Correspondence of Queen Victoria and the Crown Princess of Prussia, 1865-71* (Evans 1971)

[250] Salm Salm, Prince Felix *My Diary in Mexico Vol 2* (Richard Bentley 1868)

341

[251] Molloy, J. Fitzgerald *The Romance of Royalty Vol. 2* (Dodd, Mead & Company 1904)

[252] Harris Chynoweth, W. *The Fall of Maximilian, Emperor of Mexico* (1872)

[253] Salm Salm, Prince Felix *My Diary in Mexico Vol 2* (Richard Bentley 1868)

[254] Sheppard, Edgar (editor) *George, Duke of Cambridge – A Memoir of his Private Life Based on the Journals and Letters of His Royal Highness* (Longmans, Green & Co. 1906)

[255] Fulford, Roger (Editor) *Your Dear Letter; Private Correspondence of Queen Victoria and the Crown Princess of Prussia, 1865-71* (Evans 1971)

[256] Alice, Grand Duchess of Hesse (Editor by Princess Helena of Schleswig-Holstein) *Alice, Grand Duchess of Hesse & Princess of Great Britain & Ireland; Letters to Her Majesty the Queen* (John Murray 1885)

[257] Ponsonby, Frederick (editor) *The Letters of the Empress Frederick* (Macmillan 1928)

[258] Russell, Sir William Howard *My Diary During the Last Great War* (G. Routledge & Sons 1874)

[259] Kinlock Cooke, C. *A Memoir of Her Royal Highness Princess Mary Adelaide, Duchess of Teck* (John Murray 1900)

[260] Russell, Sir William Howard *My Diary During the Last Great War* (G. Routledge & Sons 1874)

[261] Fulford, Roger (Editor) *Your Dear Letter; Private Correspondence of Queen Victoria and the Crown Princess of Prussia, 1865-71* (Evans 1971)

[262] Ponsonby, Frederick (editor) *The Letters of the Empress Frederick* (Macmillan 1928)

[263] Ponsonby, Frederick (editor) *The Letters of the Empress Frederick* (Macmillan 1928)

[264] Ponsonby, Frederick (editor) *The Letters of the Empress Frederick* (Macmillan 1928)

[265] Mallett, Victor (editor) Life with Queen Victoria - Marie Mallet's Letters from Court 1887-1901 (Houghton Mifflin Company 1968)

[266] Marie, Queen of Roumania *The Story of My Life* (Saturday Evening Post, January 6th 1934)

[267] Marie, Queen of Roumania *The Story of My Life* (Saturday Evening Post, January 6th 1934)

[268] Fontenoy, Marquise de *The Marquise de Fontenoy's Revelation of High Life Within Royal Palaces; the Private Life of Emperors, Kings, Queens, Princes, and Princesses* (1892)

[269] Marie, Queen of Roumania *The Story of My Life* (Saturday Evening Post, January 6th 1934)

[270] Sheppard, Edgar (editor) *George, Duke of Cambridge – A Memoir of his Private Life Based on the Journals and Letters of His Royal Highness* (Longmans, Green & Co. 1906)

[271] Blachford, Frederic Rogers *Letters of Frederic Lord Blachford, Under-Secretary of State for the Colonies, 1860-1871*; (J. Murray, 1896),

[272] Sheppard, Edgar (editor) *George, Duke of Cambridge – A Memoir of his Private Life Based on the Journals and Letters of His Royal Highness* (Longmans, Green & Co. 1906)

[273] Sheppard, Edgar (editor) *George, Duke of Cambridge – A Memoir of his Private Life Based on the Journals and Letters of His Royal Highness* (Longmans, Green & Co. 1906)

[274] Sheppard, Edgar (editor) *George, Duke of Cambridge – A Memoir of his Private Life Based on the Journals and Letters of His Royal Highness* (Longmans, Green & Co. 1906)

[275] Sheppard, Edgar (editor) *George, Duke of Cambridge – A Memoir of his Private Life Based on the Journals and Letters of His Royal Highness* (Longmans, Green & Co. 1906)

[276] Nevill, Ralph *The Life & Letters of Lady Dorothy Nevill* (Methuen 1919)

[277] Lee, Arthur Gould (Editor) *The Empress Frederick writes to Sophie her daughter, Crown Princess and later Queen of the Hellenes* (Faber 1955)

[278] Louise, Princess of Belgium *My Own Affairs* (George H. Doran Co. 1921)

[279] Fulford, Roger (Editor) *Dearest Child; Letters Between Queen Victoria and the Princess Royal 1858-1861* (Evans 1964)

[280] Louise, Princess of Belgium *My Own Affairs* (George H. Doran Co. 1921)

[281] Louise, Princess of Belgium *My Own Affairs* (George H. Doran Co. 1921)

[282] Louise, Princess of Belgium *My Own Affairs* (George H. Doran Co. 1921)

[283] Fontenoy, Marquise de *The Marquise de Fontenoy's Revelation of High Life Within Royal Palaces; the Private Life of Emperors, Kings, Queens, Princes, and Princesses* (1892)

[284] Fulford, Roger (Editor) *Your Dear Letter; Private Correspondence of Queen Victoria and the Crown Princess of Prussia, 1865-71* (Evans 1971)

[285] Fulford, Roger (Editor) *Dearest Child; Letters Between Queen Victoria and the Princess Royal 1858-1861* (Evans 1964)

[286] Fulford, Roger (Editor) *Your Dear Letter; Private Correspondence of Queen Victoria and the Crown Princess of Prussia, 1865-71* (Evans 1971)

[287] Ramm, Agatha (editor) *Beloved and Darling Child Last Letters Between Queen Victoria and Her Eldest Daughter, 1886-1901* (Sutton 1990)

[288] Fulford, Roger (editor) *Beloved Mama: Private Correspondence of Queen Victoria and the Crown Princess of Prussia, 1878-85* (Evans 1981)

[289] Louise, Princess of Belgium *My Own Affairs* (George H. Doran Co. 1921)

[290] Louise, Princess of Belgium *My Own Affairs* (George H. Doran Co. 1921)

[291] Larisch, Countess Marie *My Past Reminiscences of the Courts of Austria & Bavaria* (G.P. Putnam's Sons 1913)

[292] Fulford, Roger (editor) *Beloved Mama: Private Correspondence of Queen Victoria and the Crown Princess of Prussia, 1878-85* (Evans 1981)

[293] Larisch, Countess Marie *My Past Reminiscences of the Courts of Austria & Bavaria* (G.P. Putnam's Sons 1913)

[294] Larisch, Countess Marie *My Past Reminiscences of the Courts of Austria & Bavaria* (G.P. Putnam's Sons 1913)

[295] Fontenoy, Marquise de *The Marquise de Fontenoy's Revelation of High Life Within Royal Palaces; the Private Life of Emperors, Kings, Queens, Princes, and Princesses* (1892)

[296] Fulford, Roger (Editor) *Your Dear Letter; Private Correspondence of Queen Victoria and the Crown Princess of Prussia, 1865-71* (Evans 1971)

[297] Courcy Macdonnell, John de *King Leopold II: His Rule in Belgium & The Congo* (Cassell 1905)

[298] Courcy Macdonnell, John de *King Leopold II: His Rule in Belgium & The Congo* (Cassell 1905)

[299] MacDonnell, John de Courcy *King Leopold II: His Rule in Belgium and the Congo* (Cassell 1905)

[300] Ponsonby, Frederick *Recollections of Three Reigns* (Eyre & Spottiswoode 1951)

[301] Morel, Edward Dene *Red Rubber; The Story of The Rubber Slave Trade in the Congo* (Nassau Print 1906)

[302] Casement, Roger *The Casement Report* (1904)

[303] Mallett, Victor (editor) *Life with Queen Victoria - Marie Mallet's Letters from Court 1887-1901* (Houghton Mifflin Company 1968)

[304] Mallett, Victor (editor) *Life with Queen Victoria - Marie Mallet's Letters from*

343

Court 1887-1901 (Houghton Mifflin Company 1968)

[305] Morel, Edward Dene *Red Rubber; The Story of The Rubber Slave Trade in the Congo* (Nassau Print 1906)

[306] Morel, Edward Dene *Red Rubber; The Story of The Rubber Slave Trade in the Congo* (Nassau Print 1906)

[307] Morel, Edward Dene *Red Rubber; The Story of The Rubber Slave Trade in the Congo* (Nassau Print 1906)

[308] Rappoport, Angelo S. *Leopold II, King of the Belgians* (Hutchinson 1910)

[309] Sheppard, Edgar (editor) *George, Duke of Cambridge – A Memoir of his Private Life Based on the Journals and Letters of His Royal Highness* (Longmans, Green & Co. 1906)

[310] Sheppard, Edgar (editor) *George, Duke of Cambridge – A Memoir of his Private Life Based on the Journals and Letters of His Royal Highness* (Longmans, Green & Co. 1906)

[311] Woodward, Kathleen *Queen Mary: A Life and Intimate Study* (Hutchinson & Co. 1929)

[312] Fontenoy, Marquise de *The Marquise de Fontenoy's Revelation of High Life Within Royal Palaces; the Private Life of Emperors, Kings, Queens, Princes, and Princesses* (1892)

[313] Kinlock Cooke, C. *A Memoir of Her Royal Highness Princess Mary Adelaide, Duchess of Teck* (John Murray 1900)

[314] Ramm, Agatha (editor) *Beloved and Darling Child Last Letters Between Queen Victoria and Her Eldest Daughter, 1886-1901* (Sutton 1990)

[315] Mallet Marie (edited by Victor Mallet) *Life With Queen Victoria; Marie Mallet's Letters from Court 1887-1901* (John Murray 1968)

[316] Lee, Arthur Gould (Editor) *The Empress Frederick writes to Sophie her daughter, Crown Princess and later Queen of the Hellenes* (Faber 1955)

[317] Kinlock Cooke, C. *A Memoir of Her Royal Highness Princess Mary Adelaide, Duchess of Teck* (John Murray 1900)

[318] Sheppard, Edgar (Editor) *George, Duke of Cambridge – A Memoir of His Prince Life* (Longmans, Green & Co. 1906)

[319] Woodward, Kathleen *Queen Mary: A Life and Intimate Study* (Hutchinson & Co. 1929)

[320] Hudson, Robert *George V: Our Sailor King* (Collins 1910)

[321] Lee, Arthur Gould (Editor) *The Empress Frederick writes to Sophie her daughter, Crown Princess and later Queen of the Hellenes* (Faber 1955)

[322] Kinlock Cooke, C. *A Memoir of Her Royal Highness Princess Mary Adelaide, Duchess of Teck* (John Murray 1900)

[323] Ramm, Agatha (editor) *Beloved and Darling Child Last Letters Between Queen Victoria and Her Eldest Daughter, 1886-1901* (Sutton 1990)

[324] Kinlock Cooke, C. *A Memoir of Her Royal Highness Princess Mary Adelaide, Duchess of Teck* (John Murray 1900)

[325] Sheppard, Edgar (Editor) *George, Duke of Cambridge – A Memoir of His Prince Life* (Longmans, Green & Co. 1906)

[326] Woodward, Kathleen *Queen Mary: A Life and Intimate Study* (Hutchinson & Co. 1929)

[327] Liliuokalani, Queen *Hawaii's Story by Hawaii's Queen* (Lothrop, Lee and Shepard 1898)

[328] Ramm, Agatha (editor) Beloved and Darling Child Last Letters Between Queen Victoria and Her Eldest Daughter, 1886-1901 (Sutton 1990)

[329] Sheppard, Edgar (editor) *George, Duke of Cambridge – A Memoir of his Private Life Based on the Journals and Letters of His Royal Highness* (Longmans, Green & Co. 1906)

[330] Sheppard, Edgar (editor) *George, Duke of Cambridge – A Memoir of his Private Life Based on the Journals and Letters of His Royal Highness* (Longmans, Green & Co. 1906)

[331] Nevill, Lady Dorothy *Under Five Reigns* (1910)

[332] Nevill, Lady Dorothy *Under Five Reigns* (1910)

[333] Hueffer, Francis *The Correspondence of Wagner and Liszt Vol 1* (Scribner & Welford 1889)

[334] Vasili, Paul *La Société de Vienne: Augmenté de Lettres Inédites* (Nouvelle Revue 1885)

[335] Vasili, Paul *La Société de Vienne: Augmenté de Lettres Inédites* (Nouvelle Revue 1885)

[336] Jenkins, Newell Sill *Reminiscences of Newell Sill Jenkins* (1924)

[337] Vasili, Paul *La Société de Vienne: Augmenté de Lettres Inédites* (Nouvelle Revue 1885)

[338] Reid, Michaela *Ask Sir James* (Eland 1987)

[339] Ponsonby, Frederick *Recollections of Three Reigns* (Eyre & Spottiswoode 1951)

[340] Ponsonby, Frederick *Recollections of Three Reigns* (Eyre & Spottiswoode 1951)

[341] Sheppard, Edgar (Editor) *George, Duke of Cambridge – A Memoir of His Prince Life* (Longmans, Green & Co. 1906)

[342] Records of the Columbia Historical Society Vol. 5 *"Memorandum of Sympathy and Sorrow on the Death of Queen Victoria"* (January 1st 1902)

[343] Forshaw, Charles Frederick *Poetical Tributes to the Memory of Queen Victoria* (Sonnenchein 1901)

[344] Forshaw, Charles Frederick *Poetical Tributes to the Memory of Queen Victoria* (Sonnenchein 1901)

[345] Sheppard, Edgar (Editor) *George, Duke of Cambridge – A Memoir of His Prince Life* (Longmans, Green & Co. 1906)

[346] Sheppard, Edgar (Editor) *George, Duke of Cambridge – A Memoir of His Prince Life* (Longmans, Green & Co. 1906)

[347] Sheppard, Edgar (Editor) *George, Duke of Cambridge – A Memoir of His Prince Life* (Longmans, Green & Co. 1906)

[348] Pless, Daisy, Princess of Pless *Daisy, Princess of Pless* (E.P. Dutton 1920)

[349] Pless, Daisy, Princess of Pless *Daisy, Princess of Pless* (E.P. Dutton 1920)

[350] Pless, Daisy, Princess of Pless *Daisy, Princess of Pless* (E.P. Dutton 1920)

[351] Pless, Daisy, Princess of Pless *Daisy, Princess of Pless* (E.P. Dutton 1920)

Printed in Great Britain
by Amazon